First World War
and Army of Occupation
War Diary
France, Belgium and Germany

4 DIVISION
12 Infantry Brigade
King's Own (Royal Lancaster Regiment)
1st Battalion
and Monmouthshire Regiment (Territorial Force)
2nd Battalion
4 August 1914 - 31 January 1916

WO95/1506

The Naval & Military Press Ltd
www.nmarchive.com
Published in association with The National Archives

Published by

The Naval & Military Press Ltd

Unit 10 Ridgewood Industrial Park,
Uckfield, East Sussex,
TN22 5QE England
Tel: +44 (0) 1825 749494

www.naval-military-press.com

www.nmarchive.com

This diary has been reprinted in facsimile from the original. Any imperfections are inevitably reproduced and the quality may fall short of modern type and cartographic standards.

© Crown Copyright
Images reproduced by permission of The National Archives, London, England, 2015.

Contents

Document type	Place/Title	Date From	Date To
Heading	4th Division War Diaries 1 Bn. Kings Our Royal Lancaster Reg, 1914 August To December		
Heading	12th Brigade 4th Division 1st Battalion King's Own Royal Lancaster Regiment August 1914		
War Diary	Shaft Barrah Dover	04/08/1914	07/08/1914
War Diary	Shaft Barrah Dover	07/08/1914	08/08/1914
War Diary	Cromer	08/08/1914	10/08/1914
War Diary	Norwich	10/08/1914	12/08/1914
War Diary	Horsham St Faiths	13/08/1914	18/08/1914
War Diary	Wembley	18/08/1914	20/08/1914
War Diary	Wembley Southampton	21/08/1914	21/08/1914
War Diary	At Sea	22/08/1914	22/08/1914
War Diary	Boulogne	23/08/1914	23/08/1914
War Diary	Buitry	24/08/1914	24/08/1914
War Diary	Ligny-En-Cambrensis	24/08/1914	24/08/1914
War Diary	Viesly	25/08/1914	25/08/1914
War Diary	Haucourt	26/08/1914	26/08/1914
War Diary	Catelet Roisel Hancourt	27/08/1914	27/08/1914
War Diary	Matigny Sancourt Esmery Hallon Campagne	28/08/1914	28/08/1914
War Diary	Chevilly Nayan Sempigny	29/08/1914	29/08/1914
War Diary	Sempigny Fontenoy	30/08/1914	30/08/1914
War Diary	Fontenoy Foret de Campiegne Verberie	31/08/1914	31/08/1914
Heading	War Diary 1st Bn The King's Own Ms		
Heading	12th Brigade 4th Division 1st Battalion King's Own Royal Lancaster Regiment September 1914		
War Diary	Verberie Baron	01/09/1914	01/09/1914
War Diary	Dan Martin	02/09/1914	02/09/1914
War Diary	Lagny Serris	03/09/1914	03/09/1914
War Diary	Serris Chateao Ferrieres	04/09/1914	04/09/1914
War Diary	Brie-Comte Robert	05/09/1914	06/09/1914
War Diary	Couvrote La Haute Maison	07/09/1914	07/09/1914
War Diary	La Haute Maison La Ferte Jons Jouarre	08/09/1914	08/09/1914
War Diary	Le Perte Jons Jouarre	08/09/1914	08/09/1914
War Diary	Tarterel	09/09/1914	09/09/1914
War Diary	Vaux Sous-Columbus	10/09/1914	11/09/1914
War Diary	Billy sur Ourcq Tigny Septmunts	12/09/1914	19/09/1914
War Diary	St Marguerite	20/09/1914	30/09/1914
Heading	1st Battalion King's Own Royal Lancaster Regiment October 1914		
War Diary	St Marguerite	01/10/1914	06/10/1914
War Diary	Septmont	07/10/1914	08/10/1914
War Diary	Ambrief	09/10/1914	10/10/1914
War Diary	Ambrief Le Meux	11/10/1914	11/10/1914
War Diary	In Train To Hazebrouck	12/10/1914	12/10/1914
War Diary	Hazebrouck Meteren	13/10/1914	13/10/1914
War Diary	Rough Sketch Shewing Brulin Leld By K O At Light Fall	13/10/1914	13/10/1914
War Diary	Meteren	13/10/1914	13/10/1914
War Diary	Meteren Bailleul	14/10/1914	14/10/1914
War Diary	Bailleul	15/10/1914	15/10/1914

War Diary	Petit Pont	16/10/1914	17/10/1914
War Diary	Le Touquet	18/10/1914	20/10/1914
War Diary	Meteren Bailleuv	14/10/1914	14/10/1914
War Diary	Bailleul	15/10/1914	15/10/1914
War Diary	Petit Pont	16/10/1914	16/10/1914
War Diary	Le Touquet	21/10/1914	21/10/1914
War Diary	Le Bixtet	22/10/1914	23/10/1914
War Diary	Cha D'Armentieres	24/10/1914	27/10/1914
War Diary	Chappele D'Armentieres	28/10/1914	31/10/1914
Heading	2 Sketchs Showing Location of 12th Bde		
Diagram etc	12th Brigade Position at Missy October 1914		
Diagram etc	26 Oct 1941 Onwards.		
Heading	12th Brigade 4th Division 1st Battalion King's Own Royal Lancaster Regiment November 1914		
War Diary		01/11/1914	04/11/1914
War Diary	Chapelle D'Armentieres	05/11/1914	07/11/1914
War Diary	Le Touquet	08/11/1914	29/11/1914
War Diary	Armentieres	30/11/1914	30/11/1914
Miscellaneous	Strength Return		
Heading	12th Brigade 4th Division 1st Battalion King's Own Royal Lancaster Regiment December 1914		
War Diary	Armentieres	01/12/1914	03/12/1914
War Diary	Le Touquet	04/12/1914	07/12/1914
War Diary	Armentieres	08/12/1914	11/12/1914
War Diary	Le Touquet	12/12/1914	15/12/1914
War Diary	Le Bizet	16/12/1914	20/12/1914
War Diary	Le Touquet	21/12/1914	24/12/1914
War Diary	Le Bizet	25/12/1914	28/12/1914
War Diary	Le Touquet	29/12/1914	01/01/1915
Miscellaneous	Headquarters 12th Infantey Brigade		
Miscellaneous	C Coy Hdqrs		
Heading	WO95/1506 12th Bde 4th Div 1st KORL Regt Aug 1914-Feb 1914		
Heading	4th Division War Diaries 12th Infantry Bde 1st K.O.R.L Less Feb=Mar 1915 Jan-1915 Dec		
Heading	4th Div 12th Inf Bde 1st Kings Own Royal Lancs. Regt. January 1915		
War Diary	Le Bizet	02/01/1915	05/01/1915
War Diary	Le Touquet	06/01/1915	09/01/1915
War Diary	Le Bizet	10/01/1915	13/01/1915
War Diary	Le Touquet	14/01/1915	17/01/1915
War Diary	Le Bizet	18/01/1915	21/01/1915
War Diary	Le Touquet	22/01/1915	25/01/1915
War Diary	Le Bizet	26/01/1915	29/01/1915
War Diary	Le Touquet	30/01/1915	31/01/1915
Diagram etc			
Heading	4th Div 12th Inf. Bde 1st Kings Own Royal Lancs. Regt. (War Diaries for February & March Missing)		
Heading	4th Div 12th Inf. Bde 1st Kings Own Royal Lancs. Regt. April 1915		
War Diary	Le Touquet	04/04/1915	07/04/1915
War Diary	Le Bizet	08/04/1915	11/04/1915
War Diary	Le Touquet	12/04/1915	15/04/1915
War Diary	Le Bizet	16/04/1915	19/04/1915
War Diary	Le Touquet	20/04/1915	23/04/1915
War Diary	Le Bizet	24/04/1915	27/04/1915

Type	Location	Start	End
War Diary	Le Touquet	28/04/1915	28/04/1915
War Diary	Bailleul	29/04/1915	30/04/1915
Heading	4th Div 12th Inf. Bde 1st Kings Own Royal Lancs. Regt. May 1915		
War Diary	Wieltje	01/05/1915	10/05/1915
War Diary	La Brique	11/05/1915	12/05/1915
War Diary	Wieltje	13/05/1915	15/05/1915
War Diary	Dort Hock	16/05/1915	21/05/1915
War Diary	Labrique	22/05/1915	24/05/1915
War Diary	Canal Bank	25/05/1915	27/05/1915
War Diary	Irish Farm	28/05/1915	01/06/1915
Heading	1st Kings Own Royal Lancs. Regt June 1915		
War Diary	Farm Billets Dorlhock A 23	02/06/1915	06/06/1915
War Diary	Turco Farm	07/06/1915	10/06/1915
War Diary	Belle Alliance	11/06/1915	27/06/1915
War Diary	Left Sector Times Farm	28/06/1915	01/07/1915
Miscellaneous	Key To Attached Map La. Brique		
Map	Sketch of Position on 24.5.15		
Heading	1st Kings Own Royal Lancs. Regt. July 1915		
War Diary	Belle Alliance Farm	02/07/1915	07/07/1915
War Diary	En Route to Proven	08/07/1915	12/07/1915
War Diary	Proven	13/07/1915	20/07/1915
War Diary	En Route to Forceville	21/07/1915	23/07/1915
War Diary	Forceville	23/07/1915	24/07/1915
War Diary	En route to trenches	24/07/1915	24/07/1915
War Diary	In Trenches Round & in front of Auchonviller	25/07/1915	31/07/1915
Heading	4th Div 12th Inf. Bde. 1st Kings Own Royal Lancs. Regt. August 1915		
War Diary	In Trenches Round Auchonviller	01/08/1915	09/08/1915
War Diary	En Route to Trenches	10/08/1915	31/08/1915
Map	Maps		
Miscellaneous	1st Kings Own Rgt		
Heading	4th Div 12th Inf Bde 1st Kings Own Royal Lancs. Regt. September 1915		
War Diary		01/09/1915	30/09/1915
Heading	4th Div. 12th Inf. Bde. 1st Kings Own Royal Lancs. Regt. October 1915		
War Diary		01/10/1915	31/10/1915
Heading	36th Division Transferred Nov 2nd 12th Bde.		
War Diary		01/11/1915	30/11/1915
Heading	1/Roy. Lancaster Rgt. Dec Vol XV		
War Diary	Bussus	01/12/1915	31/12/1915
Heading	4th Division 12th Brigade 1 Bn, Kings Own Royal Lancester Regt 1916 Jan-1916 Dec		
Heading	1/Roy Lancaster Rgt. Jan 1916 Vol XVI		
War Diary	Bussus	01/01/1916	05/01/1916
War Diary	Bonneville	06/01/1916	06/01/1916
War Diary	Louvencourt	07/01/1916	02/02/1916
War Diary	Colincamps	03/02/1916	03/02/1916
War Diary	Trenches Right Section Frontage of 12th Inf 13 Bde Trenches 78-86 (Both Nickname) Trenches 2 1/2 Miles E of Colincamps Boundry on right Mailly-Maillef Serre Road	04/02/1916	04/02/1916
War Diary	Trenches 2 1/2 Miles E of Colincamps	04/02/1916	09/02/1916
War Diary	Colincamps	10/02/1916	10/02/1916
War Diary	Trenches 2 1/2 Miles E of Colincamps	11/02/1916	15/02/1916

Type	Location	From	To
War Diary	Colincamps	17/02/1916	21/02/1916
War Diary	Trenches 2 1/2 Miles E of Colincamps	22/02/1916	29/02/1916
Diagram etc	Battalion Front Line		
Heading	12th Brigade. 4th Division 1st Kings Own Royal Lancaster Regiment March 1916		
War Diary	Trenchs 2 1/2 Miles E of Colincamps	01/03/1916	04/03/1916
War Diary	Bouquemaison	05/03/1916	07/03/1916
War Diary	Meleroles	08/03/1916	18/03/1916
War Diary	Halloy	19/03/1916	20/03/1916
War Diary	Baillomont	21/03/1916	22/03/1916
War Diary	Billets At Baillomont	23/03/1916	24/03/1916
War Diary	Trenches N.E of Berles	25/03/1916	31/03/1916
Diagram etc			
Heading	12th Brigade 4th Division 1st Battalion The King's Own Royal Lancaster Regiment April 1916		
War Diary	Bailluelmont	01/04/1916	05/04/1916
War Diary	Trenches 1 Mile N.E. of Berles	06/04/1916	12/04/1916
War Diary	Billets Bailleulmont	13/04/1916	20/04/1916
War Diary	Trenches-mile N.E of Berles	21/04/1916	25/04/1916
War Diary	Billets Bailleulmont	26/04/1916	29/04/1916
War Diary	Baillelmont	30/04/1916	30/04/1916
Miscellaneous	The Officer i/c Adjutant General's Office Base	18/05/1916	18/05/1916
Miscellaneous	Pipe Sap (W.24.a.4-8) Enterprise	12/04/1916	12/04/1916
Miscellaneous	Report on Minor Enterprise Carried out on Morning 12th April 1916, on German Sap (Pipe Sap) W.24.a.4-8		
Miscellaneous			
Heading	12th Brigade 4th Division 1st Battalion The King's Own Royal Lancaster Regiment May 1916		
War Diary	Sus-St-Leger	01/05/1916	07/05/1916
War Diary	Bertrancourt	08/05/1916	24/05/1916
War Diary	Beaumetz	25/05/1916	25/05/1916
War Diary	Yrench	26/05/1916	31/05/1916
Heading	12th Brigade 4th Division 1st Battalion The King's Own Royal Lancaster Regiment June 1916 Box 1506		
War Diary	Yvrench	01/06/1916	10/06/1916
War Diary	Beauval	11/06/1916	11/06/1916
War Diary	Bertrancourt	12/06/1916	01/07/1916
War Diary	Trenches E of Mailly-Maillet	02/07/1916	05/07/1916
Heading	War Diary of 1st Bn. K.O.R.L. Regt for July 1916		
War Diary		30/06/1916	01/07/1916
War Diary	Bertrancourt	30/06/1916	30/06/1916
War Diary	Assembly Area	01/07/1916	01/07/1916
War Diary	German 2nd Line	01/07/1916	01/07/1916
War Diary	Legend.	01/07/1916	01/07/1916
War Diary	Trenches East of Mailly Maillet	06/07/1916	11/07/1916
War Diary	Huts Bertrancourt	11/07/1916	18/07/1916
War Diary	Trenches E of Auchonvillers	19/07/1916	20/07/1916
War Diary	Louvencourt	21/07/1916	21/07/1916
War Diary	Authieule	22/07/1916	22/07/1916
War Diary	Cassel Herzeele	23/07/1916	23/07/1916
War Diary	Herzeele	24/07/1916	27/07/1916
War Diary	D. Camp N.E of Poperinghe	28/07/1916	31/07/1916
Miscellaneous	Disposition of 1st Batt, There kings Own Regt.		
Miscellaneous			
Heading	7th Division B.H.Q. 91st Infantry Brigade. April 1918		

Heading	12th Brigade 4th Division. 1st Battalion The King's Own Royal Lancaster Regiment August 1916		
War Diary	D Huts N.E of Poperinghe	30/07/1916	04/08/1916
War Diary	Chateau Des Trois Tours Canal Bank	05/08/1916	31/08/1916
Heading	12th Brigade 4th Division 1st Battalion The King's Own Royal Lancaster Regiment September 1916		
War Diary		01/09/1916	30/09/1916
Heading	12th Brigade. 4th Division. 1st Battalion The King's Own Royal Lancaster Regiment October 1916		
War Diary		01/10/1916	31/10/1916
Heading	12th Brigade 4th Division 1st Battalion The King's Own Royal Lancaster Regiment November 1916		
War Diary		01/11/1916	30/11/1916
Heading	12th Brigade. 4th Division 1st Battalion The King's Own Royal Lancaster Regiment December 1916		
Heading	War Diary of 1st Bn. The Kings Own Regt. From : 1st December 1916 To : 31st December 1916		
War Diary	Martaineville	01/12/1916	02/12/1916
War Diary	Camp 112	03/12/1916	03/12/1916
War Diary	Camp 16	04/12/1916	05/12/1916
War Diary	Maurepas Halte	06/12/1916	06/12/1916
War Diary	Sailly-Saillisel	07/12/1916	10/12/1916
War Diary	Support Trenches	11/12/1916	11/12/1916
War Diary	Support Trenches & Combles	12/12/1916	15/12/1916
War Diary	Sailly Saillisel	15/12/1916	18/12/1916
War Diary	Fregicourt	19/12/1916	22/12/1916
War Diary	Camp 107	23/12/1916	27/12/1916
War Diary	Belair	28/12/1916	31/12/1916
Heading	4th Division 12th Infantry Bde, 1st K.O.R.L. January to December 1917		
Heading	War Diary of 1st Bn The Kings Own Regt. From 1st January 1917 To 31st January 1917 Volume No. 1		
War Diary		01/01/1917	31/01/1917
Heading	War Diary of 1st Bn The King's Own Regt From:- 1st February 1917 To:- 28th February 1917 Volume 3		
War Diary		01/02/1917	28/02/1917
Miscellaneous	Report on Raid by the Enemy on Morning of 3rd February 1917 East of Bouchavesnes	04/02/1917	04/02/1917
Heading	War Diary of 1st Battalion The King's Own Regiment From:- 1st March 1917 To:- 31st March 1917 Volume 4		
War Diary	Corbie In Billets	01/03/1917	01/03/1917
War Diary	Corbie	02/03/1917	04/03/1917
War Diary	Villers-Bocage in billets	05/03/1917	05/03/1917
War Diary	Beauval in billets	06/03/1917	06/03/1917
War Diary	Villers-Le-Hopital in billets	07/03/1917	07/03/1917
War Diary	Villeroy-Sur-Authie in billets	08/03/1917	08/03/1917
War Diary	Villeroy-Sur-Authie	09/03/1917	22/03/1917
War Diary	Marquay in billets	23/03/1917	23/03/1917
War Diary	Marquay	24/03/1917	31/03/1917
Heading	War Diary 1st Bn The King's Own Regiment Coming Period From 1st April to 30th April 1917 Volume No. 5		
War Diary	Marquay	01/04/1917	06/04/1917
War Diary	Y Camp	07/04/1917	09/04/1917
War Diary	H 22 art	10/04/1917	18/04/1917
War Diary	Reserve Trenches Blangy	19/04/1917	19/04/1917
War Diary	British 2nd Line	20/04/1917	21/04/1917

Type	Description	Start	End
War Diary	Montenescourt	22/04/1917	22/04/1917
War Diary	Manin	23/04/1917	23/04/1917
War Diary	Etree-Wamin	24/04/1917	27/04/1917
War Diary	Sars-Lez-Bois	28/04/1917	28/04/1917
War Diary	Hermaville	29/04/1917	29/04/1917
War Diary	E of St. Nicholas	30/04/1917	30/04/1917
Miscellaneous	Attack Orders by Lt. Colonel O.C.Borrett D.S.O. Commanding 1st Battalion The King's Own Regiment	02/04/1917	02/04/1917
Miscellaneous	Appendix A		
Operation(al) Order(s)	Operation Order No. 20	11/04/1917	11/04/1917
Miscellaneous	Spar		
Miscellaneous	Try Viorl		
Map	Tracing "A"		
Heading	War Diary 1st Battn The Kings Own Regt From 1st May To 31st May 1917 Volume No 5		
War Diary		01/05/1917	13/05/1917
War Diary	Hermaville	14/05/1917	31/05/1917
Operation(al) Order(s)	12th Infantry Brigade Operation Order No. 38	01/05/1917	01/05/1917
Miscellaneous	Appendix B		
Operation(al) Order(s)	12th Infantry Brigade Operation Order No. 37	30/04/1917	30/04/1917
Operation(al) Order(s)	To Recipients of 12th Inf. Bde Operation Order No. 38	02/05/1917	02/05/1917
Miscellaneous	List of Officers and Strength of Battalion		
Miscellaneous	Appendix C		
Miscellaneous	Appendix "G"		
Miscellaneous	Appendix G		
Map	Appendix A to War Diary		
Map	Appendix A		
Map			
Miscellaneous	Appendix D		
Heading	War Diary of 1st Bn The Kings Own Regt From 1st June 1917 To 30th June 1917 Volume VI		
War Diary	Hermaville	01/06/1917	10/06/1917
War Diary	Arras	11/06/1917	11/06/1917
War Diary	In Trenches E of Fampoux	12/06/1917	15/06/1917
War Diary	Fife Camp	16/06/1917	17/06/1917
War Diary	Brown Line	18/06/1917	19/06/1917
War Diary	Rifle Camp	20/06/1917	27/06/1917
War Diary	In Trenches	28/06/1917	30/06/1917
Heading	War Diary of 1st Bn The King's Own Regt From 1st July To 31st July 1917 Volume 8		
War Diary	In the Field	01/07/1917	31/07/1917
Heading	War Diary of 1st Bn The King's Own Regt From 1-8-17 To 31-8-17 Volume No 8		
War Diary		01/08/1917	31/08/1917
Heading	War Diary of 1st Bn The King's Own Regt From 1st Sept To 30 Sept 1917 Volume No. 9		
War Diary		01/09/1917	30/09/1917
Heading	1st Bn the King's Own Regt From 1-10-17 To 31-10-17 Volume No 10		
War Diary	Hulls Farm Camp near Brielen	28/09/1917	28/09/1917
War Diary	Au Bon Gite	29/09/1917	30/09/1917
War Diary	Langemarck	01/10/1917	01/10/1917
War Diary	Redan Camp	02/10/1917	08/10/1917
War Diary	Saragossa Camp near Canal Bank	08/10/1917	08/10/1917
War Diary	Langemarck	09/10/1917	09/10/1917
War Diary	Polecappel	09/10/1917	12/10/1917

Type	Description	From	To
War Diary	Polecappel	12/10/1917	14/10/1917
War Diary	Proven	15/10/1917	16/10/1917
War Diary	St Jan Ter Biezen	17/10/1917	19/10/1917
War Diary	Harbarcq	20/10/1917	23/10/1917
War Diary	Achicourt	24/10/1917	31/10/1917
Map	Map A		
Map	Map B		
Map	Map C		
War Diary	Achicourt	01/11/1917	16/11/1917
War Diary	Monchy Le Preux	17/11/1917	30/11/1917
Heading	War Diary of 1st Bn The King's Own Regt From 1st Dec 1917 To 30th Dec 1917 Volume 12		
War Diary	Achicourt	01/12/1917	25/12/1917
War Diary	Arras	26/12/1917	31/12/1917
Heading	4th Division 12th Infy Bde 1st Bn the King's Own Roy. Lancs Jan 1918-Feb 1919		
War Diary		01/01/1918	01/02/1918
Heading	12th Brigade Herewith War Diary of this unit for the Month of February 1918		
War Diary	In the Field	01/02/1918	28/02/1918
Heading	War Diary 1st Battn. The King's Own (Royal Lancaster) Regiment March 1918		
Heading	12th Brigade. Herewith War Diary of the unit for the Month of March 1918		
War Diary	At Berneville	01/03/1918	16/03/1918
War Diary	In Trenches	17/03/1918	31/03/1918
Miscellaneous	4th Division No. G.A. 13/5	04/03/1918	04/03/1918
Heading	12th Brigade 4th Division 1st Battalion King's own Royal Lancaster Regiment April 1918		
War Diary		01/04/1918	30/04/1918
Heading	12th Infantry Brigade Herewith War Diary for the Month of May 1918		
War Diary		01/05/1918	31/05/1918
Miscellaneous	Appendix "A"		
War Diary		01/06/1918	30/06/1918
War Diary		01/07/1918	31/07/1918
Heading	12th Inf. Brigade Herewith War Diary of the unit for the Month August 1918		
War Diary		01/08/1918	31/08/1918
Miscellaneous	1st. Battalion The King's Own Regiment		
Heading	12th Infantry Brigade Herewith War Diary For the Month of September.		
War Diary		01/09/1918	30/09/1918
War Diary		01/10/1918	31/10/1918
War Diary		01/11/1918	11/11/1918
War Diary	Field	12/11/1918	31/12/1918
Miscellaneous	Returning The Colours-1st Batt. King's Own Royal Lancaster Rgt.		
Heading	12th Infantry Brigade Herewith War Diary of The Unit For The Month of April 1918		
Heading	1st Bn the KOR Lancs Jan & Feby 1919		
Heading	13th DLI Jan Oct 1916		
War Diary	Field	01/01/1919	31/01/1919
War Diary	Morlanwelz	01/02/1919	28/02/1919
Heading	WO95/1506 12th Bde 4th Div 2 Btn Monmouthshire Regt Nov 1914-Jan 1916		

Heading	War Diaries 2nd Monmouthshire Joined From U.K, Nov & December 1914 Oct 1915		
Heading	12th Brigade 4th Division Disembarked Havre 6.11.14 Joined 12th Bde 20.11.14 2nd Battalion Monmouthshire Regiment November 1914		
War Diary		31/10/1914	31/10/1914
War Diary	Northampton Southampton	05/11/1914	05/11/1914
War Diary	Havre	06/11/1914	08/11/1914
War Diary	Boulounge/Calais	09/11/1914	10/11/1914
War Diary	St Omer/Wizerne	11/11/1914	11/11/1914
War Diary	St Omer/Wizerne	09/11/1914	09/11/1914
War Diary	Wizerne	09/11/1914	20/11/1914
War Diary	Period	21/11/1914	30/11/1914
Miscellaneous	Strength Return		
Heading	2nd Battalion Monmouthshire Regiment December 1914		
War Diary		01/12/1914	29/12/1914
Heading	4th Division War Diary 12th Infantry Bde 2nd Battn Monmouth Reg. January To October 1915		
Heading	War Diary 2nd Battn. Monmouthshire Regt. January 1915		
Heading	12th Brigade 2nd Monmouthshire Rgt. Vol III 1-31.1.15		
War Diary		01/01/1915	31/01/1915
Heading	12th Inf Bde. 4th Division 2nd Battn. Monmouthshire Regt. February 1915		
Heading	12th Brigade 2nd Monmouth Regt (T) Vol IV 1-28.2.15		
War Diary	Le Bizet	01/02/1915	28/02/1915
Heading	12th Inf Bde 4th Division 2nd Battn. Monmouthshire Regt. March 1915		
Heading	12th Brigade 1/2nd Monmouthshire Rgt. Vol V 1-31.3.15		
War Diary	Le Biset	01/03/1915	31/03/1915
Heading	12th Inf. Bde. 4th Division 2nd Battn. Monmouthshire Regt. April 1915		
Heading	12th Brigade 2nd Monmouthshire Rgt. Vol VI 1.4-2.5.15		
War Diary			
Heading	12th Inf. Bde. 4th Division 2nd Battn. Monmouthshire Regt. May 1915		
Heading	12th Brigade 1/2 Monmouth Rgt Vol VII 3-31.5.15		
War Diary		03/05/1915	31/05/1915
Heading	2nd Battn. Monmouthshire Regiment June 1915 Missing		
Heading	12th Inf. Bde. 4th Division. 2nd Battn. Monmouthshire Regt. 24th-31st July 1915		
Heading	1/2nd Monmouthshire Vol VIII From 24th to 31st July 1915		
War Diary		24/07/1915	31/07/1915
Heading	12th Inf. Bde. 4th Division. 2nd Battn. Monmouthshire Regt. August 1915		
Heading	4th Division 2nd Monmouth Vol IX August 15		
War Diary		01/08/1915	12/08/1915
War Diary	Auchon Villiers	08/08/1915	24/08/1915
War Diary	Mailly	24/08/1915	30/08/1915
War Diary	France Somme Mailly, Maillet	30/08/1915	30/08/1915
War Diary		02/08/1915	31/08/1915

Heading	12th Inf. Bde. 4th Division. 2nd Battn. Monmouthshire Regt. September 1915		
Heading	2nd Monmouths Vol X Sept 10 6th Oct 15		
War Diary	Mailly	01/09/1915	02/09/1915
War Diary	Beaussart	03/09/1915	08/09/1915
War Diary	Buissart	08/09/1915	16/09/1915
War Diary	Varennes	16/09/1915	22/09/1915
War Diary	Mailly	23/09/1915	29/09/1915
War Diary	Varennes	30/09/1915	06/10/1915
Heading	12th Inf. Bde. 4th Division 2nd Battn. Monmouthshire Regt. October 1915		
Heading	4th Division 1/2nd Monmouths Vol XI Oct 15		
War Diary	Varennes	01/10/1915	08/10/1915
War Diary	Opposite Beaumont-Hamel	08/10/1915	08/10/1915
War Diary	Somme France	09/10/1915	13/10/1915
War Diary	Beaussart	13/10/1915	27/10/1915
War Diary	Mailly	30/10/1915	31/10/1915
Heading	4th Division War Diaries 1/2, Monmouths-Joined 12th Bde. 4-11-15 To L. of C, 30-1-16 November To January 1915-16 (To 29 Div Reserve)		
Heading	107th Bde 4th Division. This Battn Joined From 12th Bde. 4.11,15 1/2 Battn Monmouthshire Regiment November 1915		
Heading	4th Division 1/2 Monmouthshire Regt. Nov Vol XII		
War Diary	Mailly	01/11/1915	05/11/1915
War Diary	Trenches	07/11/1915	13/11/1915
War Diary	Beaussart	14/11/1915	19/11/1915
War Diary	Brigade Reserve	20/11/1915	25/11/1915
War Diary	Beaussart	26/11/1915	30/11/1915
War Diary	Brigade Reserve	02/12/1915	08/12/1915
War Diary	Beaussart	08/12/1915	08/12/1915
Miscellaneous	Headquarters. 107th Infantry Brigade.		
Heading	107th Inf Bde. 4th Division 1/2nd Battn Monmouthshire Regiment December 1915		
Heading	107th Bde 1/2 Monmouth Rgt. Dec. Vol XIII		
War Diary		01/12/1915	01/12/1915
War Diary	Brigade Reserve	02/12/1915	03/12/1915
War Diary	Beaussart	08/12/1915	13/12/1915
War Diary	Brigade Reserve	13/12/1915	16/12/1915
War Diary	Beaussart	17/12/1915	20/12/1915
War Diary	Brigade Reserve	21/12/1915	31/12/1915
Heading	107th Inf Bde 4th Division This Battn Was Transfered to L of C 30.1.1916 1/2nd Battn Monmouthshire Regiment January 1916		
Heading	2 Monmouth Regt. Jan Vol XIV		
War Diary	Mailly	01/01/1916	30/01/1916
War Diary	Halloy	31/01/1916	31/01/1916

4th Division
War Diaries

1 Bn. King's Own Royal Lancaster Regt.

1914 August To December

Dec 1917

12th Brigade.
4th Division.

Disembarked BOULOGNE 23.8.14.

1st BATTALION

KING'S OWN ROYAL LANCASTER REGIMENT

AUGUST 1 9 1 4

Army Form C. 2118.

1st Bn The King's Own (Royal Regiment)

WAR DIARY
or
INTELLIGENCE SUMMARY.
(Erase heading not required.)

Instructions regarding War Diaries and Intelligence Summaries are contained in F.S. Regs., Part II. and the Staff Manual respectively. Title pages will be prepared in manuscript.

Hour, Date, Place	Summary of Events and Information	Remarks and references to Appendices
5 pm 4.8.14. Shaft Barrack Dover	Telephone message received from Brigade HQ 12th Inf. Bde. "Mobilize".	WD Bridson
5.8.14 " "	1st Day of Mobilization. Progress Normal. Lieutenants Steele & Baird Douglas & Band arrived from Depot.	WD
6.8.14 " "	2nd Day of Mobilization. Draft of 105 reservists under Lieut Bookelbank 3rd Batt. arrived from Depot at 6 am. Progress "Normal"	
7.8.14 " "	3rd Day of Mobilization. Draft of 400 reservists with Lieuts Hamley & Lewis Beaumont 3rd Batt. arrived Dover 6 am.	WD
8 pm 7.8.14 Shaft Rth Dover	Received telephone message from Brigade HQ "Hold yourself in readiness to entrain at once".	
2 am – 3.30 am 8.8.14 "	4th Day of Mobilization. Battalion left Dover Town Station in 2 trains. Capts C.L. HODGSON & Lieut BRIDSON left the Details & 1st Reinforcements. Capts CLUTTERBUCK left 15 a.m.t.	Strength & see Appendix I WD

Army Form C. 2118.

WAR DIARY
or
INTELLIGENCE SUMMARY.
(Erase heading not required.)

Instructions regarding War Diaries and Intelligence Summaries are contained in F.S. Regs., Part II. and the Staff Manual respectively. Title pages will be prepared in manuscript.

Hour, Date, Place	Summary of Events and Information	Remarks and references to Appendices
10am–11.30am 8-8-14. CROMER.	Battalion arrived at CROMER and were bivouacked in field near station.	nil
6.30pm 8.8.14	Marched to billets in CROMER Town.	nil
9-8-14 CROMER.	5th Day of Mobilization. Battalion went for 7 mile route march.	
10-8-14 CROMER. 8.30am. 6am.	6th Day of Mobilization. 5 unfits dispatched to 3rd Batln at SALTASH. Orders received that Brigade would proceed to NORWICH. Captain MAYES R.A.M.C. joined as M.O. to Battalion.	Appendix 2
5.30pm – 6.30pm.	Battalion proceeded in 2 trains to NORWICH and were billeted in neighbourhood of ST ANDREWS HALL. Transport except carts went by road.	nil
11-8-14. NORWICH.	7th Day of Mobilization. — Captain JOINER joined. Battalion spent day on MOUSEHOLD HEATH at Brigade training.	
6.30pm	Capt. CLUTTERBUCK and 122 other ranks 1st reinforcements with Lieut. COULSTON 3rd Batln + base kits of Batln arrived. Base kits stored at NORWICH STATION.	nil

Army Form C. 2118.

WAR DIARY
or
INTELLIGENCE SUMMARY.
(Erase heading not required.)

Instructions regarding War Diaries and Intelligence Summaries are contained in F.S. Regs., Part II. and the Staff Manual respectively. Title pages will be prepared in manuscript.

Hour, Date, Place	Summary of Events and Information	Remarks and references to Appendices
11.8.14. NORWICH. 8 p.m.	Orders received that Brigade would move on 12th inst from NORWICH to neighbourhood of DRAYTON. Lieut E. BURKE placed on sick list & removed from Establishment.	
12.8.14. NORWICH 10.a.m.	8th Day of Mobilization. 3 medically unfit men sent to SALTASH. Brigade marched from NORWICH to billeting area. Battalion billeted at HORSHAM St PAITHS. Headquarters A & B Coys in Workhouse. C Coy in Schoolhouse. D Coy in village. Lieut Stephen JAMIESON 3rd Battn arrived to join Battn	
13.8.14. HORSHAM St PAITHS. 7.a.m. 7.30.a.m.	9th Day of Mobilization. Green Draft for service abroad despatched to SALTASH. 13 details to replace draft arrived from SALTASH. Battalion spent day at training in STRAWLESS Park	

WAR DIARY
or
INTELLIGENCE SUMMARY.

(Erase heading not required.)

Army Form C. 2118.

Hour, Date, Place	Summary of Events and Information	Remarks and references to Appendices
14.8.14 HORSHAM ST FAITHS.	10th Day of Mobilization. — Battalion spent day at SPIXWORTH training 3 medically unfit men left for SALTASH.	RSM RSM
15.8.14 HORSHAM ST FAITHS.	11th Day of Mobilization. Battalion spent day training at STANLESS HALL.	RSM
16.8.14 HORSHAM ST FAITHS.	12th Day of Mobilization. — Church of Battalion. "Day of Rest".	Appendix 3. RSM

WAR DIARY
or
INTELLIGENCE SUMMARY.
(Erase heading not required.)

Army Form C. 2118.

Hour, Date, Place	Summary of Events and Information	Remarks and references to Appendices
17-8-14 HORSHAM ST FAITHS	13th Day of Mobilization. In accordance with W.O. letter* M.D. 10-8-14 - following officers left the Battn. and went forward to depot. 2 Lieut. J.A. BEVAN. Lieuts. E.E.B. STEVENS, J.H.C. COULSTON, J.P. JAMIESON. Battn. took part in Brigade Field Day in neighbourhood of DRAYTON.	* See Appendices 4
4 P.m.	Brigade received orders to move to HARROW. 1st 2nd Reinforcements under Capt Johns to remain behind. They entrained for DOVER on 19.8.14. 14th Day of Mobilization.	
18.8.14 HORSHAM ST FAITH. 2. a.m.	Battalion marched to NORWICH and entrained for WEMBLEY in 2 trains (leaving at 6.15 am & 8.15 am).	
WEMBLEY 10.40 am to 1.40 pm	Battalion arrived at WEMBLEY & camped in neighborhood of NEASDEN. - The 12th Inf: Bde were encamped in the area. 11th Bde at HARROW and 10th Bde at HARROW WEALD.	

Army Form C. 2118.

WAR DIARY
or
INTELLIGENCE SUMMARY.
(Erase heading not required.)

Instructions regarding War Diaries and Intelligence Summaries are contained in F.S. Regs., Part II. and the Staff Manual respectively. Title pages will be prepared in manuscript.

Hour, Date, Place	Summary of Events and Information	Remarks and references to Appendices
19-8-14. WEMBLEY 2 pm	15th Day of Mobilization Batt'n: 10th Batt'n 18 recruits Rcd'n March.	end
20-8-14. WEMBLEY.	16th Day of Mobilization Batt'n: practiced the attack in morning — Medical. Last Batch of 48 men inoculated making Total of 480 inoculated since mobilization.	end
21-8-14. WEMBLEY SOUTHAMPTON.	Received order to entrain at 4 pm — left WEMBLEY 4.30 pm — arrived Southampton 9.30 pm & 10.30 pm — Batt'n in 2 trains arr. 6 pm Batt'n embarked on A.S. Saturnia same night — Lancashire Fusiliers also embarked —	end

WAR DIARY
or
INTELLIGENCE SUMMARY.
(*Erase heading not required.*)

Army Form C. 2118

Instructions regarding War Diaries and Intelligence Summaries are contained in F. S. Regs., Part II. and the Staff Manual respectively. Title pages will be prepared in manuscript.

Hour, Date, Place	Summary of Events and Information	Remarks and references to Appendices
22-8-14 AT SEA	Left Southampton at 9am. Arrived BOULOGNE 11pm – Slept on board –	end
23-8-14 BOULOGNE	Disembarked 6am marched to rest camp at St LEONARDS. Marched back to Boulogne & entrained at cet 9 pm – Strength officers 26 – 974 other Ranks	end
24-8-14 BUITRY	Left BOULOGNE 1am – Arrived BUITRY. 10am. disentrained Marched to LIGNY-EN-CAMBRENSIS – 13 miles N of village –	end
LIGNY-EN-CAMBRENSIS	Lancashire Fusiliers arrived 4pm. Received orders 10pm to march to WESLEY at 1am	end

Army Form C. 2118.

WAR DIARY
or
INTELLIGENCE SUMMARY.
(Erase heading not required.)

Instructions regarding War Diaries and Intelligence Summaries are contained in F. S. Regs., Part II. and the Staff Manual respectively. Title pages will be prepared in manuscript.

Hour, Date, Place	Summary of Events and Information	Remarks and references to Appendices
25.8.14 VIESLY	Brigade arrived VIESLY 5 a.m. Took up position facing N.W. Shelled in afternoon from direction of QUIEVY. Marched at 9 p.m. via BETHELCOURT and CAUDRY through LIGNY to HAUCOURT.	
26.8.14 HAUCOURT	Battalion arrived HAUCOURT about 4.30 a.m. halted in village. At 5.30 a.m. marched up hill due N. of HAUCOURT & formed up preparatory to entrenching position on right of Lancashire Fusiliers who had been out in chief. Themselves this since before dawn — As soon as battalion halted — about 6 a.m. heavy artillery fire was opened on them from direction of WAMBAIX Station. Followed shortly by shrapnel. Batt. and Bam; then retired to position in front of HAUCOURT village. About 8 a.m. an advance was ordered on to hill - Batt. saw Fus. & Warwickshire Regt. took part. The top of the hill was reached but (owing were enfiladed by m. gun & shrapnel from the my. left flank & forced — at am retire to HAUCOURT line.	Casualties 26.8.14 Officers Killed — Lieut. Dyke Capt. Treford " Childrick Lieut. Shirt-Pelham Lieut. Brocklebank Wounded Capt. Maren " Grece " Higgins Lt Catts 2nd/Lt. Woundal & Missing Lieut. Irvine " Barnett Darryla

WAR DIARY or INTELLIGENCE SUMMARY.

Army Form C. 2118.

Hour, Date, Place	Summary of Events and Information	Remarks and references to Appendices
26-8-14 2 am HAUCOURT	Battalion was told to take up position round HAUCOURT. One detachment went in to take up right section about 300 along HAUCOURT-LIGNY road. Left section about 300 yards along HAUCOURT-ESNES Road. Enemy's shell fire slackened from about 11 am till 3 pm when it was renewed with increased vigour. Advance on to hill due north was made about 4 pm. Lt. Collier wounded at about 6pm. Brigade was ordered to retire to SEVIGNY – left Whitchurch. Received order to retire through SEVIGNY to – billet in GOUY LE CATELET. Remainder Batt under Maj Parker remained in village – took a party of 17-18 Brigade. About 9.35 pm an attack on village was made by Germans who were finally driven out. At about 11 pm 15 party	Casualties 26-8-14 Cm Coy — Missing Capt Stephen Longe — Other Ranks Killed Wounded & Missing 431 —

WAR DIARY
or
INTELLIGENCE SUMMARY.
(Erase heading not required.)

Army Form C. 2118.

Instructions regarding War Diaries and Intelligence Summaries are contained in F. S. Regs., Part II. and the Staff Manual respectively. Title pages will be prepared in manuscript.

Hour, Date, Place	Summary of Events and Information	Remarks and references to Appendices
26-8-14 HAUCOURT	left village and after passing through German lines bivouced the Brigade near HANCOURT in afternoon of 27ᵗʰ	
27.8.14. CATELET ROISEL HANCOURT	12" Detachment of a Bde who billeted for night in GOUY marched at 5.30 am via HARGICOURT and joined remainder of Bde & 4ᵗʰ Div in Headqrs at ROISEL about noon. 4ᵗʰ Divn took up position facing N. near HANCOURT about 6 pm ~ marched at about 9.30 pm ~ 12ᵗʰ Bde acting as rear guard ~	

WAR DIARY
or
INTELLIGENCE SUMMARY.
(*Erase heading not required.*)

Army Form C. 2118.

Hour, Date, Place	Summary of Events and Information	Remarks and references to Appendices
28-8-14. MALIGNY SANCOURT	Bde arrived MATIGNY at about 6 am - Marched to SANCOURT to look up position to cover crossing of ? Divisions at HAM	
ESMERY-HALLON	Marched again at 11 am onward R. SOMME at OFFOY - through on to ESMERY-HALLON	
CAMPAGNE	where halt/ed about 2 hrs were made at 4 pm - Marched again through FRENCHES to CAMPAGNE where Bde halted billeted for night.	
29-8-14 CHEVILLY	At 8.30 am, Bde marched to CHEVILLY where they halted until 9 pm. 11" Bde was in neighbourhood of	
NOYON	SERMAIZE - 10" Bde near BUSSY. At 9 pm Division marched through NOYON - halted out	
SEMPIGNY	11 pm for 2 hrs near SEMPIGNY -	

Army Form C. 2118.

WAR DIARY
or
INTELLIGENCE SUMMARY.
(Erase heading not required.)

Instructions regarding War Diaries and Intelligence Summaries are contained in F. S. Regs., Part II. and the Staff Manual respectively. Title pages will be prepared in manuscript.

Hour, Date, Place	Summary of Events and Information	Remarks and references to Appendices
30-8-14 SEMPIGNY FONTENOY	Brigade marched from SEMPIGNY at about 1-30 a.m. Joined Division at CARLEPOINT and marched thence to FONTENOY. 12" Battn took up outpost position on heights about 1 mile north of FONTENOY.	sd/
31-8-14 FONTENOY FORÊT DE COMPIEGNE VERBERIE	Battalion at 5.30 a.m. left outpost position & halted an hour for breakfast in FONTENOY & rejoined Brigade in the FORÊT DE COMPIEGNE. Arrived at VERBERIE in evening & billeted about 1 mile S. of town.	sd/

War Diary
1st Bn The King's Own R[oyal]

12th Brigade.
4th Division.

1st BATTALION

KING'S OWN ROYAL LANCASTER REGIMENT

SEPTEMBER 1914

Army Form C. 2118.

WAR DIARY
or
INTELLIGENCE SUMMARY.
(Erase heading not required.)

Instructions regarding War Diaries and Intelligence Summaries are contained in F.S. Regs., Part II. and the Staff Manual respectively. Title pages will be prepared in manuscript.

Hour, Date, Place	Summary of Events and Information	Remarks and references to Appendices
1-9-14 VERBERIE BARON	Brigade marched from VERBERIE at 6am. Marched onto road & made look up position on hill near ? Farm for about 4 hour in middle of day. Then marched to BARON. Arrived 7pm. marched again with dawn at 11pm.	
2-9-14 DAMMARTIN	Arrived DAMMARTIN at about 10am. Battalion on outposts. Not long - marched again at 10.20pm	
3-9-14 LAGNY SERRIS	Marched through LAGNY (at 6am - arrived SERRIS about 11am - Brigade bivouacked	

Army Form C. 2118.

WAR DIARY
or
INTELLIGENCE SUMMARY.
(Erase heading not required.)

Instructions regarding War Diaries and Intelligence Summaries are contained in F.S. Regs., Part II. and the Staff Manual respectively. Title pages will be prepared in manuscript.

Hour, Date, Place	Summary of Events and Information	Remarks and references to Appendices
4-9-14 SERRIS CHATEAU FERRIERES	Halted at SERRIS until 5pm. then Rob marched on CHATEAU FERRIERES. Arrived 7pm. Marched again at 2am. 5-9-14	
5-9-14 BRIE-COMTE-ROBERT	Arrived 6am. Bivouacked 2 miles S. of Brie on bank. of R. YERRES. End of Retirement. 100 hrs. Reinforcement under Capt. Jones arrived. Advance Begun.	
6-9-14 BRIE COMTE ROBERT	Marched from Bivouac at 1 am. Dimn T.R. Saunders had a trooper on my L-54/5 on face J.O-3-19 M.Y. AT FERRIERES. Kings no Inniskilling formed a left flank guard having sighted no GERMANS. Reported Brig ade. at SERRIS and Batln. lolt up without food in pouring rain till about midday of COURRATE	Lieut Stevens & dropped on my pencil talk.

WAR DIARY or INTELLIGENCE SUMMARY.

Army Form C. 2118.

(Erase heading not required.)

Instructions regarding War Diaries and Intelligence Summaries are contained in F.S. Regs., Part II. and the Staff Manual respectively. Title pages will be prepared in manuscript.

Hour, Date, Place	Summary of Events and Information	Remarks and references to Appendices
Monday 7th Sept 14 COURROIS	Left COURROIS at about 10 a.m. - Brigade crossed Marne River at MONTARGIN and marched to key lowland of LA HAUTE MAISON where	
LA HAUTE MAISON	they bivouacked for night. 5th Inf Regt and Inniskilling were pushed out the night in to bivouac.	
Tuesday 8th Sept 1914 LA HAUTE MAISON	Brigade advance at 6am. Maitland formation through country N. of LA HAUTE MAISON as far as PIERRE LEVÉE. Then halted 1½ to	That W.E.G. Shell is wounded by report late in the day. Report from C.O. R.R. 8th.
LA FERTE SOUS JOUARRE	PETIT COURROIS. Halted here for 1 hour. Brigade then pushed on to LA FERTÉ — rear TUARRE as advanced guard. Kept up own & Divisional B. ech. forced Van Guard. Reached TUARRE about midday & saw Uhlans in village, who retired. Battalion went on to LA FERTÉ sous MARNE	

WAR DIARY or INTELLIGENCE SUMMARY.

Army Form C. 2118.

(Erase heading not required.)

Instructions regarding War Diaries and Intelligence Summaries are contained in F.S. Regs, Part II. and the Staff Manual respectively. Title pages will be prepared in manuscript.

Hour, Date, Place	Summary of Events and Information	Remarks and references to Appendices
Tuesday 8th Sept 1914 LA FERTÉ SOUS JOUARRE	Rough Sketch of LA FERTÉ showing position held by X.O. 6 pm 8.9.14 [sketch of MARNE R., PETIT MORIN R., CHATEAU, roads to JOUARRE, positions marked ①②③] Found at 1 a.m. N of R. MARNE though held by enemy who went also entrenched in being In Avenue Bridge at (1) was 50 in up before our arrival. Bullet lines to front wound (a same bridge also at (2) - Houses in neighbourhood of (3) full of snipers also woods on hill to E of. About 5 pm enemy cleaned out of town to S of river & bridges at (2) were blown up - King's own relieved by R Welsh Fus Jonied Brigade in bivouac ½ mile up W of S.M. 15 W R^d	Casualties on 8.9.14 Killed: Lieut Woodgate No 6044 CpI Pike No 8780 Pte EVERSON Wounded: Major Parker 4 Men Lieut Woodgate led party which had to push on to bridge N.E from CHATEAU. He & Major Parker accompanied by following Other ranks had to retire him 6044 CpI Pike - 8780 Pte Everson 7101 - Pte Turner. 8889 L.C.Ed. Evans 6094 Pte Henderson.

WAR DIARY
or
INTELLIGENCE SUMMARY.
(Erase heading not required.)

Army Form C. 2118.

Hour, Date, Place	Summary of Events and Information	Remarks and references to Appendices
Wednesday 9th Sept 1914 TARTEREL September 8	Brigade troops occupied heights near TARTEREL. Enter Regt. holding the Rifle Brigade covered road in evening at CHAMIGNY LA SAUSSOY. Rn. In Regt. in reserve near LUZANCY started the night	
Thursday 10th Sept 1914 VAUX-SOUS-COULOMB	Reached river King's own advanced 15 yards to bridge at LA SAUSSOY. remained there until 3 p.m. awaiting other divisions and transport. Artillery came. Then marched via DHUISSY COULOMBS & joined brigade which was in VAUX-SOUS-COULOMBS.	Lieut. Sanderson & draft of 100 joined. B Company Regimental Serjt Major having been acting as acting to 3rd Army Corps Head Quarters 2-9-14.
FRIDAY. 11th Sept 1914	Marched from COULOMBS, via MONTIGNY to BICCY sur OURCQ. There Brigade billeted for night	

WAR DIARY or INTELLIGENCE SUMMARY.

Army Form C. 2118.

Hour, Date, Place	Summary of Events and Information	Remarks and references to Appendices
Saturday 12 Sep 1914 BILLY sur OURCQ TIGNY SEPTMONTS	Marched 9 am to TIGNY — heard heavy firing to N.W. proved to be French at SOISSONS — 10th Bde were advanced guard — 12th Bde head of March Body. Billeted for night in farm ½ mile north of SEPTMONTS	
Sunday 13th Sept.	During night 1st Bde crossed R. AISNE at VENIZEL & seized heights above BUCY=LE=LONG. 12th Bde marched at 7 am & halted just west of BUCY sur AISNE & came under shell fire from direction of CROUY. Advanced axis VENIZEL & across R. BUCY=LE=LONG to ST MARGUERITE & took up a position on high ground north of 1st Bde. Enemy occupying strong position CHIVRES — VREGNY — CROUY	Casualties

Army Form C. 2118.

WAR DIARY
or
INTELLIGENCE SUMMARY.
(Erase heading not required.)

Hour, Date, Place	Summary of Events and Information	Remarks and references to Appendices
Monday 14th Sept 14	Remained in same position [illegible] batteries shelled wood all day.	Capt Wilson killed Capt Cooper & 4 men wounded.
15th Sept 14	Same position	
16th Sept 14	"	
17th "	"	Capts Von Abelle, Magram Norris Lieut Morris & Lieut Braun arrived — [illegible] 17/9/14
18th Sept		

Army Form C. 2118.

WAR DIARY
or
INTELLIGENCE SUMMARY.
(Erase heading not required.)

Instructions regarding War Diaries and Intelligence Summaries are contained in F.S. Regs., Part II. and the Staff Manual respectively. Title pages will be prepared in manuscript.

Hour, Date, Place	Summary of Events and Information	Remarks and references to Appendices
19" Sep. 1914	Position held by 12" Bde. forms enemy 7 - 13" xx /batteries German (number 15 or 3) gun our front shore gun position to front line then about 50 y Vigny	

[Hand-drawn sketch map showing positions with labels:]
- 10 & 11 Bde
- Ferme Moizy
- King'm Own Leics of Loos
- Essex Regt
- ref of flank
- L. of Fus.
- CHIVRES held by Germans
- ham. Skutlings
- ST. MARGUERITE Village
- Fahrenhein Lows

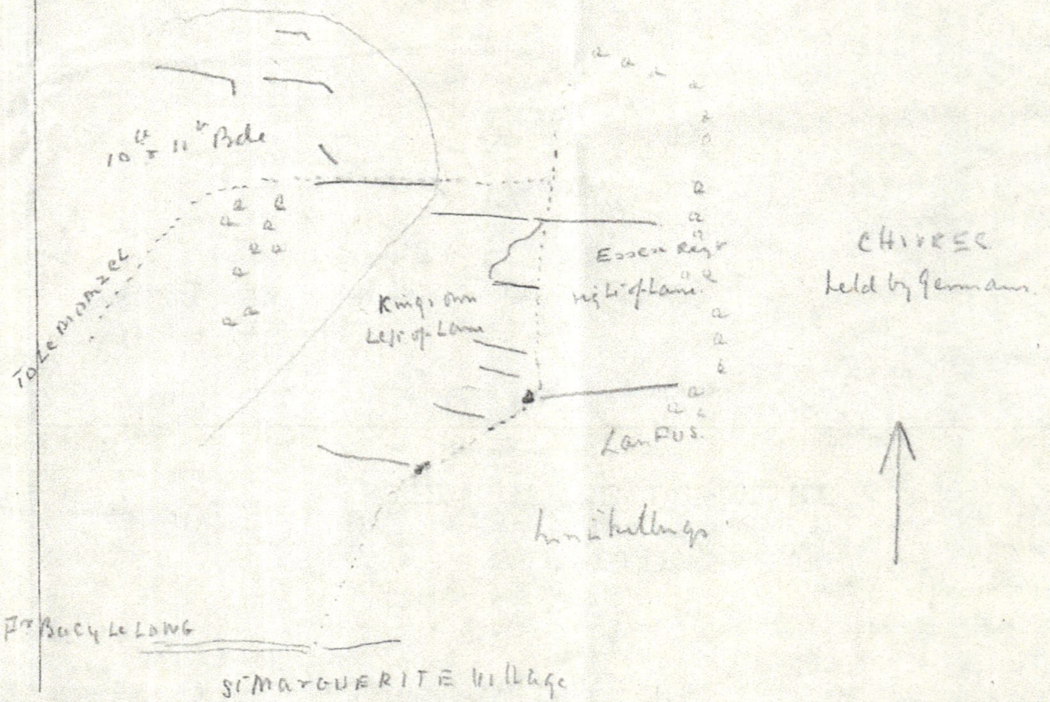

Army Form C. 2118.

WAR DIARY
or
INTELLIGENCE SUMMARY.
(Erase heading not required.)

Instructions regarding War Diaries and Intelligence Summaries are contained in F. S. Regs., Part II. and the Staff Manual respectively. Title pages will be prepared in manuscript.

Hour, Date, Place	Summary of Events and Information	Remarks and references to Appendices
20th Sep St Marguerite	Same position	
21st Sep "		
21st Sep "		

Army Form C. 2118.

WAR DIARY
or
INTELLIGENCE SUMMARY.
(Erase heading not required.)

Instructions regarding War Diaries and Intelligence Summaries are contained in F.S. Regs., Part II. and the Staff Manual respectively. Title pages will be prepared in manuscript.

Hour, Date, Place	Summary of Events and Information	Remarks and references to Appendices
23rd Sept Marquand	Same as orders	Lieut A Shan Brown & draft 16.9 have arrived also 57 shaft him
24th Sept Marquand	Village heavily shelled in evening	
25th Sept	Heavy firing heard in distance G.N.E.	

Army Form C. 2118.

WAR DIARY
or
INTELLIGENCE SUMMARY.
(Erase heading not required.)

Instructions regarding War Diaries and Intelligence Summaries are contained in F.S. Regs., Part II. and the Staff Manual respectively. Title pages will be prepared in manuscript.

Hour, Date, Place	Summary of Events and Information	Remarks and references to Appendices
26th Sept 1914 8 a.m. Sthanvents	Thing shells heard in distance BNE.	
27th September 1914 Sthanvents	Intended to dig an advanced trench 100x in from of our prev entrenchm. Enemy preparing us from about 8 p.m. to prevent & prevented work until 2 a.m.	
28th September 1914 Sthanvents	Quiet day. Evening Entrenched dug g.g in advance trench.	

Army Form C. 2118.

WAR DIARY
or
INTELLIGENCE SUMMARY.
(Erase heading not required.)

Instructions regarding War Diaries and Intelligence Summaries are contained in F.S. Regs., Part II. and the Staff Manual respectively. Title pages will be prepared in manuscript.

Hour, Date, Place	Summary of Events and Information	Remarks and references to Appendices
29th September 1914 Shanguenti 4 pm	Same position. About 4 pm. enemy's gun which had taken up position about 1000 yds N of our front line & opened as usual fire on us.	
8 pm	Heard from 11th Bde that strong columns of infantry had deployed to their front — attack expected during night. Enemy 1st 2 Coys from atars [?] 500 in front of Warnesh been chosen. Divl. Column to drop if 9's own arrived.	
11 pm 30th September 1914 Shanguenti	Quiet night. On account of expected attack did not continue in digging advanced trench — Put Philip's post. Wilks in present trench.	

12th Brigade.
4th Division.

1st BATTALION

KING'S OWN ROYAL LANCASTER REGIMENT

OCTOBER 1914

Attached:-

2 sketches shewing location of
12th Infantry Brigade.

Army Form C. 2118.

WAR DIARY
or
INTELLIGENCE SUMMARY.
(Erase heading not required.)

Instructions regarding War Diaries and Intelligence Summaries are contained in F. S. Regs., Part II. and the Staff Manual respectively. Title pages will be prepared in manuscript.

Hour, Date, Place	Summary of Events and Information	Remarks and references to Appendices
1st October 1914 Champenoux	Heard at 5pm that at 7.30pm 12th Bde would be relieved by 10th Bde and to would take our position held at M 1889 by 15th Bde — About 1 mile due West. Moves were carried out in by bus —	
2nd October 1914 Champenoux	Halt except of some snipping by day & by bus 5 by bus both by night and	
3rd October 1914 Champenoux	Position taken up by 12th Bn Cts bear M 1889 in by Lt. of 1st Battalion as described attached sheet — At 5pm Germans were totally able to able into eastern corner of Champenoux village. Not another attack by 9.30pm they few rockets into ground by left of our front & much deal of snipping throughout night.	New Colonel Cunnigh? joined from England to command

Army Form C. 2118.

WAR DIARY
or
INTELLIGENCE SUMMARY.
(Erase heading not required.)

Instructions regarding War Diaries and Intelligence Summaries are contained in F. S. Regs, Part II. and the Staff Manual respectively. Title pages will be prepared in manuscript.

Hour, Date, Place	Summary of Events and Information	Remarks and references to Appendices
4.10.14 S¹ Marguerite	Eastern end of D'hargincte shelled again at about 11 a.m. evidently trying to find our trenches.	Capt Leader M.V.C. arrived
5.10.14 D'hargincte	At 4 p.m. general bombardment of enemy's front by 4 Divisional Artillery. Part of Brigade hussars went across river to support during night.	
6.10.14 S¹ Marguerite	4 12th Brigade relieved by trench troops during night. Brigade HQ blanket via MARLIN S¹ 12 OCT to S¹ EMILY—ACY—ECUIRY—to RULLECOURT SEPT MONT arriving there at dawn on 7ᵗʰ.	

WAR DIARY
or
INTELLIGENCE SUMMARY.
(Erase heading not required.)

Army Form C. 2118.

Hour, Date, Place	Summary of Events and Information	Remarks and references to Appendices
7-10-14 SEPTMONTS	Day of Rest — Bath. went for route march 4 to 6.30pm	Lieut Benson 3rd Batt joined
8.10.14 SEPT MONT	at 2pm Brigade left SEPT MONT & went into billets at AMBRIEF (Kings Own & Essex) and CHACRISE (Iniskilling & Lancashire Regt) —	
9.10.14 AMBRIEF	Rest of Division marched away drawing eng to to broken on rail head. 12th Bde on left in support of French troops who took our firing line (previously held by 4 Div) from BUCY (5. C. R4. Went for route march in afternoon — Transport left in afternoon for rail head entraining station	Major Parkin & Lieut Bridger & Broadhurst joined Col.
10.10.14 AMBRIEF	Route march, and advance arm scheme in morning	

WAR DIARY
or
INTELLIGENCE SUMMARY.
(Erase heading not required.)

Army Form C. 2118.

Hour, Date, Place	Summary of Events and Information	Remarks and references to Appendices

11.10.14
AMBRIE R.
LE MEUX

At 9 am 12" I/ Bde left CHARLISE on route for louvain belonging to General Supply train I went via Marbéring Villers Côterets, Verbere to Le Meux — there we arrived about 3 pm, bivouced near station until evening, then entrained, Kings in mor kor left LE MEUX at 2.30 am 12 inst

12 . 13 . 14
In Train to
HAZEBROUCK

In train via AMIENS BOULOGNE. Calais to HAZEBROUCK, where we arrived at 9 pm —
Cleared out of train & went into billets in town at 11 pm.
10 " T 11" Btles already arrived & in billets —
N° 8 East of town — 6" Divsion on our right —
12" Bde in reserve in HAZEBROUCK

WAR DIARY or INTELLIGENCE SUMMARY

Army Form C. 2118.

Hour, Date, Place	Summary of Events and Information	Remarks and references to Appendices
13-10-14 Tuesday HAZEBROUCK to METEREN	At 9 am 4th Division invaded and entrained in 2 columns. 10 h.j. Rode to 32nd Bde RFA passed by L column. VIth Div'n in on our right. Brigade ordered to range CROIX then Enemy reported to be holding METEREN. Bry Lt attached this Battaye – 400 east side of R CROIX. LES ORMES. METEREN wood. Kings own and E. Lan. Regt in front line – Lan. Fusiliers & Inniskillings in 2nd line. Kings Own allotted front 400 x in rifle pits of road. Reached in this R. of METEREN W about 2 pm having first opened in on farm village & wood. Enemy had excellent field of fire. About 4 pm we were shelled at close range by 9 pdr Bty's with of village. There was a lange c.q. b. between our right & VIth Division. Lan Fus were sent to fill in gap, but a 6 way bttl? h they had not reached position. Kings Own Regt started to entrench pocket at 9 pm	C. Coy (Capt Toms) & D Coy (Capt Jackson) in front line. B Coy (kia mile?) & A Coy R Res Hodgson in 2nd line

Rough Sketch showing
position held by K.O.S.B.
night of Feb 13.10.14
K.O. shown thus —
Germans hindered thus —

+ METEREN

HQrs Headquarters
& Regt Aid Post

Germans marched up this road at 9 pm

WAR DIARY or INTELLIGENCE SUMMARY.

Army Form C. 2118.

(Erase heading not required.)

Hour, Date, Place	Summary of Events and Information	Remarks and references to Appendices
13.10.14 Lo/s METEREN	Ran Jus: marched into villages by W & found enemy had evacuated it. Kings Own stayed in billets all night. (Rough sketch of Meteren & but M Creagh attack attached)	Casualties List 4 mm KirkDaldum & 44 men killed. Kurt Walker, Kur Braden & 32 men wounded & 15 men missing.
14.x.14 Meteren. Bailleul.		
15.x.14. Bailleul.	At 6pm 12th Bde. advanced to Le LEUTTE and stayed in support of 11th Bde's attack in ERQUINGHIEM line. 11th Bde advanced towards NIEPPE. 12th Bde advanced 6.13 am 11 & went into billets.	
16.x.14 PETIT PONT	11th Brigade held line ERQUINGHIEM - NIEPPE - 12th Bde continued line to left through PLOEGSTEERT - CHAU - to D. of R DOUVE (Osten d steel) - from left to right Lan. Fus. Inns. Ever. Kings Own were in support at PETIT PONT. Cavalry Division were on left.	

Army Form C. 2118.

WAR DIARY
or
INTELLIGENCE SUMMARY.
(Erase heading not required.)

Hour, Date, Place	Summary of Events and Information	Remarks and references to Appendices
17-X-14 Petit Port	Same position until evening when 12" Belg. line advanced to line Le Touquet station - Le Gheer - then a farm – limited fuel through Chau. - to F. F. P.W. S.W. of St Douvé. – Bn. Fus. about 9¼" – Irons. Fus on their left and Enc.r from Le Gheer to left of bn. – K.O. in support at Petit Port.	
19.10.14 Le Touquet	At 5.30 a.m. 13" ordered to attack Le Touquet in conjunction with Som. Fus. marched by via Ploegsteert to F.r. King's Own ordered to attack from Le Bizet – Le Touquet – road to R.248. – Som. Fus. from road in Chavire to down to left. Line of railway gained with no actual opposition, but bey. and enemy brought strong fire to bear from outskirts of Frelun across river – Machine. By evening Le Touquet was held as lay our Coys were out C. Coy being sent.	

WAR DIARY
or
INTELLIGENCE SUMMARY.
(Erase heading not required.)

Army Form C. 2118.

Hour, Date, Place	Summary of Events and Information	Remarks and references to Appendices
18.10.14 Le Touquet	Ordered to left - to fill up gap in line. The 18th Bde made attack on Ephlighien during day from other side of river but could not reach railway. much casualty.	Cancelled Killed Major J.H. Marsh Wounded 5 men.
19.10.14 Le Touquet -	Position stationary - 10" Brigade attacked ag'in to make an attack Radinghem. In evening our company on left (C) ordered to advance to Wim x Y Z (on shell)	
20.10.14	Our column advancing was made on this coy on left. & enemy getting right in round their flank. They were forced to retire to orig'l ad'vs in Le Touquet road. A coy was sent up to reinforce this line - and 1 Coy F noisily placed in support at F.	

WAR DIARY
or
INTELLIGENCE SUMMARY.
(Erase heading not required.)

Army Form C. 2118.

Hour, Date, Place	Summary of Events and Information	Remarks and references to Appendices
14.10.14. METEREN. 13 MILLEUL	At 10 a.m. left trenches & went into billets in farms in neighbourhood. 11" advanced eastward towards Bois. 13 Milleul. 10" Bde in reserve in rear. At 2 p.m. 13" Bde marched into 13 Milleul into billets for the night.	
15.10.14. 13 MILLEUL	11" B'nights towards holding line ERQUINGHEM. WIEPPE. PLAEGSTREET. At 7 pm 12" Bde advanced to LE LENTRE & halted in road for night.	
16.10.14. PETIT PONT.	4" Divn took up defensive line from Te buried from ERQUINGHEM. through NIEPPE PLOEGSTEERT. C.H.Q. E. Farm near D. of ROUVE — 11" Bde a/far as NIEPPE. Divn 12" Bde in left — Regt. 6 in fillary indu-Lan: PUS. Inm: PUS. Envn. Regt — King's Own Regt & went into billets in Reserve at PETIT PONT. 10" Bde is in Reserve near LE LENTRE	

Army Form C. 2118.

WAR DIARY
or
INTELLIGENCE SUMMARY.
(Erase heading not required.)

Hour, Date, Place	Summary of Events and Information	Remarks and references to Appendices
21.10.14. LE TOUQUET.	At dawn a very strong attack was made on Lt. G.H.E.E.R. position by enemy. Inniskillen on left of R.F. Coy were forced to retire. Enemy now got right around flank of their 2 coys to their by ones who were in command behind them from road to position 200 x in rear. When they tried to dig themselves in. 1/2 Bey & 1/2 Coy was sent up to reinforce. Trench was railway line at one. Retaken - but 2 advances during day to try to retake trench are + roads proved unsuccessful. A combined attack was made in afternoon by portion of 1 min R. Inf. 2 mi Fus: 1st Lan. through Bors de Ploegsteert on Le G.H.E.E.R. which was retaken. Gap between R. KARNAVE + Le G.H.E.E.R. filled in by 1 Coy Innis. 1st Coy E. Lanc.	Casualties 20th + 21st inst. Killed - Major Byrne 3+4 Capt. Landon Capt. Heaving Wounded Lieut Smith De Robinson 4+ Kent. 76 Capt Worrallde. Wounded & missing 2+76 Lieut Brown Lieut Coulton. Otto Ranks. Killed. 21 Wounded 78 Missing. 76.

WAR DIARY
or
INTELLIGENCE SUMMARY.
(Erase heading not required.)

Army Form C. 2118.

Hour, Date, Place	Summary of Events and Information	Remarks and references to Appendices
22.x.14. L.E.B. & T=T.	Trenches as & roads were found vacated by enemy. At 2.am - 1 Rifle down, the Batln were relieved by Hants Regt & marched into Billets at Le Bizit.	

Army Form C. 2118.

WAR DIARY
or
INTELLIGENCE SUMMARY.
(Erase heading not required.)

Hour, Date, Place	Summary of Events and Information	Remarks and references to Appendices

2.3.X.14
Le Bizet.

In billets at Le Bizet.
Evening Brigade crossed R. Lys by pontoon bridge at Le Bizet + took over line set CHAPELLE D'ARMENTIERES formerly held by 17th Bde (?). Lantern to Ermeer front out into front line - Kais tun from near Rue du Bois to tram LILLE road - E側 in this (left to railway Kings Own Frs) : Bn preme arrived in billets in CHAP: D'ARMENTIERES. (D Coy KOR sent out for 24 hrs to help Enrea Reg t on left of this line

24 – X – 14

Army Form C. 2118.

WAR DIARY
or
INTELLIGENCE SUMMARY.
(Erase heading not required.)

Hour, Date, Place	Summary of Events and Information	Remarks and references to Appendices
24 - X. 14 CHA. DARMENTIERES	As my hi Kings Own relieved Hampshire in front line relief was delayed until I am owing to attack made by enemy on 18th Brigade who was holding line to my left of Rue du Bois. Balin was kept in reserve at Jes Nanques - Artillery opening with their bomb -	
25. X. 14 CHA. DARMENTIERES	Enemy shelling Rue du Bois to my right line all day. The Batt held this line his retired slightly to the evening - Trench inundated front of Trenches held by K.O.R.R. to be re-dug during night.	

Army Form C. 2118.

WAR DIARY
or
INTELLIGENCE SUMMARY.
(Erase heading not required.)

Hour, Date, Place	Summary of Events and Information	Remarks and references to Appendices
26. X. 14	Enemy shelling Rue du Bois - made infantry attack at dawn which was repulsed - Occasional shelling of our trenches during day.	
27. X. 14	At dawn heavy shell fire sent on to Rue du Bois neighbourhood followed by infantry assault - 1 section of "D" Coy (which was in support of D.L.I.) called on to reinforce D.L.I. sent to left of section - This party was much put to [?] cannon who played on their all day. Both officers of D.L.I. & all men in the trench caught about 2 dozen were killed or wounded but infantry attack was repulsed with great loss - All our front trenches were also shelled during day. At 6 p.m. Bn. relieved King's Own & by 11 p.m. the line - battalion between to Billets in D'ARMENTIERES.	Casualties. Killed - 3 N.C.O.s men. Wounded. Capt. Vivian Lieut Bamm. 22 other ranks.

Army Form C. 2118.

WAR DIARY
or
INTELLIGENCE SUMMARY.
(Erase heading not required.)

Hour, Date, Place	Summary of Events and Information	Remarks and references to Appendices
Chapelle D'Armentières 28.x.14	In billets in Armentières	
29.x.14	Battalion relieved the Lancashire Fusiliers in trenches in evening	
30.x.14	In trenches	
31.x.14	In trenches - Lancashire Fus: and Innis killings were sent to Ploegsteert wood	1/4

2 Sketches
Shewing location
of 12" Bore

Instructions regarding War Diaries and Intelligence Summaries are contained in F. S. Regs., Part II. and the Staff Manual respectively. Title pages will be prepared in manuscript.

WAR DIARY
or
INTELLIGENCE SUMMARY.
(Erase heading not required.)

Army Form C. 2118.

Hour, Date, Place	Summary of Events and Information	Remarks and references to Appendices
	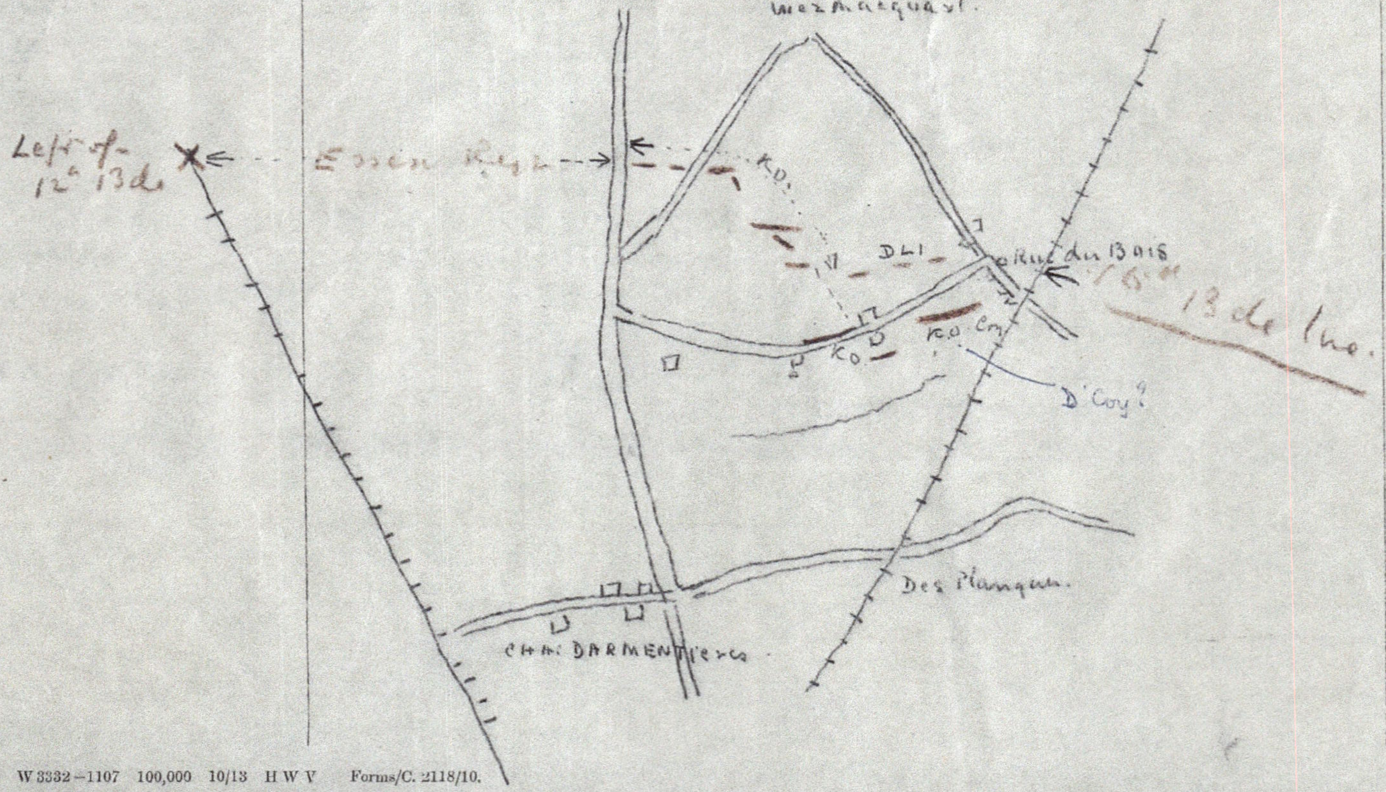Mezmacquart Left of 12th Bde Essex Regt K.O. DLI Rue du Bois 16th Bde line K.O. Coy K.O. D Coy? Des Planques Chin D'Armentieres	26 Oct 1914 onwards. This is probably position from night 26/10 when 16 Bde (? 18 Bde) withdrew somewhat making it necessary to re-dig some KO trenches on their right.

12th Brigade.
4th Division.

1st BATTALION

KING'S OWN ROYAL LANCASTER REGIMENT

NOVEMBER 1914

1. 1·11·14
2. 1·11·14
3. " 11 14
4. 11 14

h heinke
h heinke
h heinke
h heinke

WAR DIARY or INTELLIGENCE SUMMARY

Army Form C. 2118.

Hour, Date, Place	Summary of Events and Information	Remarks and references to Appendices
Chapelle D'armentieres		
5.11.14	In billets	
6.11.14	[illegible]	
7.11.14	Relieved tonight by Essex Regt & went into billets in Chapelle D'armentieres	
	At 6pm Battn was sent out to be in support of 12th Bde Brigade who were holding line from R.2 & S.6 own trench N½ E of Warneton. Since about 2.30pm. They shelled same trench as were dug by King's Own Many Tpm when 1st August was relieved in 18 October & Germans on left of line had rapped up to within 30 to 40 's of our trenches. C. Coy King's Own were left in support of rifle Bde at Chiès Peendu [illegible] at invaders	
	D Coy " Farm in rear of crossroads 13 Bn Coys were in reserve in LE NIEZE.	
8.11.14 – 20 August	Same position A Coy relieved D in evening.	

Army Form C. 2118.

WAR DIARY
or
INTELLIGENCE SUMMARY.
(Erase heading not required.)

Hour, Date, Place	Summary of Events and Information	Remarks and references to Appendices
Le Touquet	Same position	
9.11.14		
10.11.14	Battalion relieved Rifle Brigade in trenches from R. Lys. to Cross roads. at 6h	
	In trenches	
11.11.14		
12.11.14	Coy to man: trenches both on line from Cross roads to railway.	wounded Capt De Pury & Irving

Army Form C. 2118.

WAR DIARY
or
INTELLIGENCE SUMMARY.
(Erase heading not required.)

Instructions regarding War Diaries and Intelligence Summaries are contained in F. S. Regs., Part II. and the Staff Manual respectively. Title pages will be prepared in manuscript.

Hour, Date, Place	Summary of Events and Information	Remarks and references to Appendices
Le Touquet 26.11.14	Where can I write this	
Le Touquet 27.11.14	Quiet day. A Coy relieved B Coy in left half in evening.	
Le Touquet 28.11.14	Quiet day	
29.11.14	Karn. Jur. relieved us in trenches in evening. Batln. moved into billets in reserve in	
Armentières 30.11.14	In Billets	

STRENGTH RETURN.

Detail.	Officers Number.	Other ranks Number.	Remarks.
Strength of Unit on 30th Nov. 1914.	24	864	
Details, by arms attached to unit as in War establishment) A.S.C.) R.A.M.C.) A.O.C.) etc.		4 4 1	
Total	24	873	

Signature Barker Major
Unit Comdg 1st Bn The King's Own Regt

Date
3/12/1914.

URGENT.

This return to be completed and forwarded through the usual channel to reach Div. H.Q.'s by 12 M.D. on 3rd Dec. 1914.

(Sd) G. Smyth Osborne
for
Lt. Col.
A.A. & Q.M.G. 4th Div.

2/12/14.

12th Brigade
4th Division.

1st BATTALION

KING'S OWN ROYAL LANCASTER REGIMENT

DECEMBER 1 9 1 4

1st "B" Bn Kumar Regt

Army Form C. 2118.

WAR DIARY
or
INTELLIGENCE SUMMARY.

(Erase heading not required.)

Instructions regarding War Diaries and Intelligence Summaries are contained in F.S. Regs., Part II. and the Staff Manual respectively. Title pages will be prepared in manuscript.

Hour, Date, Place	Summary of Events and Information	Remarks and references to Appendices
Armentières 1.12.14	In Billets. 2.50 men inoculated - Draft of 49 men and 6 officers arrived to-day - Capt F R Scott Lieut Bem Vey Cheshire Regt (a tts) Lieut Taylor - to "relieve" gains and to govern	
2.12.14	In Billets In afternoon Batln marched to Government Baths at Nieppe and were there in platoons by H.R.H. the King The Prince of Wales was also present	1/1
3.12.14	In Billets The Batln relieved Kan Zey in trenches in the evening. All comn. in-road in trench for wire and in proper mds.	
de 7 Aug wed 4.12.14	In Trenches.	
5.12.14	In Trenches. Heavy rain all day - All comn. in-ard. Trenches flooded and breastworks	

F.J.

Army Form C. 2118.

WAR DIARY
or:
INTELLIGENCE SUMMARY.
(Erase heading not required.)

Instructions regarding War Diaries and Intelligence Summaries are contained in F.S. Regs., Part II. and the Staff Manual respectively. Title pages will be prepared in manuscript.

Hour, Date, Place	Summary of Events and Information	Remarks and references to Appendices
Le Touquet 6.12.14	In Trenches still wet	
7.12.14	Batln relieved by Lan Fus in the evening. Returned to billets in Armentières	1/1
Armentières 8.12.14	In Billets	
9.12.14	" "	
10.12.14	" "	
11.12.14	Batln relieved Lan Fus in trenches. Trench began	
Le Touquet 12.12.14	In Trenches	
20½ 13.12.14	" " Lieut Aitchison killed working at Listening Post. Command Trench	

Army Form C. 2118.

WAR DIARY
or
INTELLIGENCE SUMMARY.
(Erase heading not required.)

Instructions regarding War Diaries and Intelligence Summaries are contained in F.S. Regs., Part II. and the Staff Manual respectively. Title pages will be prepared in manuscript.

Hour, Date, Place	Summary of Events and Information	Remarks and references to Appendices
Le Touquet 14.12.14	To Trenches.	
15.12.14	In Trenches. Relieved by 2 F. in evening and went into billets in 2 E 131 2 E 1	
Le 13 ujet 16.12.14	In Billets	
17.12.14		
18.12.14		
19.12.14	Battn. should have relieved Norfolks in the Trenches evening of 19.inst. but postponed owing to an attack which "B" Coy made in afternoon. Regt. lent 1 Sub., 1 Sergt. & 20 men.	1st
20.12.14	Battn. went to trenches in afternoon — left two Coys in and had four in billets and garrisoned with a platoon.	
Le Touquet 21.12.14	Been there good deal of rain during day.	

Army Form C. 2118.

WAR DIARY
or
INTELLIGENCE SUMMARY.
(Erase heading not required.)

Instructions regarding War Diaries and Intelligence Summaries are contained in F.S. Regs., Part II. and the Staff Manual respectively. Title pages will be prepared in manuscript.

Hour, Date, Place	Summary of Events and Information	Remarks and references to Appendices
Le Touquet 22.12.14	In trenches. Fine day	
23.12.14	In trenches.	
24.12.14	2 Fusiliers relieved us in evening	
Le Bizet 25.12.14	In Billets (Xmas day - fine & frosty day)	1/15.
26.12.14	In Billets	
27.12.14		
28.12.14	Relieved Kensingtons in evening - Right High Command being by R F	
Le Touquet 29.12.14	In Trenches. Fine day. Enemy shelled barricade on railway at about 2.30 p.m. - 11. H.E shells dropped in and around barricade. Casualties 3 men wounded. Essex Regt had 3 killed & 3 wounded. Not much damage done except to barricade.	

WAR DIARY
INTELLIGENCE SUMMARY.

Army Form C. 2118.

Hour, Date, Place	Summary of Events and Information	Remarks and references to Appendices
Le Touquet 30.12.14	In trenches. Cold fine day. R. LVS employed its tanks — Enemy very active in sniping at working parties during day. 5 casualties.	
31.12.14	In trenches. Fine cold day. Enemy dropped about 11 H.E. shells behind Headqrs Farm. Very little sniping all day — At 11 pm (Tuesday i.e. by Berlin time) Enemy opened rapid fire all along their line which lasted for an ½ hour.	
Le Touquet 1.1.15	In trenches. Fine day — an artillery shelled Fulinghem in morning. Enemy replied by shelling about 30 H.E. shells round our Headqrs & shied the building. They also shelled hospital in Le Bizet and Bois Houblon. Am Fus relieved us in evening — bit — enght	

Headquarters
12th Infantry Brigade.

With reference to the man of this Battn: who was reported missing on the 23rd inst — I attach report of the O.C. Coy.

A Smith (?)
Captain
Comdg 1. The King's Own Regt

26.12.14.

10.45.

C Coy HQrs.

III.

This man is a Coy cook — I saw him in my barricade about 10 am. talking to the Sentry — I asked him what he was doing and he said he was going to see our Snipers — I thought the man strange, and thought for the moment he had been drinking. I walked past him to call the Corpl of the Barricade, and when I came back perhaps a minute later, I saw him about forty or fifty yards away walking towards the Snipers — The Corpl. had previously shouted to him, but he refused to come back. — I was afraid of drawing attention to him, and as it was beginning to snow hoped he would reach the Snipers in safety. This he managed to do — & from further information this evening I find he spoke to the Snipers & they allowed him to go forward alone to forage in some house in front. He has not been seen since, although they tried to locate him. He may possibly still be in one of the empty

(2).

Contd.

Houses, and fallen asleep - as I gather, he had been working pretty hard all night in the cookhouse - The man was well known to the Sentry on barricade guard - he said he tried to stop him but the man brushed past him - It all happened in a short space - while I was calling the Corporal from the room adjoining the Barricade. - The man appeared to me to be strange in his manner, and I do not think from questioning the Cooks, that he had been Drinking. - No shot of any kind was fired as he walked across to the Snipers Houses, and as it was very foggy and snowing I do not think he was fired at. - but probably taken prisoner by the German Snipers. - I gather that he did this once before & visited the Snipers by day. - He was quite rational at 5am this morning, and I attribute his action to his having gone suddenly mad.

T.R. Scott Capt.
O.C. C Coy.

WO95/1506

12th Bde
4th Div

1st KORL Regt
Aug 1914 - Feb 1919

4th Division
War Diaries
12th Infantry Bde
1st K.O.R.L. LESS Feb + Mar

~~January To October~~
1915

1915 JAN — 1915 DEC

4th Div.
12th Inf. Bde.

WAR DIARY

1ST KINGS OWN ROYAL LANCS. REGT.

J A N U A R Y

1 9 1 5

Army Form C. 2118.

WAR DIARY
or
INTELLIGENCE SUMMARY.
(Erase heading not required.)

Instructions regarding War Diaries and Intelligence Summaries are contained in F.S. Regs., Part II. and the Staff Manual respectively. Title pages will be prepared in manuscript.

Hour, Date, Place	Summary of Events and Information	Remarks and references to Appendices
Le Bizet		
2.1.15	In Billets – great deal of rain	
3.1.15		
4.1.15		
5.1.15	Returned down from to evening	
Le Touquet		
6.1.15	In trench we had an attack of various kinds acts from Enemy, River Lys rising	
7.1.15	In trenches. Very heavy bombardment about 5 pm. (A.m.) Gaps were flooded out of part of Steenbecque. Men were placed in high command, and Wolf Block houses. In trenches.	
8.1.15	In trenches	
9.1.15	In trenches Lieut. Fry relieved Western Yeomanry	

Army Form C. 2118.

WAR DIARY
or
INTELLIGENCE SUMMARY.
(Erase heading not required.)

Instructions regarding War Diaries and Intelligence Summaries are contained in F.S. Regs., Part II. and the Staff Manual respectively. Title pages will be prepared in manuscript.

Hour, Date, Place	Summary of Events and Information	Remarks and references to Appendices
Le Brunt		
10.1.15	Ch. Biller	
11.1.15		
12.1.15	Went to trenches in evening	
13.1.15		
Le Touquet		
14.1.15	In trenches Germans shelled Cordon Farm area	
	bombed us up til dawn.	
15.1.15	In trenches Quiet day but no-	
16.1.15	Quiet day	
17.1.15	Quiet day relieved by Hamshires in evening	

Army Form C. 2118.

WAR DIARY
or
INTELLIGENCE SUMMARY.
(Erase heading not required.)

Instructions regarding War Diaries and Intelligence Summaries are contained in F.S. Regs., Part II. and the Staff Manual respectively. Title pages will be prepared in manuscript.

Hour, Date, Place	Summary of Events and Information	Remarks and references to Appendices
Le Bizet		
18.1.15		
19.1.15	In Billets	
20.1.15		
21.1.15		
L'armentières		
22 Jan 1915	Went to trenches in evening	
23 Jan 1915	K. Trenches. Quiet day. German shelled houses in left of trenches town was held by housewife	1/4
24 Jan 15	K. trenches. quiet day	
25.1.15	Enemy dropped 27 H.E. shells in & around barracks in rear nway. No casualties - men took refuge in cellars & mines	

Army Form C. 2118.

WAR DIARY
or
INTELLIGENCE SUMMARY.
(Erase heading not required.)

Instructions regarding War Diaries and Intelligence Summaries are contained in F.S. Regs., Part II. and the Staff Manual respectively. Title pages will be prepared in manuscript.

Hour, Date, Place	Summary of Events and Information	Remarks and references to Appendices
Le Brioc		
26.1.15		
27.1.15	In Billets	
28.1.15		
29.1.15		
Le Touquet		
30.1.15.	Relieved Essex Regt in trenches in evening. Quiet day, ground dried up wonderfully, weather almost dry.	
31.1.15.	Quiet day. Reports of being concentration of enemy opposite E. D. D. coys.	

WAR DIARY
or
INTELLIGENCE SUMMARY.
(Erase heading not required.)

Army Form C. 2118.

Instructions regarding War Diaries and Intelligence Summaries are contained in F.S. Regs., Part II. and the Staff Manual respectively. Title pages will be prepared in manuscript.

Hour, Date, Place	Summary of Events and Information	Remarks and references to Appendices
	Attacked & Shelled of L'nes held by Kings Own N'lancaster Fusiliers during December & January	
	Key: British trenches, fortified houses etc. shown thus ———	
	German " " " " "	
	Portions of British front line in reserve trenches which became flooded in Dec & then shown thus - - -	
	Names of trenches	
	① Railway Barricade	
	② Ashram Trench } Garrisoned by A773 Coy. Kings Own Regt.	⑪ Barkenham "Farm" not permanently held by D.Coy.
	③ Left High Command During 4 days tour in trenches each of	Farm was Barricaded. (Kings Own Regt)
	⑥ Centre " these Coys. spent 2 days in trenches and	⑬ Cashio Farm permanent
	⑦ Right " " 2 in reserve in Bn. Headqrs Farm or ⑮	Support trench
	⑭ North Block	M.M. Portion of machine guns.
	④ Dreadnought trench }	
	⑤ Salient Trench.	
	⑧ Tree Trench	
	⑨ Tom brown Trench } Held by C. Coy Kings Own Regt	
	⑩ Snipers House	
	⑫ Barricade & Centre Coy Headqrs	

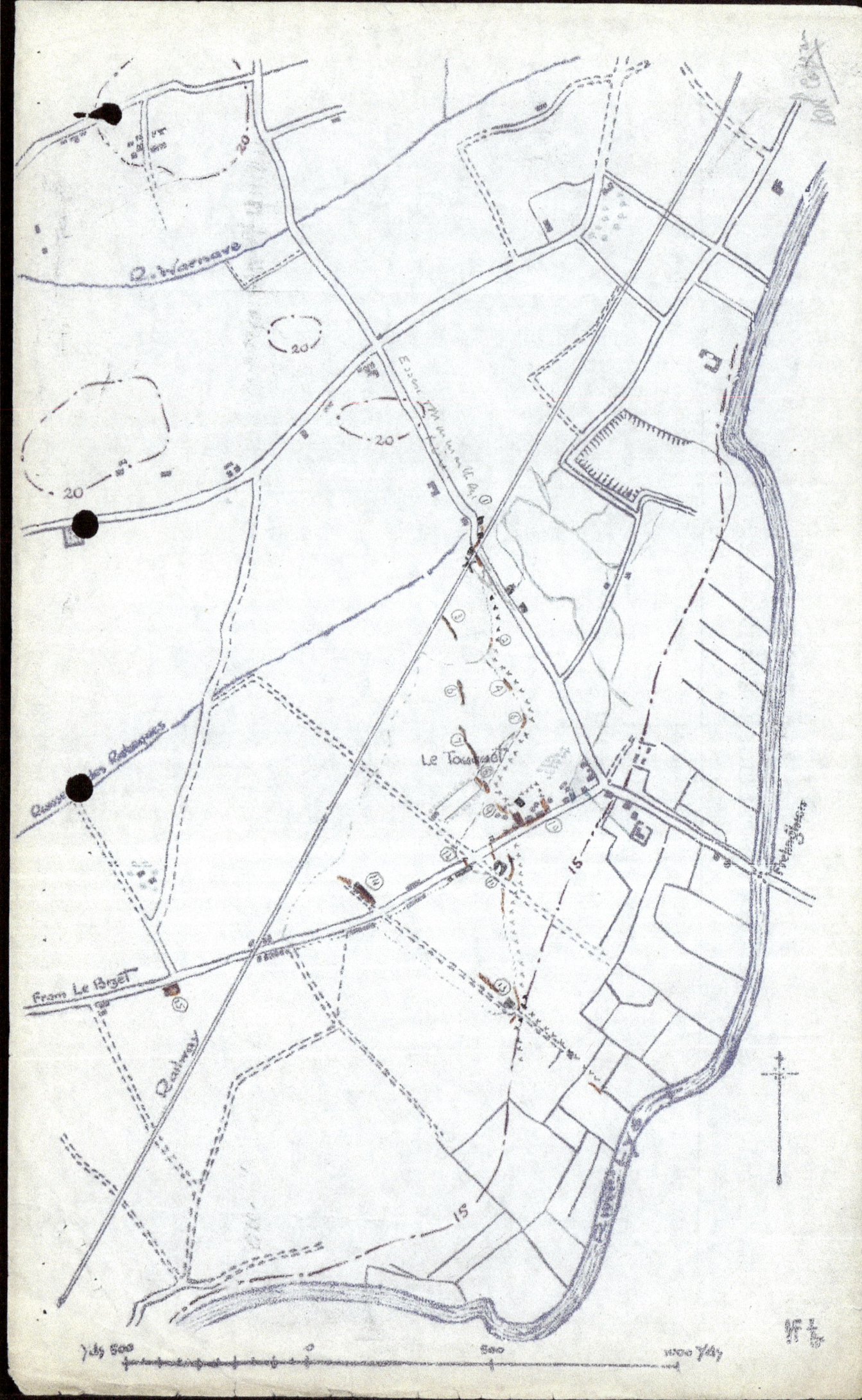

4th Div.
12th Inf. Bde.

1ST KINGS OWN ROYAL LANCS. REGT.

(WAR DIARIES FOR F E B R U A R Y & M A R C H MISSING)

4th Div.
12th Inf. Bde.

WAR DIARY

1ST KINGS OWN ROYAL LANCS. REGT.

A P R I L

1 9 1 5

WAR DIARY
or
INTELLIGENCE SUMMARY.
(Erase heading not required.)

Army Form C. 2118.

Hour, Date, Place	Summary of Events and Information	Remarks and references to Appendices
Le Touquet 4.4.15	In trenches. Very quiet day - at dusk enemy dropped rifle grenades into Railway Barricade, which killed 3 men, wounded 1 officer (Napier Clavering) and 5 men.	
5.4.15	In trenches. Good deal of rapid Com[munication] wire admin[?] head up railway. Has completed also Blencowe head saved[?] passed on to Ennis line -	
6.4.15	In trenches. Showery day - sniping very active round outer lines - also several rifle grenades we replied with rifle grenades and 1 lb. from 2 gdr. at 10 pm.	
7.4.15	Quiet day - deal of rain during day but trenches wet. Quiet day - Relieved by Leicesters in evening.	sgd

WAR DIARY or INTELLIGENCE SUMMARY.

(Erase heading not required.)

Army Form C. 2118.

Hour, Date, Place	Summary of Events and Information	Remarks and references to Appendices
La Bizet 8.4.15	In billets. During night it was found War Germans were continuing forward on line from southern trench - It was decided to blow one more up.	
9.4.15	In billets. Raid was exploited at 8.30am. Trench parties by a bombardment of our artillery & repaid fire from Men. Fire in the trenches. Two heavy mortars also bombarded 1/6 school house wall. huns died great damage to Enemy front wall. also blistered wire entanglements. 2/0 Battalion from 9 army also 2pm - Enemy replied by rifle, high commands also R.A Platoon & RF Howitzer in afternoon until 5.9 hrs. Post pos 5.9 shells into Bizet.	
10.4.15	In billets. Enemy shelled to Ployt (Ridge) Church this morning at 9am until 5.9 hrs. Also shelled bombs to Cherry Lane ridge.	

Army Form C. 2118.

WAR DIARY
or
INTELLIGENCE SUMMARY.
(Erase heading not required.)

Hour, Date, Place	Summary of Events and Information	Remarks and references to Appendices
11-4-15	In Billets. In afternoon enemy shelled with heavy shells front support & two home & reserve trenches - they damaged a few of support lines & set fire to one hut in pugh 13 Coy - No relieved Essex 7th in trenches in evening. In Trenches	
12-4-15	At 2 pm enemy put 39 S.Q. shells into trenches - have 14 casualties - knocked down parapet by twice head which was repaired at night	
13-4-15	In trenches. Enemy very busy with L.M.G. bullets all day. no damage.	
14-4-15	In trenches - Quiet day.	
15-4-15	In trenches. Van Tuc mortars & reserve arts. From entries today - We been relieved at night by East Lancs this from 11 & 13 Cos	

(9 29 6) W 4141-463 100,000 9/14 H W V Forms/C. 2118/10

WAR DIARY
or
INTELLIGENCE SUMMARY.
(Erase heading not required.)

Army Form C. 2118

Hour, Date, Place	Summary of Events and Information	Remarks and references to Appendices
Le Biget 16-4-15	In Billets - at 8 am enemy put few heavy shells round the Biget Church -	Lieut Grimley admitted to hospital
17.4.15	In Billets	
18.4.15	In Billets. Enemy shelled La Biget Church heavily with S.G. hun. Had to change our Headqtrs. Lt returned to Kames in hounds in evening.	
19.4.15	In trenches. at about 4 pm Mr Kyle him in at "Berlin" tunnel reported that they saw electric flashes down trench from my LG gallery. Capt Woodgate went to investigate and also saw them.	Lance Corp injured to the arteries
Le Touquet 20.4.15		

WAR DIARY or INTELLIGENCE SUMMARY

Army Form C. 2118.

Hour, Date, Place	Summary of Events and Information	Remarks and references to Appendices
Le Touquet 20 - 4 - 15 Cont.	Shortly afterwards when Lieut L Fulton and 2 men were watching from listening gallery, they saw flashes again and then many head & shoulders came in & formed "let into" man gallery. Three shots were fired in our Stylis dis appeared. Capt Woodgate & No Sergt Rentals followed by No Capt Edwards (men stop) went up line as far as listening gallery fired 3 rounds - placed a lamp and in this manner worked up to the enemy. Short way down right gallery found their enemy had pulled down sandplanks & east. They fired two rounds over this and in a few minutes this fire was replied to by German - Firing & was kept up, and a sandbag barricade began	German Trench [sketch with labels: R&L Gallery, Listening Gallery, ?-17, Railway barricade] Shell of time - 13 am each received at ×

WAR DIARY
or
INTELLIGENCE SUMMARY.
(Erase heading not required.)

Army Form C. 2118.

Hour, Date, Place	Summary of Events and Information	Remarks and references to Appendices
Le Touquet 20.4.15 Cont'd	At about 6.30 pm when barricade was nearly finished the Germans exploded a charge at that end. We had four men in trench — two Three managed to get out — but one, Pte Stephens was overcome by the fumes — Several efforts were made to rescue him by Capt Woolryche - No other, but these were defeated by the fumes. Capt Woolryche became unconscious & was taken to hospital. The Germans had evidently stored up my L/Gallery when working along this tunnel and were discovered only point in time. Sentries were left at "my his own end down to cellar from which the tunn. was started —	and

WAR DIARY
or
INTELLIGENCE SUMMARY.
(Erase heading not required.)

Army Form C. 2118.

Hour, Date, Place	Summary of Events and Information	Remarks and references to Appendices
Le Touquet 21.4.15.	Where Lieut. Brennan gave in tired at Rudry Barracks had considerably diminished this morning and by 11 am it was possible to enter mine again – Body of Sp. Stephenson was recovered and it was found that no damage had been done to our main gallery. At 12 noon. 3 horses were heard which proved that Germans were counter mining & had approached within 2 yards of one of the galleries of my turn from the "Juypers Home". It was decided to change its end of this gallery to face it as soon as possible & note at changing it was continued throughout the night.	

WAR DIARY
or
INTELLIGENCE SUMMARY.

Army Form C. 2118.

(Erase heading not required.)

Hour, Date, Place	Summary of Events and Information	Remarks and references to Appendices

Lt Leinster

22.4.15

The mine at Sinken Home was fired at 7.15 a.m. It was followed by 10 seconds rapid fire from neighbouring trenches — German front loopholed wall was a good deal damaged. The mine also unexpectedly blew up a drain (D) which extended across the road —

Enemy replied by shelling our Sinken house heavily, both S. 9 and Little Willie. They also shelled moved 18" Howitzer, and L. Bget.

At 12 noon. They began heavy bombardment of Railway barricade bombing 4.5, 5.9 shells in and around it. Both barricades were badly breached. And huts damaged. Casualties 2 men killed. 1 wounded.

Remarks column:
≈≈≈ Mine fired by our mine in morning of 22nd
----- Drain (D) blown up by our mine.
X Mine exploded by Enemy evening 22nd.

German trench
X
Sinken House

Army Form C. 2118.

WAR DIARY
or
INTELLIGENCE SUMMARY.
(Erase heading not required.)

Hour, Date, Place	Summary of Events and Information	Remarks and references to Appendices
Le Touquet (Contd.) 22-4-15	At dark work on repairing trench was begun & completed by daylight. At 2 after noon damage to hut furnaces done by shells in morning was begun to be repaired. Work delayed by enemy shelling at ar 9hrs with "Little Willie". At about 12 midnight enemy exploded a mine at point X (see sketch previous page). Reason why mine was exploded is unknown — it did no damage.	
23.4.15. Le Bizet	Quiet day. Relieved by E Lancs in evening	L Billets
24.4.15		L Billets
25.4.15		L Billets

Army Form C. 2118

WAR DIARY
or
INTELLIGENCE SUMMARY.
(Erase heading not required.)

Instructions regarding War Diaries and Intelligence Summaries are contained in F. S. Regs., Part II. and the Staff Manual respectively. Title pages will be prepared in manuscript.

Hour, Date, Place	Summary of Events and Information	Remarks and references to Appendices
Le Bizet 26.4.15	L Billets	
27.4.15	L Billets. Relieved E Lancs in trenches in evening. At 9pm heard that 1/2 "Hants" Bde is going to Ypres. 10 pm 1/Bde had gone Motor Bus to Ypres some days previously.	
Le Touquet 28.4.15	L trenches. Nax. Inns. E Lancs and Essex Regt. marched off to Billets at 1 pm. E Yorks (1/13ds) relieved us in trenches in evening. At 11.30 pm Battln to march to Billets arrived 3.30 am. Went into billets – however Hqrs. and L Lancs moved also.	

WAR DIARY
or
INTELLIGENCE SUMMARY.
(Erase heading not required.)

Army Form C. 2118

Instructions regarding War Diaries and Intelligence Summaries are contained in F.S. Regs., Part II. and the Staff Manual respectively. Title pages will be prepared in manuscript.

Hour, Date, Place	Summary of Events and Information	Remarks and references to Appendices
Bailleul 29.4.15.	Spent day in billets in Bailleul	
30.4.15.	12: Bde marched at 8am via LOCRE to about 2 miles S of VLAMERTINGHE — reached 1.30 pm. Then marched via LA BRIQUE (5 late up line of trenches north of YPRES held by 13" Inf Bde. Line adv anced 150 Yards East. King's Own, & Lan Fus in front trench. Rest had been in support. Heavy cannonade hem wards & Shares New Canal. Bad march as road was shelled the whole way.	

4th Div.
12th Inf. Bde.

WAR DIARY

1ST KINGS OWN ROYAL LANCS. REGT.

M A Y

1 9 1 5

Army Form C. 2118.

WAR DIARY
or
INTELLIGENCE SUMMARY.
(Erase heading not required.)

Instructions regarding War Diaries and Intelligence Summaries are contained in F.S. Regs., Part II. and the Staff Manual respectively. Title pages will be prepared in manuscript.

Hour, Date, Place	Summary of Events and Information	Remarks and references to Appendices
WIELTJE.		
1 - 5 - 15	At 2 pm after heavy bombardment by artillery & both scales finished Belts & French made attack on hill 29. Sixth & Belts Coms advanced through Essex trenches. Attack apparently failed — we now held to East — passage things/ no news — but in attaching troops came through.	Lieut Pryn killed while cutting wire. Capt Woods returned from hospital at Boulogne.
2 - 5 - 15	At about 4:30 pm enemy were approaching gas agam. Line held by 12" & 10" Pates o - Essex kept their trenches but retained Knoll — with exception of about 10 yds where Kings pen stayed in their trenches. Nam Fus retired from this line & suffered heavily from enemy's artillery fire — though keeping in the retiring clouds of gas. Shortly after this gas the enemy attacked our centre in a half hearted way but were stopped by rifle &	

WAR DIARY or INTELLIGENCE SUMMARY

Army Form C. 2118

(Erase heading not required.)

Hour, Date, Place	Summary of Events and Information	Remarks and references to Appendices
WULVERGHEM		
2.5.15 contd	Machine gun fire. They however got into "Lisbeiring Petitt" Farm, but on being charged by Cpl Cosby & about 20 men fled - Our own artillery then shelled the but of farm. 2 & & Miss Bulli & 2 & Hughs came up & reoccupied trenches vacated by Leins, Zinn & & S. Lemen. 10% men their trenches air wight.	Lieut Greenwood } killed Lieut Taylor } Capt Hodgson wounded Capt Hay a R.A.M.C. " Lieut Dakin Bishop (gassed)
3.5.15	At day break it was discovered Germans had again occupied trenches Petitt Farm. Lieut h Cullord & bombing party tried to turn them out unsuccessfully (Lieut h was bombed up to top of our line (held by D Coy)) very heavily.	Lieut h Cullord killed
4.5.15	Heavy bombardment of right of our line to Shell Trap Farm nearly all day.	Lieut Hearle to Hosp. gassed.

WAR DIARY
or
INTELLIGENCE SUMMARY.

(Erase heading not required.)

Army Form C. 2118

Hour, Date, Place	Summary of Events and Information	Remarks and references to Appendices
Wulverghem		
5.5.15.	Quiet morning. About 5 pm heavily shelled by Shrapnel & heavily bombarded and a good number of Obus left their trenches.	
	4 m wilt Regt relieved S. Lancs in evening.	
6.5.15.	Heavy artillery bombardment went of day.	
7.5.15.	Artillery bombardment went of day.	
8.5.15.	Very heavy bombardment out of whole line began at 7am and continued until 4pm. Enemy reported to have broken through in two trenches to right of Shell Trap Farm and to have reached W.I.E & T.J.E. 11th by Rein were being brought up in night & E Lancs reoccupied line of trenches N of W.I.E LITTLE village.	Lieut Coode Adams wounded.

WAR DIARY or INTELLIGENCE SUMMARY.

(Erase heading not required.)

Army Form C. 2118.

Hour, Date, Place	Summary of Events and Information	Remarks and references to Appendices
9.5.15.	Enemy shelled our left- Very heavy morning -	Capt Scott killed Lieut Timbs was wounded
10.5.15	Comparatively quiet day - Hants Regt relieved us at night and Batt went into Bde reserve in dugouts at LA BRIQUE	
LA BRIQUE 11.5.15	Quiet day spent in dugouts at LA BRIQUE	
12.5.15	In dugouts at LA BRIQUE	
WIELTJE 13.5.15	Very heavy bombardment by enemy began at 3.30 am - line then held by London Rifle Bde & Cavalry Bde across WIELTJE - FORTUIN and WIELTJE - ST JULIEN roads. In pm Cav left their line then - Essex Regt who occupied Divisional Support line were ordered to cover its attack - to be supported by Kings own -	

WAR DIARY or INTELLIGENCE SUMMARY

Army Form C. 2118.

Hour, Date, Place	Summary of Events and Information	Remarks and references to Appendices
WIELTJE		
13.5.15 contd.	German aim were found not to have advanced. Essex occupied their trenches with 1 Coy Kings Own - Remainder des Batt. occupied trenches which Essex had been in - At night Kings Own relieved Essex Rd R B in front line. Taking 9 om trenches from 100th Regt WIELTJE - St Julien Rd + Fortuin Road - WIELTJE - 9 St Julien Fortuin Road. He also took over 2 defended posts in WIELTJE village - During whole night of this very trying day	Lieut O B Breen went to hosp sick with influenza
14.5.15	Fairly quiet day and firm	
15.5.15	Quiet day - he was relieved in evening by A & S Highlanders Terr: force. And then in marched to dug outs in I 3 27 (perhaps 28 @ Survey) where we arrived at 2.30 am	

WAR DIARY
or
INTELLIGENCE SUMMARY.
(Erase heading not required.)

Army Form C. 2118

Instructions regarding War Diaries and Intelligence Summaries are contained in F.S. Regs., Part II. and the Staff Manual respectively. Title pages will be prepared in manuscript.

Hour, Date, Place	Summary of Events and Information	Remarks and references to Appendices
Oost-hoek. 16.5.15	Batt" marched at 2 pm to billets [in farms in burg Khood out of] OOSTHOEK (A 23 G 22. See Map 28 Sewi 13 N W)	
17.5.15	In Billets - one day	
18.5.15	"	
19.5.15	"	
20.5.15	Fine day. (A Company of 6" North Fus (T.F.) arrived to be attached to Batt" during tour low in trenches.	

WAR DIARY or INTELLIGENCE SUMMARY.

(Erase heading not required.)

Army Form C. 2118.

Hour, Date, Place	Summary of Events and Information	Remarks and references to Appendices
21-5-15.	Batt'n left billets in A 23 T marched to 4" Don Headqr at Château Vlamertinghe - bivouaced in grounds until 7 pm when we marched via LA BRIQUE and relieved 1" Rifle Brigade in centre section trenches between B5T (see LA BRIQUE map). Relief was carried out or expected by Batt'n from 30 %. Saus trenches on or expected by Batt'n from 30/5/15.— 16-10 6/15.—	
LA BRIQUE 22. 5. 15.	In trenches. Fine day. Very little shelling except from 2. M.G.'s & little rifle. Heavy thunderstorm about 9 pm which made trenches very wet. Remainders of 12th Brigade returned to trenches this evening:— This line is now held by 10 men Regt & 6.15. King's Own 13.6.T.C. Royal Irish & C 15 Shell Trap Farm 10 " My 13 due left on from "Shell Trap Farm — Dublin Tree 7 " Argylls & Sutherland ete.— Men Tys. casualty left of) 1 wounded supporting line a & 7 Argyle. 2 nights	

Army Form C. 2118.

WAR DIARY
or
INTELLIGENCE SUMMARY.
(Erase heading not required.)

Instructions regarding War Diaries and Intelligence Summaries are contained in F.S. Regs., Part II. and the Staff Manual respectively. Title pages will be prepared in manuscript.

Hour, Date, Place	Summary of Events and Information	Remarks and references to Appendices
2.3. 5/12	In trenches - Trench & general duty	
2.4. 5/12	In trenches. Just before dawn at about 2.30 a.m. Enemy attacked with gas - there was a good deal of shelling & rifle fire but no attempt at infantry attack. The Coy. of Royal Irish on our right remained but the rest of the 13th attached. between this & SHELL TRAP FARM retired from this trench - part of 16 & "A" H.H. from the supports line went also. The remaining Coy. of Royal Irish were moved down to occupy its vacant trench and we moved our 2 reserve platoons into it. At about 3.3 a.m. enemy advanced by SHELL TRAP FARM, and captured trenches held by Royal Irish - Enemy now tried to bomb down our trenches but were held up by [?] Capt. Brophy etc. and a bombing party when close Irish took T [?] recaptured about 50 yards of [?] and Irish trench.	

WAR DIARY or INTELLIGENCE SUMMARY

Army Form C. 2118.

(Erase heading not required.)

Instructions regarding War Diaries and Intelligence Summaries are contained in F.S. Regs., Part II. and the Staff Manual respectively. Title pages will be prepared in manuscript.

Hour, Date, Place	Summary of Events and Information	Remarks and references to Appendices
24.5.15 contd	They captured a flag on his left which was used by the Germans to show their artillery their position in trench and erected a barricade. Enemy also captured the trenches on right of 5th Trap. occupied by D us Fusiliers, and they also held the R. of 2nd Communication trench or in right Flank – 20 of us were now placed between steady & dug out to hold this in this flank. Enemy were now holding every alt. or two – A counter attack by other 5ns. to succeed, & should have been held up in being behind end of Coon Road Farm. At about 1 pm enemy advanced in force to right of Well T. roof & occupied portion of trench held by A. ?. M. H. 4 b. At 2 pm enemy began to shell us with gas shells from large bore (5cm?) which continued until	

WAR DIARY
or
INTELLIGENCE SUMMARY.
(Erase heading not required.)

Army Form C. 2118.

Hour, Date, Place	Summary of Events and Information	Remarks and references to Appendices
24.5.15 Cuinchy	6 p.m. — Some of our own field guns also dropped their shells into our trenches with great accuracy for about 1½ hours. The {input?} of our burial from the burying Petit Fosse to night was nearly all flattened. Then shelling ceased at about 8 p.m., about 10 of enemy got out of this trench opposite us and advanced to the barbed wire — they were all killed. Afterwards we were informed that a counter attack was going to be made. 16 men his than lost by Royal I wish not, and almost immediately afterwards their counter attack would were to have and that King's our Reserve were to relieve him when blowing & unarmed support — but should were being killed by our own trench {mortars}.	

Army Form C. 2118.

WAR DIARY
or
INTELLIGENCE SUMMARY.
(Erase heading not required.)

Hour, Date, Place	Summary of Events and Information	Remarks and references to Appendices
24. 5.15 contd	King's own 1st relief first followed by Lincs. All our wounded were sent back and at about 10.30 pm battalion retired by Coys, a covering party of men to keep up rushing being left behind. Everything was very quiet and retirement was carried out successfully. The battalion went back to the canal bank for the night. Casualties for day. Lieut Leach & Lieut Blackets wounded. Other ranks killed wounded missing about	Capt Lawson & Lieut Pollinot of 5" K.R. were killed.

WAR DIARY
or
INTELLIGENCE SUMMARY.
(Erase heading not required.)

Army Form C. 2118.

Hour, Date, Place	Summary of Events and Information	Remarks and references to Appendices
Canal Bank 25.5.15.	13th alln arrived at canal bank at about 2.30 a.m. At 9 p.m. marched & relieved Lan: Fus: (Half Reserve in Divisional support line) (now front line) in being hundred of Cross Roads Farm. The Divisional support line is there in rear on map is now held as from line forming up with French (where right rests on TURCO Farm) by 1st French (reserve right rests on TURCO Farm) by 1st French switch - Cross Roads Farm is held as an advanced post.	
26.5.15.	In trenches - Our right side supped to its right and 10th ave some trench occupied by hanxoets.	Lieut Bennett E. James (killed) Sent to hospital suffering from gas poisoning -
27.5.15.	In trenches - Relieved at night by South Lanes. 13th occupied support trench will my term Irish Farm.	

WAR DIARY
or
INTELLIGENCE SUMMARY.
(Erase heading not required.)

Army Form C. 2118

Hour, Date, Place	Summary of Events and Information	Remarks and references to Appendices
Irish Farm 28.5.15	In support trenches. Good deal of shelling in evening caused by French on our left, making an attack in retd. of us. Captured some trenches from enemy.	
Irish Farm 30.5.15	In support trenches - quiet day	
Irish Farm 31.5.15	In support trench - quiet day -	
Irish Farm 1.6.15	In support trenches - quiet day. Relieved by Royal Irish Fus: (1st Bde) in evening. Batt'n marched back to billets in farm at A.23.	

4th Div.
12th Inf. Bde.

WAR DIARY

1ST KINGS OWN ROYAL LANCS. REGT.

J U N E

1 9 1 5

(Note; This diary includes an entry for 1.7.'15.)

WAR DIARY
or
INTELLIGENCE SUMMARY.
(Erase heading not required.)

Army Form C. 2118

Instructions regarding War Diaries and Intelligence Summaries are contained in F. S. Regs., Part II. and the Staff Manual respectively. Title pages will be prepared in manuscript.

Hour, Date, Place	Summary of Events and Information	Remarks and references to Appendices
From Billets Oolhoek A.23		
2. 6. 15	In Billets. —	
3. 6. 15		
4. 6. 15		
5. 6. 15		
6. 6. 15	In Billets — 6" Division have taken over trenches formerly held by 4" Division — 4" Division taken over from 1st French line of trenches from TURCO Farm to Canal. 12" Bde on right (reading 6") on) 10th & 13th do in centre 11th Bde on left. — Night of 6" 11th Batt. 1052 men trench round TURCO Farm. 2 Coys I have allotted	

WAR DIARY
or
INTELLIGENCE SUMMARY.
(Erase heading not required.)

Army Form C. 2118

Hour, Date, Place	Summary of Events and Information	Remarks and references to Appendices
6.6.15 contd	Saw Div. Comdr. & lunch in our left. Essex Regt. went into support trenches between Belle Alliance Farm and Fort Farm. 2 Coys I Leinsters + Roy. of I nish in canal Bank. Trenches in very bad state, not bullet proof - no parados, and very dirty, bodies buried in parapet -	
Turco Farm 7.6.15	In trenches - quiet day. Good deal of sniping at night.	
Turco Farm 8.6.15	In trenches, quiet day.	

Army Form C. 2118.

WAR DIARY
or
INTELLIGENCE SUMMARY.
(Erase heading not required.)

Instructions regarding War Diaries and Intelligence Summaries are contained in F.S. Regs., Part II. and the Staff Manual respectively. Title pages will be prepared in manuscript.

Hour, Date, Place	Summary of Events and Information	Remarks and references to Appendices
Farm Farm 9.6.15.	In trenches. Quiet day. Thunderstorm in evening. Trench heads very wet.	(Capt.) Oldfield Jnr. + Bradbury rejd
Farm Farm 10.6.15.	In trenches — quiet day — Enemy Mg. + Mr Lewis in evening + we returned his support. Trenches at Belle Alliance Farm. Pouring wet night, all communication trenches flooded out.	
Belle Alliance 11.6.15.	In support trenches.	

Army Form C. 2118.

WAR DIARY
or
INTELLIGENCE SUMMARY.
(Erase heading not required.)

Instructions regarding War Diaries and Intelligence Summaries are contained in F.S. Regs., Part II. and the Staff Manual respectively. Title pages will be prepared in manuscript.

Hour, Date, Place	Summary of Events and Information	Remarks and references to Appendices
Bellawaire		
12.6.15	In support trenches - Worked at completion of	
13.6.15	2nd line fire trenches - Quiet days - Good	
14.6.15		
15.6.15	deal of sniping at night	
16.6.15		
17.6.15		
18.6.15		
Bellawaire		
19.6.15	Units new division of trenches 12 Bns are allotted trenches from Tunes Farm to 100 yards East of Boesinghe road - These trenches divided into 2 sectors. Right sector allotted to Slow Feo & Essex Regt. Left sector to Kings Own & Lancs	

Forms/C. 2118/10

Army Form C. 2118.

WAR DIARY
or
INTELLIGENCE SUMMARY.
(Erase heading not required.)

Instructions regarding War Diaries and Intelligence Summaries are contained in F.S. Regs., Part II. and the Staff Manual respectively. Title pages will be prepared in manuscript.

Hour, Date, Place	Summary of Events and Information	Remarks and references to Appendices
Belle Alliance 19.6.15 Cont.	Royal visit to be permanently a Cavalry Bank. On Bath in support, trenches at "Belle Alliance" and one Bath" relieving in billets. On the eveng of 19.6.15 Battalion relieved 5 Leurs in left section — 3 coys in front line 1 in support.	
20.6.15 21.6.15 22.6.15 23.6.15	} 4 front trenches. quiet time On evg 23.6.15 I have relieved Bath oth proceeded to billets in A.21.	

Army Form C. 2118.

WAR DIARY
or
INTELLIGENCE SUMMARY.
(Erase heading not required.)

Instructions regarding War Diaries and Intelligence Summaries are contained in F.S. Regs., Part II. and the Staff Manual respectively. Title pages will be prepared in manuscript.

Hour, Date, Place	Summary of Events and Information	Remarks and references to Appendices
24. 6. 15	In Billets at A.2.1.	
25. 6. 15		
26. 6. 15		
27. 6. 15	Paraded (5" ELVERDINGE at 4 pm hallied this for tea — Then marched on & relieved S Lancs in front trenches.	
Supt. Potts. Turco Farm		
28. 6. 15	In front trenches.	
29. 6. 15		
30. 6. 15	S. Lancs relieved us in front trenches in evening. Batt went to support trench — Belle Alliance Fork Farm.	
1. 7. 15		

WAR DIARY
or
INTELLIGENCE SUMMARY.
(Erase heading not required.)

Army Form C. 2118

Instructions regarding War Diaries and Intelligence
Summaries are contained in F. S. Regs., Part II.
and the Staff Manual respectively. Title pages
will be prepared in manuscript.

Hour, Date, Place	Summary of Events and Information	Remarks and references to Appendices
	Key to attached map L.A. BRIQUE.	
A. B. C. D. -	Line of trenches (taken up by 12" hy Bde on mg: br. of 30 - sp 1.5".	
French were on left of A. 10" hy Bde on my br. of D. -		
A 15.13	held by E 8 terr Regt. 13.65°C held by Kin 20 Arm. C (& D) held by Kein Terr.	
E to F.	line of trenches held by Kings own Reg: on y br. 13/14" to mg br 15" 16" hvy	
G to H.	Defended Posts held in NIEUTTE village	

Army Form C. 2118

WAR DIARY
or
INTELLIGENCE SUMMARY.
(*Erase heading not required.*)

Instructions regarding War Diaries and Intelligence Summaries are contained in F. S. Regs., Part II. and the Staff Manual respectively. Title pages will be prepared in manuscript.

Hour, Date, Place	Summary of Events and Information	Remarks and references to Appendices
	Sketch of Position on 24.5.15.	Trenches held by us. Original German Trenches Trenches of R I taken by Germans

Line held by men.
Canadian Farm
Winnipeg Patrol F.m
K.u.13.a
Shell Trap Farm

4th Div.
12th Inf. Bde.

WAR DIARY

1ST KINGS OWN ROYAL LANCS. REGT.

J U L Y

1 9 1 5

(Note: See end of JUNE diary for entry dated 1.7.'15.)

Army Form C. 2118

WAR DIARY
or
INTELLIGENCE SUMMARY.
(Erase heading not required.)

Instructions regarding War Diaries and Intelligence Summaries are contained in F.S. Regs., Part II. and the Staff Manual respectively. Title pages will be prepared in manuscript.

Hour, Date, Place	Summary of Events and Information	Remarks and references to Appendices
Belle Alliance Farm		
2. 7. 15	In support trenches	Lt Morris arrived to command Coy. Taylor on leave — B. 3rd
3 " "	" "	Capt Munro was transferred to 2nd Batln.
4 " "	" "	
5 " "	" "	
6 - 7. 15	In support trenches — 11" hof 13th made an attack at 6 am and captured some German trenches — German counter attack failed — 8a.m. Too strong. Put in in evening to hold trench captured. —	
7. 7. 15	In support trenches. Men led by Lieut Fenton were heavily shelled & attacked by Germans — All attacks were beaten off — Batln relieved in evening by Batln of 49 Division & marched to camp A.16.c.	

Army Form C. 2118

WAR DIARY
or
INTELLIGENCE SUMMARY.
(Erase heading not required.)

Instructions regarding War Diaries and Intelligence Summaries are contained in F. S. Regs., Part II. and the Staff Manual respectively. Title pages will be prepared in manuscript.

Hour, Date, Place	Summary of Events and Information	Remarks and references to Appendices
En route to PROVEN 9.17.15	Whole 4th Division is being relieved by 49th Div. And is going to rest near PROVEN. Batt marched from A 16.a in afternoon and went into billets in PROVEN village.	
9 – 7 – 15	In billets in town of Proven.	
10 – 7 – 15	Draft of 71 men arrived in evening, no Officer	
11 – 7 – 15	} In billets in PROVEN. Usual parades.	
12 – 7 – 15		

WAR DIARY
or
INTELLIGENCE SUMMARY.

(Erase heading not required.)

Army Form C. 2118.

Hour, Date, Place	Summary of Events and Information	Remarks and references to Appendices
PROVEN 13-7-15	Inspection of Brigade by Gen. Plumer KCB G.O.C 2nd Army Brigade was inspected at 2. after which a short address was given. While inspecting having The King's Own was mentioned as having done especially well in Gas attacks The Brigade was complimented on excellent work done in the Ypres salient. This was due entirely to the fighting qualities of the troops and had nothing to do with the Generalship. The Gen. then informed the Brigade that it was leaving the 2nd Army and 6th Corps & was going to the 7th Corps & 3rd Army. He expressed his regret at losing the Brigade The parade was dismissed	

WAR DIARY
or
INTELLIGENCE SUMMARY

Army Form C. 2118.

Hour, Date, Place	Summary of Events and Information	Remarks and references to Appendices
PROVEN		
14-7-15	⎫ In billets.	
15-7-15	⎬	
16-7-15	⎭	
17-7-15	Presentation of D.C.M's to Sergt Mann & Sergt Watts by Gen Wilson C in C 4th Division	
18-7-15	Church Parade	
19-7-15	Inspection of Brigade by Sir John French Commander in Chief, G.C.B. O.M. G.C.V.O. K.C.M.G After the Inspection, the C in C gave a short address. He had come especially to the 12th Bde to congratulate them on the splendid work done by them at Ypres, especially that of the Essex Regt.	

Army Form C. 2118.

WAR DIARY
or
INTELLIGENCE SUMMARY.
(Erase heading not required.)

Hour, Date, Place	Summary of Events and Information	Remarks and references to Appendices
PROYEN 19-7-15 (cont)	Not only had the Bde held their trenches against the gas attack but had kept together as well. The Bde had arrived at a place where all war-confusion & had the heaviest artillery turned onto them. It was for this purpose he had come to the Bde & he wanted every Officer, N.C.O. & man to understand that he as Commander in Chief appreciated deeply the work done. He was sure that the 12th Bde would continue their glorious record. The Parade was dismissed	

WAR DIARY
or
INTELLIGENCE SUMMARY.
(Erase heading not required.)

Army Form C. 2118.

Hour, Date, Place	Summary of Events and Information	Remarks and references to Appendices
Proven 20-7-15 en route to FORCEVILLE 21-7-15	In billets At 6.45 am the Batt" marched out of Proven, reaching GODYAERSVELDE at 9.45. Bivouacking started at 2.11.45 p.m. The rain started at 2 arriving at DOUHENS at 10 pm. The Batt" then marched to billets in FRESHVILLE	
22-7-15	Batt" marched out of billets at 10.45 a.m. A halt was made for dinners from 2 pm - 3 pm. Batt" marched into billets at FORCEVILLE.	
23-7-15	CO & Company commanders went round trenches that Batt" would take over the following day. Good trenches, cut out of the chalk. Scrupulously clean & good shell proof dugouts including large ones for men	

WAR DIARY
or
INTELLIGENCE SUMMARY.

Army Form C. 2118.

Hour, Date, Place	Summary of Events and Information	Remarks and references to Appendices
FORCEVILLE 23-7-15 (cont)	Parapets on the whole bullet proof. Good number of loopholes. Listening posts all connected up by trenches. 2 Lieut Worth joined on reaching his appointment in R.F.C.	
24-7-15	Brigade inspected by Brigadier Gen Sir Onley. After which he made a short speech saying that Sir John French had sent a letter in which he said how much he regretted having omitted to mention the good work done by The Kings Own Regt & he had pleasure in telling the Brigade about it. Also how much he appreciated it. The Parade was dismissed	

Army Form C. 2118.

WAR DIARY
or
INTELLIGENCE SUMMARY.
(Erase heading not required.)

Instructions regarding War Diaries and Intelligence Summaries are contained in F.S. Regs., Part II. and the Staff Manual respectively. Title pages will be prepared in manuscript.

Hour, Date, Place	Summary of Events and Information	Remarks and references to Appendices
FORCEVILLE 24-7-15 En route to Leuchen	Brigade inspected at 3 o'clock by Lt Gen C C Monro KCB Batt'n marched out of Gulch to take over trenches from French at 8.45 Relief was successfully carried out.	

Army Form C. 2118

WAR DIARY
or
INTELLIGENCE SUMMARY.
(Erase heading not required.)

Hour, Date, Place	Summary of Events and Information	Remarks and references to Appendices
In trenches round & in front of AUCHONVILLER 25-7-15 26-7-15 27-7-15 28-7-15 29-7-15 30-7-15 31-7-15	Trenches. Quiet days. No shelling except few "little willies". Work done consisted principally of digging large shelters for men proof against shells. Resetting up inside of parapets & generally making it bullet proof roof	

4th Div.
12th Inf. Bde.

WAR DIARY

1ST KINGS OWN ROYAL LANCS. REGT.

A U G U S T

1 9 1 5

WAR DIARY
or
INTELLIGENCE SUMMARY.
(Erase heading not required.)

Army Form C. 2...

Instructions regarding War Diaries and Intelligence Summaries are contained in F. S. Regs., Part II. and the Staff Manual respectively. Title pages will be prepared in manuscript.

Hour, Date, Place	Summary of Events and Information	Remarks and references to Appendices
In Henchen Camp AUCHONVILLER		
1-8-15	In trenches. Wet day	
2-8-15	Batt'n relieved by same two in evening. Relief slow on account of heavy rain that fell throughout the day. Marches into billets at MAILLY-MAILLET. One Coy at AUCHONVILLER	
3-8-15	In billets.	
4-8-15	Large working parties required for digging new line of trenches & cutting of wood for trenches	
5-8-15		
6-8-15	Still in billets. Parties required every day. About 400 men used per day. Band of the Bn. played in square on Sunday. Very wet day, heavy thunderstorm	
7-8-15		
8-8-15		
9-8-15		

Army Form C. 2118.

WAR DIARY
or
INTELLIGENCE SUMMARY.
(Erase heading not required.)

Instructions regarding War Diaries and Intelligence Summaries are contained in F.S. Regs., Part II. and the Staff Manual respectively. Title pages will be prepared in manuscript.

Hour, Date, Place	Summary of Events and Information	Remarks and references to Appendices
En Route to Henches		
10-8-15	Batt'n relieved came fire in trenches leaving MAILLY-MAILLET at 7.45 & proceeding (by platoons) to AUCHONVILLERS.	
11-8-15	In trenches. Bad condition on	
12-8-15	just night. but soon dried up	
13-8-15	Continued on work building large	
14-8-15	dugout, revetting up front line	
15-8-15	& putting up traverses. Shelling	
16-8-15	more frequent than before & Sniping	
17-8-15	slightly more active.	
18-8-15	Several Wilson Q.O.E 4th Division	
19	Sevrl. Round trenches	
	Batt'n relieved by same fire starting	
	at 9 & marched into billets at FORCEVILLE	

WAR DIARY
or
INTELLIGENCE SUMMARY.
(Erase heading not required.)

Army Form C. 2118.

Hour, Date, Place	Summary of Events and Information	Remarks and references to Appendices
19th	ttttt 1st day in billets at FORCEVILLE	2nd Lt R.C. Matthews joined 2 H.Q. 15 Co took over Adjutant
20th	Parties of 250 men required for digging	
21st	each day. Also running Drill and route marches	
22nd	Brigadier general Onsley addressed 11th Battalion	
23rd		
24th		
25th		
26th	Right of 4th Co marched from FORCEVILLE at 7.30 pm via MAILLY- MAILLY to take over front line trenches occupied by 1/Royal Warwickshire Regt and 1/4 Company of 2/Seaforth Highlanders (10th Inf Bde). Relief completed at 10 pm. for positions see sketch map. Line held as follows:- front line trenches X.75 to 85. 3 platoons per company, 1 platoon in BURROW trench, 3 platoons in LEGEND trench Battn headquarters marked "A"	

WAR DIARY
or
INTELLIGENCE SUMMARY.

(Erase heading not required.)

Army Form C. 2118

Hour, Date, Place	Summary of Events and Information	Remarks and references to Appendices
27th	Started work on communication trenches and strengthened front line trenches. A very quiet day. Weather fine.	
28th	A very quiet day. Work on trenches continued	2/Lt A. R. Kerr 3/Norfolk Regt joined 179 Coy R.E. 28.8.15.
29th	A very quiet day. Work on trenches continued. 1 Coy of R/E. Kings Regt attached to the battalion for instruction. Distribution ½ platoon with right Company. 1 Platoon with entire Coy. ½ platoon with left Coy, 2 platoons with Reserve Coy. Rain commenced 8 p.m. Thunderous.	
30th	Enemy trench mortars active early in the morning, only one man wounded. Rain commenced 6.30 p.m. but ceased by 9 p.m.	
31st	Enemy trench mortars again active. 3 men of left Coy wounded early in the morning. A great deal of work done to communication trenches.	Reinforcement 2/Lt W. J. Litherland 1/the Kings Own Regt.

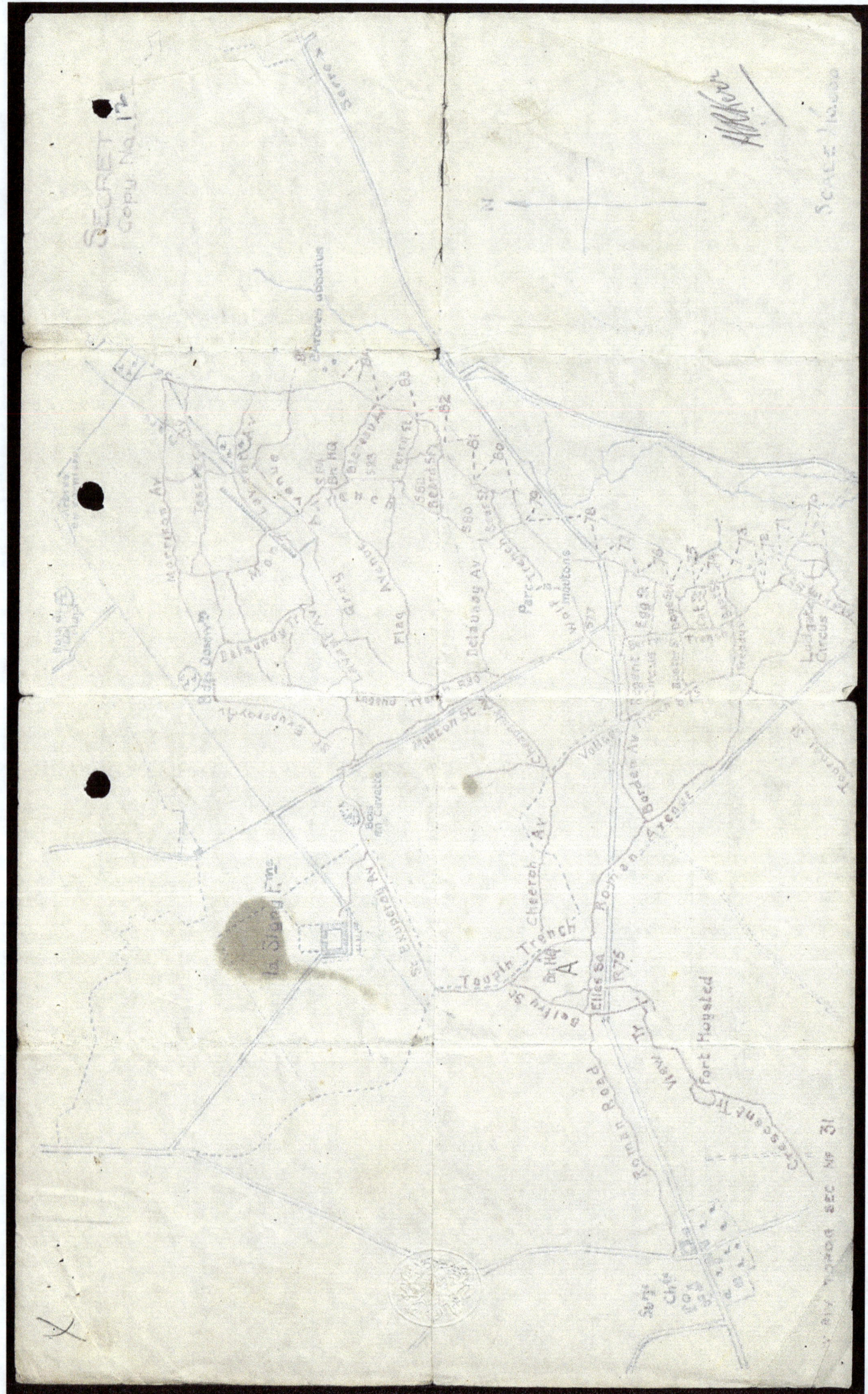

H. Kerr Lt.
1st King's Own Rgt.

4th Div.
12th Inf. Bde.

WAR DIARY

1ST KINGS OWN ROYAL LANCS. REGT.

SEPTEMBER

1 9 1 5.

WAR DIARY
or
INTELLIGENCE SUMMARY.
(Erase heading not required.)

Army Form C. 2118.

Hour, Date, Place	Summary of Events and Information	Remarks and references to Appendices
September 1915 1st	Enemy guns and trench mortars again active especially on the left Coy. three men killed in the morning by Mn. Ehrenes Ref. 2 Kings bury) two E. knee wounded in the morning. Active again in the enemy an aerial torpedo hitting the parapet in the centre of the centre Company and burying six men, two of whom were killed and two slightly injured. Rain in the evening made trenches very wet	2/L Gardner joined Bn from Scots Guards
2nd	A quiet day. Much work done towards drainage of the trenches. 1/Royal Warwickshire Regt relieved the Battalion. Relief completed 10.30pm Companies marched to billets at MAILLY - MAILLET	
3rd	Quiet day in billets. Battalion baths at MAILLY - MAILLET	

Army Form C. 2118.

WAR DIARY
or
INTELLIGENCE SUMMARY.
(Erase heading not required.)

Instructions regarding War Diaries and Intelligence Summaries are contained in F. S. Regs., Part II. and the Staff Manual respectively. Title pages will be prepared in manuscript.

Hour, Date, Place	Summary of Events and Information	Remarks and references to Appendices
4 E	Large digging parties found both by day and night. About 4.00 am until all digging finished.	Lt Colonel T.D. Pilcher MVO DSO took over command of 2nd Bn. Temporarily Captain C.R. Lester assumed command of the company temporarily.
5 E / 6 E	Digging parties as before, billets heavily shelled. Only one man wounded. About 100 shells fired by the enemy between 5.30 pm and 7.30 pm.	
6 E - 7 E	Enemy shelled billets about midday. 36 shells in all. Difficult to interfere with enemy's gun, bombarded enemy billets in the evening.	
7 E - 9 E	Digging as usual.	
9 E	Relieved 1/Royal Warwickshire Regt. Relief completed 10 pm. D Coy right C. B Coy Centre, A Coy on left. "C" Coy in Reserve.	
10 E	First day in trenches. A quiet day except for a fine aerial torpedo seen by the enemy.	
11 E	Quiet day. A Coy commenced a safe climb to that. A Kbres. D Coy continued 3.30 pm one of our TBDs bombarded approaches to DOPS	

WAR DIARY
or
INTELLIGENCE SUMMARY.

(Erase heading not required.)

Army Form C. 2118.

Hour, Date, Place	Summary of Events and Information	Remarks and references to Appendices
12th	A few aerial torpedoes at dawn, very little damage done. 11 Coy, 12 Cheshire Regt came up in the evening to be attached to the battalion. Distributed as follows 1 Platoon to D Coy, 1 Platoon to B Coy, ½ Platoon to A Coy, 2 Platoons to "C" Coy. Aerial torpedoes again active in the evening. Work ongoing in front of A & D Coys continued, also pulldown MONK and communication trenches drains.	
13th	A quiet day. Work on aerial torpedoes especially the MILLS [?] to life company, but Sap continued.	
14th	Again worried by aerial torpedoes. B Coy and C Coy trench down in MONK Trench. Saps work carried on.	
15th	A quiet morning, artillery bombarded salient. Enemy retaliation in MT. top of B Coy and right of A Coy Sap finish. Work on MONK TRENCH and communication trenches. Firing ditches cut on north side of BLENAU.	
16th	A few aerial torpedoes. MONK Trench much work done to finish, work continued in BLENAU. An officer (Roy Inniskilling Regt) killed by trench mortar. 1 Royal Inniskilling Regt attachment [?] actor. The enemy bombed very Trench mortars very active. Little damage to trenches. 1 Royal Inniskilling Regt	
17th		

WAR DIARY
or
INTELLIGENCE SUMMARY.

(Erase heading not required.)

Army Form C. 2118.

Hour, Date, Place	Summary of Events and Information	Remarks and references to Appendices
	arrived in the evening. Relief completed 10 pm. Battalion marched to billets in ACHEUX, last Company arrived about 1.30 am 17th.	
17th	First day in billets. 40-a-men and baths in the morning.	
18th	More baths. Battalion parade 12.30 pm for march inspection by G.O.C. 51st Army Corps via LOUVENCOURT. G.O.C. V.O.C. and returned for Inspection. Battalion carried out practice attack back to ACHEUX. Battalion returned to billets 6.15 pm. G.O.C. IV Div. watched attack.	
19th	Working parties 450 strong found for work on Corps line. Church. Reveille at 8 am to again this battalion.	
20th	Working parties 300 strong found daily	
21st	Guards, fatigues, training, Kitchens and general Jobs found at Army H.Q. by draw. Work with mules from XIV HE DIV. by Companies Battalion marched from ACHEUX to ACHEUX to relieve 1/Royal Warwicks in the line Relief completed 10.15 pm. Relief carried out without opposition. Night quiet, A & C Companies in front line, B in support, D in reserve.	2/5 Pte 2/ammunition attached for instruction in the duty of Adjutant for one month. 2/5 Graham to Hospital 2/5. Kent joined from Brown.

(9 29 6) W 4141—463 100,000 9/14 H W V Forms/C. 2118/10

Army Form C. 2118.

WAR DIARY
or
INTELLIGENCE SUMMARY.
(Erase heading not required.)

Instructions regarding War Diaries and Intelligence Summaries are contained in F.S. Regs., Part II. and the Staff Manual respectively. Title pages will be prepared in manuscript.

Hour, Date, Place	Summary of Events and Information	Remarks and references to Appendices
23rd	Enemy Trench mortars active at dawn. Worked on communication trenches and renewing MONK	
24th	Beginning of active preparations for another reconnaissance in force against enemy strongpoint started at left Coys Hdqrs, work on MONK R—. Continuation of preparations. A wet morning. Trench mortars active about midnight. Nothing commenced	
25th	Cutting wire Scheme opposite Trench 77. two strong points pushed up to trenches 78 and 79. Bn HR changed to ROMAN VILLA to make room for G.O.C. 13th Rd., Preparations Continued, enemy very quiet except for a few whizz bangs which had no effect. Work on MONK and strong point continued. Sent out in front of BURROW Redoubt	
26th	a wet morning. Nothing transpires and continued cutting wire scheme. Went as previously by A quiet day, three aerial torpedoes fired by enemy at the centre Company on all previous days.	Captain Woodger D.S.O. to Hospital.
27th 28th	Patrols sent out without any ill from enemy had enemy, no attempt by the enemy to replenish the wire to a certain extent although	

(9 29 6) W 4141—463 100,000 9/14 H W V Forms/C. 2118/10

WAR DIARY
or
INTELLIGENCE SUMMARY.
(Erase heading not required.)

Army Form C. 2118.

Hour, Date, Place	Summary of Events and Information	Remarks and references to Appendices
28th	Heavy rain in the morning, trenches very wet. Fine in the afternoon, but heavy rain again in the evening. A quiet day. Patrols sent out as on the previous night. Work (continued) on the strongpoint at CATTCOMBE and MONK FEAT dugouts.	Lt Colonel T.J. Jackson D.S.O. rejoins from the Command Depot to the Bn. Major-General Lambton took over the Command of 4 Division.
29th	A quiet morning. Bn. H.Q. moved back to old dugout. 1/Royal Warwickshire Regiment relieves the Battalion. Relief complete 10.30 pm. Battalion marched by companies to billets at FORCEVILLE. First day in billets. Bn paraded 2 pm for inspection and was marched by G.O.C. 3rd Army, who did not inspect. The march was follows:— FORCEVILLE – ACHEUX turning on a practice attack on VARENNES. Battalion reached billets 5 pm. The first occasion on which the Drums played to the Battalion. German aeroplane brought down close to billets by British machine. R.C. Matthews Lt. A.D.C. for Lieut Colonel Comdg. 1/4th King's Own Regt.	

4th Div.
12th Inf. Bde.

WAR DIARY

1ST KINGS OWN ROYAL LANCS. REGT.

OCTOBER

1915.

WAR DIARY
or
INTELLIGENCE SUMMARY.

Army Form C. 2118.

Hour, Date, Place	Summary of Events and Information	Remarks and references to Appendices
October 1st	Large working parties found about 330 in all. 50 by day the remainder by night. Battn. in the morning for 200 men and four N.C.O's acted as pall bearers to German officer and mechanic killed in the aeroplane the previous day, also party of 1 Officer and 40 men. funeral with full military honours.	Drums play working parties out to MAILLY daily.
2nd 3rd 4th 5th	Working parties as previous day. " " "	Captain Woodgate D.S.O. returned from LEALVILLERS (15 Divn. Convalescent home for Officers) 2/Lt Pepraham rejoined from Hospital. Lce/Cpl M. Browne 3/ the King's (L.Pool Regt) joined 1st Battalion.
6th	Battalion marched from FORCEVILLE & then withdrawn to relieve 1/Royal Warwickshire Regt. Drums played Battalion as far as the entrance to MAILLY MAILLET. The Battalion relieved 1/Royal Warwick Regt. in BURROW, C COY left, B COY in support in trenches. Relief complete 9.15 p.m. Casualty A COY Rankin A COY 1 less.	

WAR DIARY
or
INTELLIGENCE SUMMARY.
(Erase heading not required.)

Army Form C. 2118.

Hour, Date, Place	Summary of Events and Information	Remarks and references to Appendices
7th	First day in trenches. A quiet day, work on MONK and CATTACOMBE. Wire put out in front of BURROW.	
8th	A quiet morning. Between 3.50 and 4.30 pm enemy fired between twenty and thirty aerial torpedoes at the centre company, knocking in several dug outs and causing a number of casualties. Little wire was developed at the same time in large numbers by the enemy. The centre company's parapet breached in several places, left company's parapet breached in six places. All promptly repaired same night. Work on main trench running from BIENAU to GREY, also on MONK and CATTACOMBE.	
9th	A quiet day. Work on MONK, CATTACOMBE. Main trench running from BIENAU to GREY. Wire put out by all companies in the front line.	

WAR DIARY
or
INTELLIGENCE SUMMARY.
(Erase heading not required.)

Army Form C. 2118.

Hour, Date, Place	Summary of Events and Information	Remarks and references to Appendices
10th	A quiet day. work as on 9th	
11th	A quiet day. A number of shells fired between 3 and 4.30 pm at the left of our left Company but little damage done. Slept that the nest of a Lewis weapon of "C" Coy's Royal Irish Rifles sticks for instruction distribution	1 Platoon to D Coy. ½ platoon to C coy. ½ " to B Coy 2 platoons to A Coy.
12th	A quiet day. work as on 10th. A few rifle grenades fell near BRENA V. Road at night	
13th	A quiet day. A few rifle grenades at night. 2 Platoons of 8/Royal Irish Rifles receive relieved those 2 platoons who marched to billets in MAILLY. 11 Royal Warwicks in left of Battalion. Relief complete 9.10 pm. marched to billets by Companies in MAILLY-MAILLET. Present in billets at 10.30 pm.	
14th	First day in billets. 150 men per batln.	
15th	Large work parties found both day and night. To Cal 568.	

WAR DIARY or INTELLIGENCE SUMMARY

Army Form C. 2118.

(Erase heading not required.)

Hour, Date, Place	Summary of Events and Information	Remarks and references to Appendices

16th Large working parties out for starting work. Aidinville.

17th Do. for do. Working parties and other fatigues.

18th 1/2 Bn Royal Irish Rifles (Ulster Division) attached to the Battalion in billets for instruction. Issued parties about 300 strong.

19th First day of Instruction in trench work. One Company Commander and four M.C. Sentries for each Company of 11 R.I.R. Inspected trenches. D.G. E. 2 & 3 being dug by us in future. Platoon Routes MAILLY + MAILLET— BEAUSART BERTRANCOURT— FORCEVILLE MAILLY MAILLET

20th Further Instruction of 11/R.I.R. in the morning. Battalion marched out by billets to trenches by Acheux commencing 5.15 pm to Relieve 1/R. Warwick R. in trenches. Relief complete 8.15 pm. Dispositions A Company on right + 2 Companies to follow. "B" Coy in support in C Coy + 2 Coy — BURROWS C Coy in Eutrehuide. B Coy on left. 8 less 1 Platoon in reserve in LE BASUIDE.

(9 29 6) W 4141—463 100,000 9/14 H W V Forms/C. 2118/10

WAR DIARY
or
INTELLIGENCE SUMMARY.
(Erase heading not required.)

Army Form C. 2118.

Hour, Date, Place	Summary of Events and Information	Remarks and references to Appendices
21st	Quiet day in the area. Work on MONK and CATTA COMB F.E. Every M.R.R. Coy to find instructional distribution parties to A, B platoons.	
22nd	"B" & "A" platoons to "C" 2 platoons to "D".	
22nd	Enemy bombarded our line from BLENAU to BOARD STREET and Platoon Sgt Ranks and Sentries and much little shelling during respite no 5 g's and rifle. Bombardment lasted from 10.15am to 10.15pm. Most on MONK, also much enemy shell activity south of A.10 line. It was heavier in new trenches.com Relieved for duty, but in a convent, the whole night from BLENAU, PERRY, and from 3 OAKE, COPPER. State 2 platoons "WRIR" in reserve exchanged with new trenches Platoon.	
23rd	A quiet day except for enemy flying signals. Work on Defence line (cutting wire) and on new trench connecting "B" Coy in R.F.R.7000. Enemy trench mortar active without firing. A bombard of 3 by enemy infantry tried enter in 10 Casualties, Enemy apparently driven off by accurate rifle. Aircraft BOARD and RESS Evid operational at 9pm for 24 hours away. Capt Rawn	

WAR DIARY
or
INTELLIGENCE SUMMARY.
(Erase heading not required.)

Army Form C. 2118.

Hour, Date, Place	Summary of Events and Information	Remarks and references to Appendices
25th	On march to VARLADE and BORDON. A quiet day, very wet. Snow showers when our night Billets on Apt 18 "A" R.I.R. instructed cos. 60, Coy being marched to Billets. NAILLY MAILLY ET. Work as on 24th. 1 Platoon of D Coy out to enemy on account of casualties.	Lt. Colonel V.J. parker went to hospital sick. Command of 2nd R.I.R. taken over by Lt Col ?? Cooper upon Command O of Bn.
26th	A quiet day. A few wild Willie and Rifle grenades. Work as on 25th.	E. Col. ?? Parker ?? Comd. B.Gen Pryce Comm. 9th R.I.R ?? Capt Geere e R Carter taff on a Committee. Bn.
27th	Quiet day. Very wet. Work as on 26th. 9 Pioneers in VALLADE and BORDON complete.	2/R.E. Stewart 2/Lt Kemp Basey. Pr/Lieut to Br. 2nd R.I.R ?? R. Lt. ?? from Reg. ?? A H S Company Bn.
28th	A Quiet day. Very wet. Work as on 27th. English Prisoners commence in FLAG.	
29th	A quiet day. Rain a Day. Instruments and Ammunition Works out to Brigade of LEGENDRE Completion Commenced	Captain A.B. Wright D.S.O left on join E.Coy R.I. being invalided off R? R. 2/5. D.M. Burran took over Comm as A? Coy
30th	A quiet day. Fine. Work as on 29th. During the day the Engr crew of duty a large number of wire pickets out of all Coys in the front line.	

Forms/C. 2118/10

WAR DIARY
or
INTELLIGENCE SUMMARY.
(Erase heading not required.)

Army Form C. 2118.

Hour, Date, Place	Summary of Events and Information	Remarks and references to Appendices
	Interior Econ. Routine Company Ex. Bn marched to billets in ACHEUX. Bn. relieved 1/4 Essex in command by	Col. Olive Major D.B. Clarke to his train. Independently on command by Bn
31st	First day in billets at ACHEUX. Bn. inspected by the GOC XXXIII Bde, & being behind for up by GOC (His Army). Preparation for impending Church parade at SUCRE DE ACHEUX. Brown Bays B Bn to church. 4 D Coin Band Bays Brass band to church.	

R.C.Ma.Reinolds Adjt.
1/The King's Own Regt.

36th Division 12/36

King's Own Regt.
(Roy. Lancaster)

Transferred Nov 2nd

12th Bn

Army Form C. 2118.

WAR DIARY
or
INTELLIGENCE SUMMARY.
(Erase heading not required.)

Instructions regarding War Diaries and Intelligence Summaries are contained in F.S. Regs., Part II. and the Staff Manual respectively. Title pages will be prepared in manuscript.

Hour, Date, Place	Summary of Events and Information	Remarks and references to Appendices
Nov 1st	Still in billets, shipping parties about 250 per diem found.	
2nd	6 men received for attachment of 2nd R.E. Bde to 36th (Ulster) Division for instructional purposes.	
3rd	Magazines packed for move. 300 men to Baths.	
4th	Battalion marched from ACHEUX to RUBEMPRE and billeted there for night, about ten mile march. Good billets.	
5th	Battalion marched at 9.30 am from RUBEMPRE to ST LEGER about 12 mile march. 12th Bde split up. Essex Regt to 10th Bde. Lanc. Fus. to 108th Bde. Kings Own and 1/5 Shrops. remaining with 12th Bde. Billetted at ST LEGER two. 12 F.Boo.	
6th	Joined 36th Division. Adjutant & Transferre Officer returning to train in the afternoon.	

WAR DIARY
or
INTELLIGENCE SUMMARY.

Army Form C. 2118.

(Erase heading not required.)

Hour, Date, Place	Summary of Events and Information	Remarks and references to Appendices
7th	Day spent in improvement of billets and settling down.	at ST LEGER
8th	Company Training. Lecture by O.C. to Officers.	
9th	Brigade Operations (Rehearsal of how battery LE CATEAU should have been fought.)	
10th	Battalion Route March. G.O.C. 36 Div inspected billets	
11th	Company Training. Rain.	
12th	Brigade Route March. Very wet.	
13th	C.O's paraded a Company. Training	
14th	C.O's target. Improvement of billets, battalion then marched to Church. Improvement of billets during the week. Incinerators, latrines built	
15th	Company Training.	
16th	Snow in the morning. Bn. Route march. 1. 30 pm returned to billets in afternoon marched off. 7 pm. Snow now. Training difficult	

WAR DIARY
or
INTELLIGENCE SUMMARY.

Army Form C. 2118.

Hour, Date, Place	Summary of Events and Information	Remarks and references to Appendices
18th	300 men to baths at ST OUEN. Company training	
19th	Brigade pld exercise. Attack carried out from ST OUEN on VIGNACOURT. Left billets 9.15am, returned via HALLOY at 3.15pm.	2/Lt McWalter rejoined Bn from BUFFS.
20th	B and A Coys grouping on the range in the morning. H & D Coys to baths. B and A Coys found sundry Company ?? in the afternoon	2/Lt Patterson to hospital 2 R.W. Kent Regt. Billets at ST LEGER.
21st	C O's parade then Battalion marched to Church. No work in the afternoon.	
22nd	2 Companies on the Range. Kit inspection.	
23rd	Brigade Route march.	
24th	Battalion field operations	Major J.A. ?? ?? to Reserve. ?? eye ?? and to ?? ??

Army Form C. 2118.

WAR DIARY
or
INTELLIGENCE SUMMARY.
(Erase heading not required.)

Instructions regarding War Diaries and Intelligence Summaries are contained in F.S. Regs., Part II. and the Staff Manual respectively. Title pages will be prepared in manuscript.

Hour, Date, Place	Summary of Events and Information	Remarks and references to Appendices
25th	Company Inspection. Drill smoke Helmet parades. Rations for 300 men.	
26th	Battalion rested from St LEGER Battle. BUSSUS- Field Operation	
27th	Battalion marched from ST LEGER to BUSSUS-BUSSUS to new billets. much better than ST LEGER.	
28th	Improvement of Billets and sanitation. Inspection of Billets by C.O.	
29th	Company training. and Improvement of Billets. Battalion parade, Lewis machine gun and rifle all the new improvements	
30th	A very wet day. Improvement of Billets, and lectures by O.C. Coys	L.C. Deakin, Z = thickens 2/L Brown & pears for duty. Reuter Kings Capt & who 1/and Alphons Comdt of the Kings own Rest

Forms/C. 2118/10

1/Roy. Inniskilling Regt.

Dec / XV / vol

13.J.
7.

Army Form C. 2118.

WAR DIARY
or
INTELLIGENCE SUMMARY.
(Erase heading not required.)

ORDERLY ROOM,
1ST BATTALION
THE KING'S OWN REGT.
Received 19
Forwarded 2/1/16. 19
No. ....

Instructions regarding War Diaries and Intelligence Summaries are contained in F.S. Regs., Part II. and the Staff Manual respectively. Title pages will be prepared in manuscript.

Hour, Date, Place	Summary of Events and Information	Remarks and references to Appendices
BUSSUS		
1.12.15.	Battⁿ carried out field Exercises starting 9 pt. Point #9.	
2.12.15	Coy horn wg. Battⁿ Classes carried on as per usual	# Sent Captⁿ A. McGown left Battⁿ for the Mediterranean Ex. Force
3.12.15		
4.12.15	Brigade Route March. Route Pt 57 E of Bussus - GORENFLOS - Ymrds 1300 yds E of U in Chou - pt 105 - Y rods 700 yds S of M in HESMIL - Billets Improvement (Week) General cleaning up. Voluntary C of E Service.	
5.12.15.	Wood cutting party detailed to parade every day for the purpose of clearing wood.	# Major Jones loved Battⁿ

(73989) W4141—463. 400,000. 9/14. H.&J.Ltd. Forms/C. 2118/10.

Army Form C. 2118.

WAR DIARY
or
INTELLIGENCE SUMMARY.
(Erase heading not required.)

Instructions regarding War Diaries and Intelligence Summaries are contained in F.S. Regs., Part II. and the Staff Manual respectively. Title pages will be prepared in manuscript.

Hour, Date, Place	Summary of Events and Information	Remarks and references to Appendices
6:12:15	Batt" continued Route March & field exercises. Batt" marched off at 9.30 hrs VAUCOURT & towards ST MAUQILLE. Batt" then carried out movements of counter attack	
7:12:15	Coy training before by O.C. to Batt" & Coy Commdrs. One Coy on range.	
8:12:15	O.O.C. inspected A Coy in full marching order. He then ordered platoon to carry out various maneuvers. B Coy on range. Coy training for remainder of Batt".	
9:12:15	Wet day. Coy training as usual	

WAR DIARY
or
INTELLIGENCE SUMMARY.
(Erase heading not required.)

Army Form C. 2118.

Hour, Date, Place	Summary of Events and Information	Remarks and references to Appendices
10:12:15	Batt¹ route march Route STRIQUIER - VADCHELLES - VAUCOURT In Gunners on range.	
11:12:15	Coy training. One Coy bathed in Batt¹ Baths	
12:12:15	No parades. Voluntary C of E Service.	
13:12:15	Gen Nugent ROC 36th Div inspected Bde bombing School. He then inspected the billets of the Batt¹. He appeared to be satisfied with everything & especially pleased with the Sanitary arrangements.	

WAR DIARY
or
INTELLIGENCE SUMMARY.
(Erase heading not required.)

Army Form C. 2118.

Hour, Date, Place	Summary of Events and Information	Remarks and references to Appendices
BUSSUS 14:12:15	Coy Training & Improvement of Billets. One Coy bathing & inspection of two Coys by Armourer Sergt. Machine Gunners on Range. Studde making parties also paraded	
15:12:15	Brigade Route march. Route of march AILLY-BUIGNY-ST. MAULLE-ST. RIQUIER-NEUVILLE EN MAISON-BOSSUS. After route march inspection arms & feet	
16:12:15	Coy Training. One Coy on sanger drum & two Coys inspected by Armourer Sergt.	
17:12:15	Batt'n field Operations- Batt'n performed various exercises including the attack, artillery formation &c	
18:12:15	Coy training. Woodcutting party & party for making studdes paraded. One Coy on Range	

Army Form C. 2118.

WAR DIARY
or
INTELLIGENCE SUMMARY.
(Erase heading not required.)

Hour, Date, Place	Summary of Events and Information	Remarks and references to Appendices
BUSSUS 19.12.15	Woodcutting party paraded. No parade for rest of Batt., except Church parade & kit inspection	Capt Carter appointed instructor at 3rd Army School
20.12.15	G O C 8th Bde inspected one Coy in full marching order. Various platoons were put through exercises ie Putting on of Smoke Helmets, taking tuning with dummy cartridges, positions for taunting attack & one platoon was ordered by the O C to line the stages of the attack. The G O C remarked on the steadiness of the men. Remainder of Batt Coy training & sound of inter platoon football competition commenced	
21.12.15	Coy training	

WAR DIARY
or
INTELLIGENCE SUMMARY.
(Erase heading not required.)

Army Form C. 2118.

Hour, Date, Place	Summary of Events and Information	Remarks and references to Appendices
22.12.15	Brigade Route March.	
23.12.15	Route BUIGNY - Pt 98 - AH.Y - B Web. Batt" marched well. Weather was bad. Coy training. One platoon practised an attack out of trenches with the use of dummy bombs. New pattern helmets were worn.	
24.12.15	Coy training. One coy on range. Two coys bathing.	
25.12.15	Xmas Day. Church Parade at 8.15. Officers v Sergts football match at 10.30. Officers won 4-1. Coy udg officer went round dinners. All officers dined together. Major Higgins, Major Cowley, Lt Beaumont, Lt Slaght. We also had Lt Bradley. 5 o other ranks arrived. No Officers.	

Army Form C. 2118.

WAR DIARY
or
INTELLIGENCE SUMMARY.
(Erase heading not required.)

Instructions regarding War Diaries and Intelligence Summaries are contained in F.S. Regs., Part II. and the Staff Manual respectively. Title pages will be prepared in manuscript.

Hour, Date, Place	Summary of Events and Information	Remarks and references to Appendices
26/12/15	Church Parade at 9.15. No parades, except woodcutting party	
27/12/15	Coy training. Range allotted to one Coy. Woodcutting party.	Lt. C Turner & Lt J Rouser taken over strength of Batt'n
28/12/15	Coy training. Coy on range commenced firing practice I & II tables of Musketry as laid down by B.de	
29/12/15	Brigade Route March. Route BUSSUS – Rd Junction 200 yds N of Q in ST MAUGILLE – Railway crossing S of A in ST RIQUIER – Pt 57 – GORENFLOS – FRANIES – AILLY. Foot & rifle inspection on arrival back. Coy training. One Coy on Range. Two coys failing.	
31/12/15	Muster Parade by Coys. Comnda Officer inspected D Coy at 10 A Coy at 2.30 pm	

(73989) W4141–463. 400,000. 9/14. H.&J.Ltd. Forms/C. 2118/10.

4 DIVISION
12 BRIGADE

1 BN. KING'S OWN ROYAL LANCASTER REGT

1916 JAN — 1916 DEC

Box 1506

1/1 Roy Lancaster Rgt
Jan 1916
vol XVI

A/PTE MOTEL 12th Bde 36th Div
GLOV

Army Form C. 2118.

WAR DIARY
or
INTELLIGENCE SUMMARY.
(Erase heading not required.)

1st The Kings Own Reg

Hour, Date, Place	Summary of Events and Information	Remarks and references to Appendices
BUSSUS 1.1.16		
Jan 2nd	Coy training. Two Coys arrange to carry on with practice I Two Coys bathing	
3rd	Company training musketry on the Range	
4th	Company training musketry on the Range	
5th	Preparations for move	
BONNEVILLE	The Battalion marched from BUSSUS again 2/Lt. P.M. Melly joined BUSSUS-LONGPLOS-DOMART-BERNEUIL the Battalion at -BONNEVILLE. billeted at BONNEVILLE for BONNEVILLE the night	
6th	The Battalion marched from BONNEVILLE at 9am via BONNEVILLE-BEAUVAL- BEAUQUESNE-MARIEUX-VAUCHELLES- LOUVENCOURT arrived LOUVENCOURT 3.15pm went into billets. Draft of 50 joined Battalion attached to A&B Coys	
LOUVENCOURT	7th Day in Billets. Improvement of billets	

Army Form C. 2118.

WAR DIARY
or
INTELLIGENCE SUMMARY.
(Erase heading not required.)

1st The King's Own Reg

Hour, Date, Place	Summary of Events and Information	Remarks and references to Appendices
January 8th LOUVENCOURT	Following working parties found for work on the Corps line and quarry work. 200 for Corps line, 200 for Quarry work near COIGNEUX.	
9th	Working parties as yesterday. Battalion grenade course recommenced. Coys at disposition of one company.	
10th	Working parties as on 8th. One company Company training	
11th	Working parties as on 10th. One company Company training	
12th	do on 11th	
13th	do 12th	
14th	" " 13th	
15th	Battalion Baths opened. 240 men bathed at VAUCHELLES. 175 men BUS. 100 men bathed at Battalion Baths. No working parties.	
	Commanding Officer inspected D Coy in fighting order.	
16th	Working parties as on 14th.	

Army Form C. 2118.

1/7 The King's Own Reg

WAR DIARY
or
INTELLIGENCE SUMMARY.
(Erase heading not required.)

Hour, Date, Place	Summary of Events and Information	Remarks and references to Appendices
January 17th LOUVENCOURT	Working Parties as on 16th. "C" Coy Inspected in Fighting order by the Commanding Officer.	
18th	Working Parties as on 17th. Base company Maths at B U S	
19th	Working parties as on Jan 18th. New Battalion Grenade Class formed	
20th	Working Parties as on 19th	
21st	No Working Parties. Companies at Disposal of Coys	
22nd	Working Parties as on previous 20th	
23rd	" " " " 22nd Church Parade	
24th	For company not digging Working Parties as on 23rd. Interviews by 50 for No 10 Labour Battalion.	
25th	Working parties on 24th. 4 Officers and Subalterns sent to 56th Divisional School of Instruction	

Army Form C. 2118.

1st The Kings Own Reg.

WAR DIARY
or
INTELLIGENCE SUMMARY.
(Erase heading not required.)

Instructions regarding War Diaries and Intelligence Summaries are contained in F.S. Regs., Part II. and the Staff Manual respectively. Title pages will be prepared in manuscript.

Hour, Date, Place	Summary of Events and Information	Remarks and references to Appendices
LOUVENCOURT		
Jan 26th	Working Parties as R.	
27th	No Working Parties. Inspection of Billets by Commanding Officer	
28th	Working Parties as on 26th	
29th	" " 2 Ph	
30th	" " 2 gh	
31st	No Working Parties. Companies prepare for move.	

Jackson Lt Colonel
Comd 1 Batn King's Own Regt

WAR DIARY or **INTELLIGENCE SUMMARY**

Army Form C. 2118.

18th The King's (Liverpool Reg)

Hour, Date, Place	Summary of Events and Information	Remarks and references to Appendices
LOUVENCOURT 1st Feb.	Battalion in billets cleaning up generally. Orders received for move to reinforce 8th Div.	4½ C.R.S.O'rs and upkeep until 36 Victoria trench. Engineers and 4 trench mortars and machine gun sections. 4 hours period to be retained Supply of 3 schemes tactical to forward.
2nd "	Battalion marched from LOUVENCOURT at 9 a.m. to COL IN CAMPS. Billetted at COLINCAMPS. C.O. Adjutant and M. Coys went up to trenches to see those held by 1st Royal Irish Fusiliers in the afternoon. The 12th Brigade reopened HQ Services.	
COLINCAMPS 3rd "		
Trenches. H.Q. Ripleswood fronting opposite of 12 Bat. Bde. (Trench B.86 (Unfinished) Trenches 2½ miles E of COLINCAMPS. Boundary on right MAILLY-MAILLER SERRE road.	Battalion marched by Companies from COLIN CAMPS positions from to relieve 1st Royal Irish Fusiliers. Relief complete 10.30 p.m. B Company and C Company held the front line. A Company in reserve to B and D Company in reserve to "C" Rey and LEGEND. "D" Company lay in LEGEND at LYGSUM. Distribution of Band C Companies the front line was a line of fighting and a second line of Posts numbered from the right to night. B Company Nos 1 to 7 Posts but exchanged "C" Company Nos 8—13 Posts between Boissy	

WAR DIARY or INTELLIGENCE SUMMARY

1st Bn. Kings Own Regt.

(Erase heading not required.)

Hour, Date, Place	Summary of Events and Information	Remarks and references to Appendices
Trenches 2½ miles NE of COLINCAMPS	Keeping one in reserve in LEGEND. See attached. 1 inch map for position of huts and other reference. 4 emissaries being taken into LEGEND in place of NYREEN & WYTHEN guns and one to the B. [M?]G. Company having been [?]	
5th	1st day in trenches. A quiet day. Work commenced on MUNGSTONIAN LEGEND to a second line of defence. Drills to clear the front line trenches being kept up. NYPEWORT dug in mud, and quite the posts of 2 platoons from both A & D coys for this work. Considerable progress made. The remaining platoons from the A and D companies employed on working the Railway from EUSTON - CHARING CROSS and up from carrying ration parties hut we compound and timber stores. Tramping trump at EUSTON. Trench dump CHARING CROSS. Patrol received 2nd Watershed movement from trench 6 to discover strength of enemy wire and put out if the German patrols were active. One reconnaissance patrol and raiding party found no two positions but our own wire found to be weak.	
6th	A quiet day. Engaged in the morning ordinary routine of the afternoon A and D Companies relieved the Companies they were supporting. Working [...] [?].............................	

WAR DIARY or INTELLIGENCE SUMMARY.

(Erase heading not required.)

1st. The Kings Own R.L.

Hour, Date, Place	Summary of Events and Information	Remarks and references to Appendices
Tuesday to with 26.7.16 to Colincamps	A quiet day. Very warm the morning. Telephonic communication has been established at posts with but communication has been entirely reliant on despatch riders. Germans very quiet in LA SIGNY FARM and railway line. Carrying parties on 8½. A party of N.C.O. and 3 men went out with hand to try and drive a sniper from DEAD MAN'S TRENCH (first in front of nearest corner of THE QUADRILATERAL not marked on trench map) They found DEAD MAN'S TRENCH manned by at least a dozen men, who on seeing our patrol endeavoured to come out of the trench and endeavoured to surround it, but the patrol was able to regain its own trenches without any difficulty without firing hardly a certain amount if shelling of communication trenches especially (BEAUMONT and LEGRAND LITTENTHIA (?) and nothing more was done. Enis. relieved the Battalion in trenches on night 26/27/7/16. Relief complete 9.30pm. Companies marched independently to billets in COLINCAMPS. Marching Parties found 120 by A Coy. First day in billets.	25 + 9. C. Company left the Battalion to go to England on leave. 140 by B Coy

First day in billets. 140 by B Coy

WAR DIARY
or
INTELLIGENCE SUMMARY.

(Erase heading not required.)

1st Kings own

Hour, Date, Place	Summary of Events and Information	Remarks and references to Appendices
COLINCAMPS Jan 10th	Working parties as in g.k. 136 men to B.2 & B.5. Bullets whistled about & our men wounded, except the other damage done about 40 shells and owr in all.	
11th	Next day, no shelling	
12th	Batt. relieved 2nd B. Lanc Fus in trench	
Trenches 2 Kilometres E of COLINCAMPS 13th	Next day, no shelling. Men employed in clearing up & tidying out trench	
14th	Next day, patrol went out on night of 13th & 14th Object. Barricade Serre Rd X35 A 61. 12 midnight, to ascertain if DEAD MAN'S trench was occupied.	opposite Post 13
	Men who found unoccupied. Lines of patrols climbed this front row & taught were	
	not were challenged when close to trench.	
	They were fired on at about 10 yds range	
	They relied under the Sev. bombs were	
	thrown by enemy.	
15th	Quiet day trench in very bad state.	
	Front line com. power forced to retreat	
	on top as communication trench were	
	impassible. Batt. relieved by 2nd Lanc Fus	
	on night of 15th/16th.	

WAR DIARY
or
INTELLIGENCE SUMMARY.
(Erase heading not required.)

Hour, Date, Place	Summary of Events and Information	Remarks and references to Appendices
COUYCAMPS		
17th	CO's Inspection of A Coy.	
18th	Baths. 320 bathed at HEBUTERNE. Working Parties under field Coy. RE Day 20 Left B" Support line 50 Second line 20 Rt B" Support line 26 Laying water pipes to SUCRERIE to C Night 86 Rt B" Support line 86 Lt B" Support line 20 Second line 16 R.E. fatigue	
19th	Working Parties as for 18th. 2 F's attacked.	
20th	Church Parade. Relieved LF's by night &	
in 21st		
21st	Six aerial torpedoes were distributed about K.9.C.b.4 (Behind posts 4 + 5) Sniping very active. Report on bombing attack on LF's on 19th finding tapes were laid down a [illegible] by enemies. Many were killed. Bomb slung in front of m/chine. Seat today of a German Warrant Officer brought in.	

WAR DIARY
or
INTELLIGENCE SUMMARY.
(Erase heading not required.)

Instructions regarding War Diaries and Intelligence Summaries are contained in F.S. Regs., Part II. and the Staff Manual respectively. Title pages will be prepared in manuscript.

Hour, Date, Place	Summary of Events and Information	Remarks and references to Appendices
Trenches 2½ miles E of COUIN CAMPS.		
22nd	Quiet day. Mobile Artillery in action.	
23rd	Quiet day.	
24th	Bath relieved by LF's	
25th	Working party of 270	
26th	Working parties 270 & 18th C.O.'s inspection of "A" Coy.	
27th	270 men bathed at BUS Working parties 270 & 18th Church parade C.O.'s inspection of "C" Coy.	
28th	Bath relieved 2 LFs in trenches.	
29th	Quiet day. Artillery quiet. Very wet day.	

Johnson Lt Col.
Comdg 1/12th Regt. Cmdr.

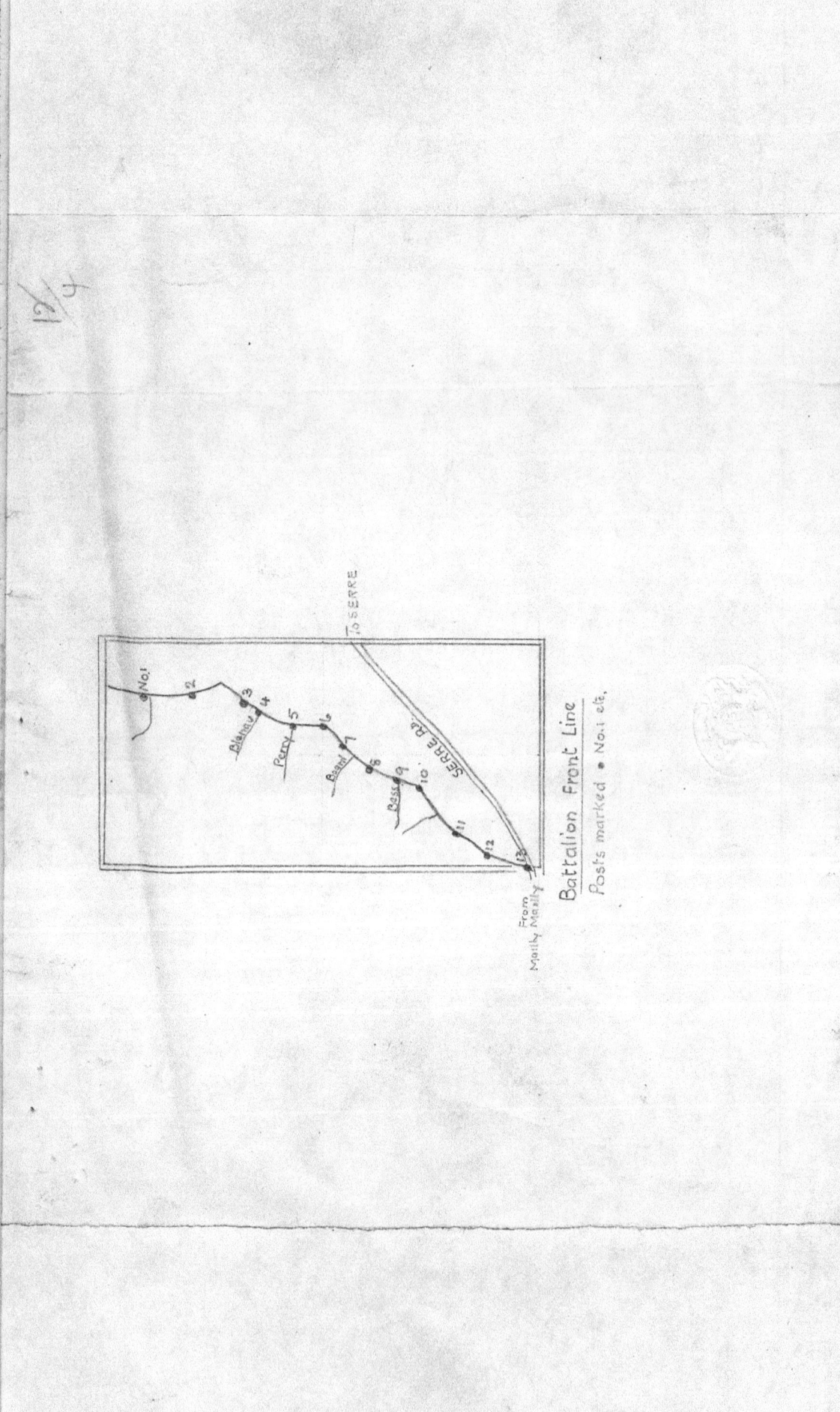

12th Brigade.

4th Division.

1st BATTALION

KING'S OWN ROYAL LANCASTER REGIMENT

MARCH 1916

Army Form C. 2118.

1st H. Kings Inf Reg

WAR DIARY
or
INTELLIGENCE SUMMARY.
(Erase heading not required.)

Hour, Date, Place	Summary of Events and Information	Remarks and references to Appendices
Trenches 1/2 mile E. of COLINCAMPS March 1st	Extremely wet day. Trenches in very bad state. All men employed in cleaning trenches. Bad state due to thawing of snow which fell during 48 hrs in lieu of the 1 to F8.	
2nd	Quiet day. Trenches still very bad	
3rd	Batt" relieved by the Worcesters. Bad weather still prevailing. Trenches in very bad state & much work is required to drag legs with leg weather. Rations being sent of the question. Batt" billeted at SAILLY-AT-BOIS for night	
4th	Batt" marched to MONDICOURT a billeted there for night. Route via COIGNEUX - SOUASTRE - PAS. Heavy snow storm. Road in extremely bad state	

Army Form C. 2118.

WAR DIARY
or
INTELLIGENCE SUMMARY.
(Erase heading not required.)

Hour, Date, Place	Summary of Events and Information	Remarks and references to Appendices
BOUQUE MAISON 5	Battⁿ marched to BOUQUE MAISON via LUCHEUX. One day but mens Still Suffering from foot state of weather.	
6th	Day spent in general cleaning up of equipment clothing etc	
7th	CO inspects all Coys in full marching order	
MEZEROLLES 8	Battⁿ marched to MEZEROLLES via ME UVILLETTE - 60 COCHES. Roads in terrible state but men DOULLENS Road Good Improvement of billets. All companies commenced to construct rifle ranges.	
9th 10th	Battalion Route march LEMBILLARD - OUTRE BOIS- MEZEROLES.	
11th	Battalion Ceremonial Parade.	

WAR DIARY
or
INTELLIGENCE SUMMARY.

(Erase heading not required.)

Army Form C. 2118.

R.B. Kings Own Roy[?]

Hour, Date, Place	Summary of Events and Information	Remarks and references to Appendices
MEZEROLES March 12th	Church Parade. Battalion Hockey. Inspection of Billets by Major General Hon W. Lambton G.O.C. 4th Div.	
13th		
14th	Training and Musketry. Revise Company arrangements Project.	
15th	Brigade "Route march and field operations"	Lt. Hunt & 2/Lt. Levin joined (note Bn.)
16th	Training as on 14th	
17th	" "	
18th	Battalion Memorial Parade.	
19th	Battalion moved from MEZEROLES to HALLOY via DOULLENS and billeted there and its way to trenches	Lt. Colonel J.A. Hitchinson to England invalided. Captain Mathew Lloyd given command of the Battalion temporarily.
" 20th	Physical Training by Companies.	
HALLOY 21st	Battalion marched from HALLOY at 10 am to billets at BAILLEMONT. Route via POMMERA and LA HERLIERE against 1 pm	
BAILLEMONT 22nd	Cleaning of kits. A and B Coys inoculated	

WAR DIARY
or
INTELLIGENCE SUMMARY.

Army Form C. 2118.

12th R. Kings Liverpool Regt

Hour, Date, Place	Summary of Events and Information	Remarks and references to Appendices
Billets BAILLEULMONT 23rd	Working Parties 150 by night 50 by day.	
24th	Working Party 100 by day.	
Trenches N.E. of BERLES 25th	The Battalion relieved 2/Hampshire Fusiliers in trenches East of BERLES. Boundaries Northern:- a tramway line drawn due East from EASTINEAU to front line. Southern Boundary not at present discernible. Both these boundaries from POINT 147 to front line. Battalion reports to on BERLES-ARRAS road. Battalion:- 3 Companies in front line 1 Company in reserve Position of Bryn. Distribution :- in front line as follows:- D Coy Right from trenches 113 to 117 inclusive. A Coy Centre from 118 to 122 inclusive. B Coy Left front from Trenches 123 to 127 inclusive. C Coy HQ and 2 Platoons at POINT 147 2 Platoons at FORT EASTINEAU. Battalion HQ at quarries FORT EASTINEAU. in local Battalion Reserve. Front about 2000 yds.	Reference trench map marked 6.
26th	First day in trenches a quiet day. Workmen to new Battalion HQ at Western end of RENFREW Work on front line parapet. Work on front parapet and on front line communications. Working parties from other Companies improving trenches in the month and	

WAR DIARY
or
INTELLIGENCE SUMMARY.

(Erase heading not required.)

1st The King's Own Rl. Rgt.

Army Form C. 2118.

Hour, Date, Place	Summary of Events and Information	Remarks and references to Appendices
Trenches N.E. of BERLES (21st cont)	One in support about 50 yards in rear.	Reference trench map marked Q
27th	Day of 30 O.R. joined the Battalion. Snipers at work on enemy network. a quiet day.	
28th	27th Battalion continued. Battalion headquarters shelled. Work on trenches in the front line continued. Companies employed.	
29th	A quiet day. Our own snipers active. Working parties continued.	
30th	2 O.R. continued. Patrol sent out, no enemy met with. Our snipers accounted for several enemy snipers.	
31st	A fairly quiet day. Work of 2 O.R. continued. Battalion relieved a quiet day, 2nd Cheshire Rers. relieved the Battalion in trenches. Relief completed 9.15 p.m. Companies marched independently to billets in BAILLEULMONT.	

Rematthews Captain
Comm 1/4th King's Own Rp.

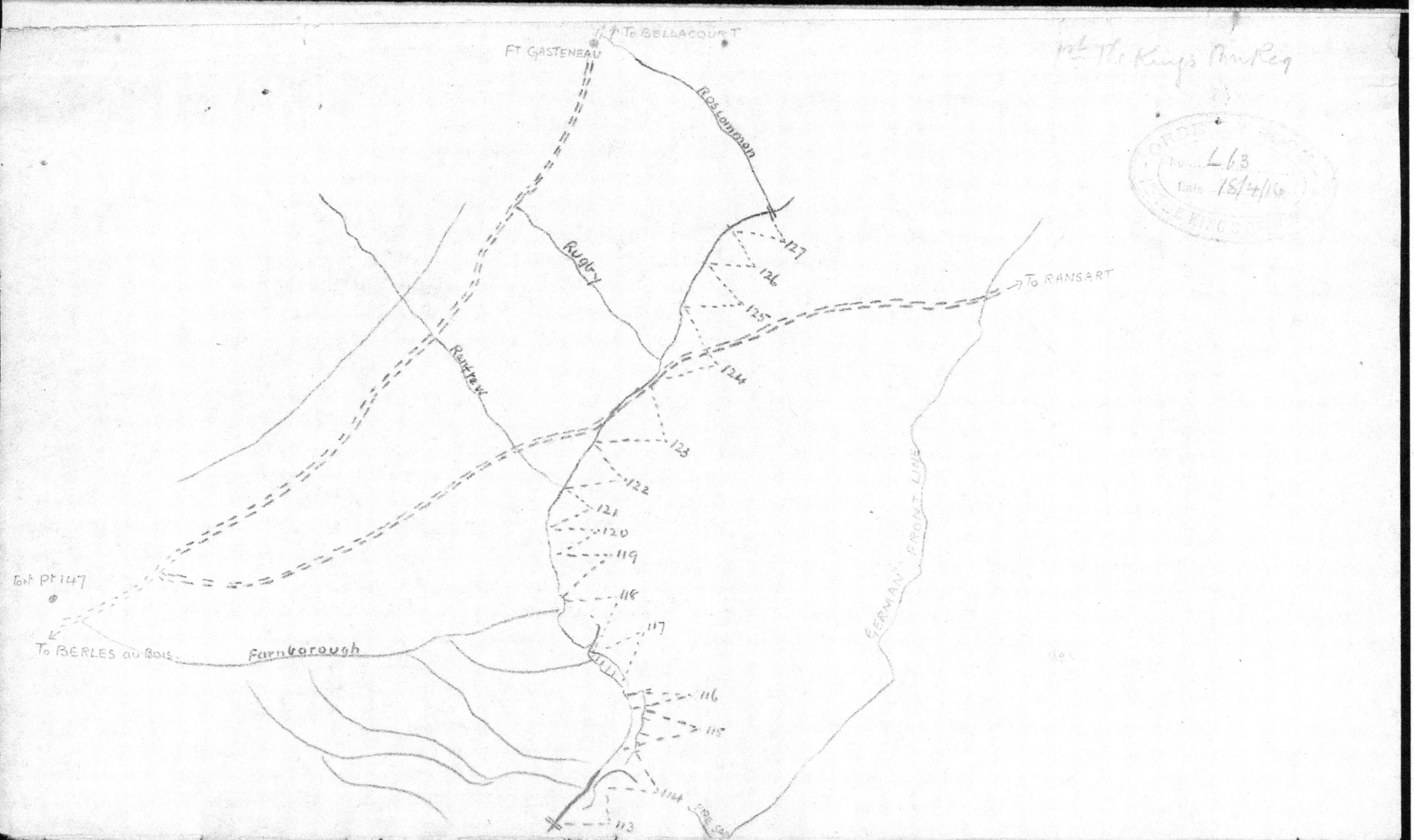

To BELLACOURT
FT GASTENEAU
ROSCOMMON
Rugby
Renfrew
To RANSART
127
126
125
124
123
122
121
120
119
118
117
116
115
114
113
FIRE SAP
GERMAN FRONT LINE
Fort Pt 147
To BERLES au BOIS
Farnborough

12th Brigade.

4th Division.

1st BATTALION

THE KING'S OWN ROYAL LANCASTER REGIMENT

APRIL 1 9 1 6

Appendices :- Report on Minor Operations 16th,
             on PIPE SAP.

Army Form C. 2118.

WAR DIARY
or
INTELLIGENCE SUMMARY.
(Erase heading not required.)

1st The King's Own R.L.

Instructions regarding War Diaries and Intelligence Summaries are contained in F.S. Regs., Part II and the Staff Manual respectively. Title pages will be prepared in manuscript.

Hour, Date, Place	Summary of Events and Information	Remarks and references to Appendices
BAILLEULMONT April 1st	First Day in Billets. Inspection of Equipt. Battalion Baths	
" 2nd	Church Parade. 270 men found for Working Parties	
" 3rd	Baths. Working Parties and 2nd Musketry for Coys.	
" 4th	No one working Parties	
" 5th	Baths. Training under Company arrangements.	
" 6th	Commanding Officer's Inspection of E Company. Commanding Officer's Inspection of "C" Company. The Battalion relieved Spare Two. Relief completed 9.4pm C Company Right Front Company. B Company Centre Front Company. A Company left Front Company. D Company in Reserve Garrisons FORT 147. 2 platoons FORT GASTINEAU. Bn HR MAISON GASTINEAU in FORT GASTINEAU	
Trenches 1 mile N of BERLES. 7th	A quiet day. Battalion Headquarters shelled. Working Company Supplied and Battalion Headquarters relieved by REDFREW Inn Platoon of B Company told off to supply working Party all the enemy Rail Affairs Systems to guns round the Inspection	Representative Trench mortar forwarded with March 1916 War Diary.
8th	A quiet day. Working on a T.T. Communication Patrols out all night between our line and enemy line	

Forms/C. 2118/10.

Army Form C. 2118.

12th K.R.R King's Own Regt

WAR DIARY
or
INTELLIGENCE SUMMARY.
(Erase heading not required.)

Hour, Date, Place	Summary of Events and Information	Remarks and references to Appendices
April 9th Trenches 1 Mile N.E. of BERLES.	A quiet day but Artillery active. Endeavour to induce enemy to disclose his position to the rail. Our patrols again active. One man entered the enemy's wire & returned & reported condition. The information obtained by him was useful in the planning of our raid. Work of B & C Companies & Company commenced wiring in front of their wire near BERLES trenches.	
10th	A quiet day. Our Artillery active but hostile artillery supremely quiet. Enemy shots absolutely nil. A patrol into Bayonet trench and into FORT BASTIN BAY (Both) visited and no enemy seen. Lent Preston for his patrol in totally cooperation for our attempt to mine patrols & run ration.	A draft of 54 Men Rank & File to Battalion from 21st Entrenching Battalion 25 N.C.O.s & 29 men being the draft one Battalion.
11th	A quiet day. Raid on enemy trenches out at 2.10am night M.2. Account raid and preparement of Artillery operation attached. Raid successfully carried out up to objects and Prisoners were taken.	M.W.R.E.A. Z Casualties Officer (Lt ?) Brown wounded 4 Other Ranks wounded

WAR DIARY
or
INTELLIGENCE SUMMARY.
(Erase heading not required.)

Army Form C. 2118.

1st The King's Royal Rifles

Hour, Date, Place	Summary of Events and Information	Remarks and references to Appendices
Trenches M.16 N.E. of BERLES. 12th	A quiet day. Work of Reconstruction since Tour relieved the Battalion in trenches. Relief completed 9.10 p.m. Companies marched back and billeted to billets in BAILLEULMONT	L.O.R. Jones Rn from No 6 Entrenching Battalion
Billets BAILLEULMONT 13th	First day in billets Baths. Cleaning generally. Working Parties 320 strong. C.O.s inspecting D Coy Baths. The following message received from the Corps Commander on a trial of gas on night of 11/12th:- "The Corps Commander wishes you to inform General ? his Battalion the enterprise planned by 8th Bn Middlesex was well conceived and gallantly carried out by all concerned on the night of 11/12th.	
14th	C.O's inspection of A Coy and Machine Gunners. Baths. Working Parties as on 14th.	
15th	Church Parade. Working Parties 200 strong.	
16th	Musketry on range 2 Companies. Remainder Inspection of Company. Working Party of 340.	Lt Colonel J.A. Bircon returned from sick leave and took over Command from Captain Matthews

Army Form C. 2118.

WAR DIARY
or
INTELLIGENCE SUMMARY.
(Erase heading not required.)

1st The King's (Liverpool)

Hour, Date, Place	Summary of Events and Information	Remarks and references to Appendices
Billets BAILLEULMONT 19th April 1916	General Unley by O. the Brigade inspected "C" Company by Platoons. Range two Companies on right of 18/19 to the Battalion relieved time in trenches. "E" Company left front sector. D Company Centre front sector. A Company left front sector. B Company Coy HQ was Platoon, at FORT POINT 147. 2 Platoons FORT EAST INEAU. Bn HQ MAISON EASTINEAU in FORT EASTINEAU.	See trench map in march WAR DIARY
19th		
20th	Considerable Enemy Artillery activity against the Rugeton. Quiet day. One Sniper shot a German. Our Lewis Gun Rangers Enemy working Party in front of SAT M No. 358 Bingham at the angles	See trench map in march WAR DIARY
Trenches hill N.E. of BERLES 21	Enemy Artillery active. One of our Patrols Met a German Patrol and tried to shake them. the later retired in a driving party which came to stand to be attacked.	2Lt S.I.R. O'Shea is sick in England between leave sick & strength.
22	Enemy fired 30 shells into RUGBY RD. Two Pigeons seen to fly over our lives in direction of ADINFER Wood. A Patrol been between Rugelon and 9.12.15 am reports "all quiet".	2nd Lt Ricketts to Hospital Sick. 5621 CSM Thomson Branched A Company in Ap 21. and posted to Rifle Pups or own Regt.

Army Form C. 2118.

1st Bn The King's Own R. Regt

WAR DIARY
or
INTELLIGENCE SUMMARY.
(Erase heading not required.)

Hour, Date, Place	Summary of Events and Information	Remarks and references to Appendices
Trenches April 23rd N.E. of BERLES	Enemy reported our wire opposite the left Coy. Enemy shelled our trenches heavily - appeared to be trying to find machine gun emplacements.	Pres. O. R's improved
24th	Rea.Rn has very bad the whole of this time in the trenches. The front lines of the Bn were frequently swept with M/c gun fire.	
	Progressland	
	Relieved 9 p.m. (reliev) Says No 7 &15 trench taped. the wire kins greatly improved off & until the Battalion was relieved —	
	Left and C in the Coys — 2nd Bn Lancashire Fusiliers relieved on trenches by No 2 — Baks D & C Coys.	
Billets 25th BAILLEULMONT. 26	Coys under OC Coys — Baths Arts B. Battalion Company training. — Lewis Parties Bombing Class reopened.	
27.	Bn Strength of B 270 been been seen furnished by the Bn. Lt Col Bn Bombing Officers inspectors to Battalion Bombers — Lewis Parties 270.	Lt Col Nixon left the Bn Sick
28.	G.O.C. Division inspected 1st Line transport - Physical training and "B" Attack — training. Working parties found. Strength B 270	
29	Coy training —	

Army Form C. 2118.

1st The King's Own Regt

WAR DIARY
or
INTELLIGENCE SUMMARY.

(Erase heading not required.)

Instructions regarding War Diaries and Intelligence Summaries are contained in F.S. Regs., Part II. and the Staff Manual respectively. Title pages will be prepared in manuscript.

Hour, Date, Place	Summary of Events and Information	Remarks and references to Appendices
BAILLEUMONT 30th	The Battalion marched by night from BAILLEUMONT to Billets in SUS-ST LEGER. The Battalion top marched at 8.15 p.m. and reached SUS-ST LEGER at 11.30 a.m 31st Close Billeting — Route — BAILLEUMONT, L'ARBRET, WARLUZEL, SUS-ST LEGER.	

Jn Bromilow
Major
Comdg 1st The King's Own Regt

The Officer i/c

Adjutant General's Office,

Base.

                Herewith please find "War Diary" of the
Battalion under my Command for the month of April 1916.

18/5/16.

                                  ~~Captain.~~ Major
                Commdg 1st The King's Own Regt.

PIPE SAP (W.84.a.4-6) ENTERPRISE.

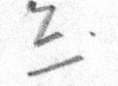

18th April 1916.   Time Table.

Time.

2.10 a.m.   Artillery open slow fire on Sap, and on Front Line.

2.12 a.m.   Fire on Sap Ceases.
             Slow fire continues on Front Line.
             Wire Cutting party (8 men) move out from Listening Post
             12, and place two Bangalore Torpedoes under wire at N.W.
             end of Saphead, and return to our wire.

2.41 a.m.   Torpedoes fired.
             Artillery fire on Sap and increase rate on Front Line
             trenches and communication trenches.
             Howitzers fire on Pt.W.18.d.4-7 and W.18.a.3-4.*

2.43 a.m.   Artillery fire lifts off Sap and continues on Front Line
             and Communication Trenches.
             Wiring party moves forward to clear gaps made by Torpedoes
             followed by Assaulting Party, (2 Officers & 20 men) who
             enter sap and divide into two parties (each 1 Officer &
             10 O.R.). One party move around Right and the other to
             Left. The party arriving first at Entrance to Communi-
             cation trench moves up about 40 yds towards enemy's ~~post~~
             Front Line leaving a stop at entrance.
             The other party clears saphead of any enemy etc.
             Covering Party follow Assaulting Party as far as old
             French Trench and then divide into three parties.

2.51 a.m.   Artillery drops to slow fire.

2.58 a.m.   Claxon Horn sounds for Assaulting Party to retire if they
             have not already returned.
             Covering Party cover the withdrawal.

     *   Maxim fired from this place last night so it requires
             special attention from Artillery.

                                                  Captain.
                                   Commdg 1st The King's Own Regt.

REPORT ON MINOR ENTERPRISE CARRIED OUT ON
MORNING 12TH APRIL 1916, ON GERMAN SAP
(PIPE SAP) W.24.a.4-8.

OBJECT.
(I).(i). a. To kill Germans.
b. To take prisoners who did not offer resistance.
c. To find out strength of enemy post in the Sap.
d. To capture suspected Machine Gun.
e. To obtain articles of equipment and clothing.
f. To endeavour to locate Unit holding enemy trenches in front of our lines.

(ii). RESULTS. (references to above headings).

a. Six Germans were accounted for certain, being bombed in their mined dug-outs. It is probable there were other men in these dug-outs who were not seen.

b. No prisoners were taken. Enemy refused to leave their dug-outs, and threw bombs at our Assaulting Party from the dug-outs, consequently a large number of grenades were thrown into these dug-outs.

c. The Post was not so strong as was believed. There were firing positions for about ten men in the strong post at the head of the sap. There were practically no revetments and very few trench boards. The trenches were muddy and there was a good deal of water in places. The trenches were about 12 feet deep, and 4 feet wide.

d. No Machine Gun, or emplacement was found.

e. The following articles were brought back:-
Smoke Helmet in satchel complete marked with date of issue 26/2/16.
Mowser Rifle dated 1899.
Two German Hand Grenades.
No articles of clothing were obtained.

f. It was not possible to identify unit holding the trenches.

Manner of CARRYING OUT ATTACK.

(2). Attached Time Table was adhered to.
The programme worked without a hitch. (Marked & attached).
2nd Lt.Hayes   The Wire cutting Party however placed the Bangalore torpedoes
R.E.   under enemy wire and returned to point of exit in our trenches
8 Batth Scouts. at 2.34 a.m., this operation taking 7 minutes less than
previously estimated. 2 Lewis Machine Gunners were therefore ordered to open fire on the sap from 2.34 a.m. to 2.41 a.m. to prevent the enemy from tampering with them.
The following is a detailed account of manner in which attack was carried out.
The Wire Cutting Party left at 2.12 a.m. and placed torpedoes in position, returning to the point of exit in our trenches at 2.34 a.m. During this operation two Lewis Machine Gunners were detailed to fire over the German sap and so deaden any noise that might be made in putting the torpedoes through enemy wire.
From 2.34 a.m. to 2.41 a.m., these same Machine Guns were ordered to lower their fire in order to prevent enemy from tampering with the torpedoes.
The Bangalore Torpedoes were exploded at 2.42 a.m.

The Wire Cutting Party left at 2.43 a.m. On arrival at gap in enemy wire, they found a gap 16 feet wide by 5 feet deep, there still remained about 6 feet to cut, which was at once done by the wire cutting party with wire cutters.

Over.

2.

No opposition was met with. The wire cutting took about two minutes.

The Assaulting Party left at 2.44 a.m. and were held up at enemy gap for about a minute whilst the wire cutting party were doing their work.
The Assaulting Party entered trench in file. Party A on the right. Party B on the left.

```
        B       A
        ¡       ¡
        ¡       ¡
        ¡       ¡
```

On entering the sap Party A turned to their right along the southern arm of enemy strong post at the head of the sap. Party B along the northern arm, as had been previously arranged.

1 Officer.
10 O.R.

Party A. This party had no difficulty in entering the sap. Soon after they entered they found a mine dug-out, a German dived into this dug-out before he could be caught, his rifle was however taken. The enemy threw grenades from the dug-out but without effect, the party immediately threw about a dozen grenades into the dug-out. Three Germans were seen in the dug-out. The roof fell in and a hurdle fell across one of the openings. The party then proceeded to the southern point of the sap, here another mine dug-out was found and two Germans were seen half-way up the steps, one apparently badly wounded in the face. About 8 grenades were thrown into the dug-out and the roof fell in. There was only one entrance to this dug-out. The party then went about 20 or 30 yards up the communication trench to the enemy front line and found an empty mine dug-out, which was searched but nothing found.
The Officer Commanding the Party then gave the order to retire, going at the same time himself to get into touch with Party B.
Officer Commanding Party A, 2nd Lieut.O.C.MacWalter.

1 Officer.
10 O.R.

Party B. This party entered sap at the same point as party A and simultaneously. The Party turned to its left on entering and found a mine dug-out, from which a number of grenades were thrown, wounding the Officer Commanding the Party and four other Ranks. The grenade thrown had a very black smoke and peculiar smell. About a dozen grenades were immediately thrown into this dug-out which collapsed. The Party then proceeded up the trench and met 2nd Lieut. MacWalter who ordered them to retire.
One dead German was in the bottom of the trench at the point of entry trampled into the mud. The elan of the Assaulting Party on entering prevented 2nd Lieut.MacWalter from searching him and cutting off epaulettes and other badges.
Officer Commanding Party B, 2nd Lieut.J.I.Mason.

Covering Party. The Covering Party left our trench immediately in rear of the Assaulting Party. This party consisted of 1 Officer and 12 Other Ranks.
The Party was split up into three:-
Two flanking parties and a centre party, to cover retirement of the Assaulting and Wire Cutting Parties and attack any enemy patrol.
Assaulting & Wire Cutting Parties returned 2.58 a.m.
Covering Party 2.59 a.m.

COMMUNICATIONS.
(3).

Battalion H.Q. was established at Right Coy H.Q. about 20 yards from Point of Exit. Trench 115, 1.45 a.m.
The Second in Command remained at FORT GASTINEAU with the Reserve Company.

OVER.

Captain A.H.Read Commanding the Company carrying out the Enterprise established his Headquarters at head of Sap No. 12 (Point of Exit) Trench 115, and was in telephonic communication with Battn H.Q. He was responsible that parties left the Point of Exit according to scheduled times, and communicated all arrivals and departures to Battn H.Q. All matters of policy were referred to Battn H.Q.
The order to fire torpedoes was given from Battn H.Q.
Artillery wires were run into Battn H.Q.
There was communication all the time that parties were out between Wire Cutting & Covering Parties back to Point of Exit Sap 12.

Liaison. (4).

Liaison between the Artillery and ourselves was very good. And Lieut.Radcliffe Commanding "C" Battery (The Battery detailed to fire on the sap) was present with me at Battn H.Q. during the operations.

GENERAL NOTES.

The Time Table was strictly adhered to, Artillery support was most effective, and the whole enterprise was carried out as a drill movement.

Captain.
Commdg 1st The King's Own Regt.

POINT OF EXIT.   Sap No.12.   W.18.c.2-0.   Trench 114.

POINT OF ATTACK.   German Sap northern corner.   W.24.a.4-8.

VICKERS MACHINE   2 Vickers Machine Guns fired during the
GUNS.   operations on Point 4373 W.18.d.5-7. most
                        effectively.

STOKES GUN.   2 Stokes Guns fired on W.24.a.4-4.

12th Brigade.

4th Division.

1st BATTALION

THE KING'S OWN ROYAL LANCASTER REGIMENT

M A Y 1 9 1 6

WAR DIARY
or
INTELLIGENCE SUMMARY.
(Erase heading not required.)

Army Form C. 2118.

Hour, Date, Place	Summary of Events and Information	Remarks and references to Appendices
Sus-St LEGER	**May**	
	1st. Cleaning Billets. The 8th Bedfords moved out. Billets passing to Battalion better Billets.	
	2nd. Physical Training – Battalion Parade 10.15am	
	3rd. Physical Training – Coy O Training – Musketry Matters – Sick and Bayonet fighting – Batting for A & B Coy. Afternoon Football	
	4th. Battalion Cleans. Physical Training. Bowling also Reg Youth Cadets (3 prs) for Transport Bounties. Physical Training – Range A & B Coy 0 – C Coy Batten. 9-12 – D Coy Coy Training Classes 1 a 3. Also Lewis gun Classes. A short Musketry Course started. A & B Coy. Range. Two Lectures. Two Practices afternoon Football	Games & officials
	5th. Musketry Course C.D. HQ 1st two June Sets. A & B Coy. Company Training – afternoon Myo	Sir Cpt I.N. Brunden assumed Cmd of the Battalion and took over Command from Capt R Etherden
	6th. Physical Training – Coy Training – by Drill Musketry Coy Training. Bayonet fight. Afternoon Marching Thrus (being a short distance by Lorie) was released	
	7th. Football – (being a short distance by Lorie) was released. The Battalion marched out of S.u.S. St LEGER at 5.10 pm and marched to BERTRAN COURT arriving there at 11.30 pm Route. Sus-St LEGER – HUMBERCOURT – PAS – Buster Ariles BERTRAN COURT. The Bus was driven	

Army Form C. 2118.

1st The King's (L'pool Reg)

WAR DIARY
or
INTELLIGENCE SUMMARY.
(Erase heading not required.)

Hour, Date, Place	Summary of Events and Information	Remarks and references to Appendices
BERTRANCOURT May	Cleaning up Billets. The Battalion was billeted in Huts.	
9th		
10th	Physical Training - 9.30 - 10.30 am. Musketry.	
11th	Every even. lecture given by the Battalion bomb. and digging. Total Strength of Parties 640 men - Rest physical exercise	Every day drill Smoke Helmets were allotted to each Company.
12th	Digging - Strength of Parties 585 men - ditto	
13th	Digging - Strength of Parties 730 men - ditto	
14th	Digging - Strength of Parties 730 men - ditto	
15th	Digging - Strength of Parties 780 men - ditto	
	Owing to brighter Skies hourly Enforcing the front line area, we had to keep digging	2 O R Slightly wounded
16th	Digging - Strength of Parties 730 men - ditto	
17th	Digging - Strength of Parties 730 men - ditto	
18th	Digging - Strength of Parties 683 men - ditto	
19th	Digging - Strength of Parties 683 men - ditto	
20th	Digging - Strength of Parties 683 men - ditto	
21st	Digging - Strength of Parties 685 men - ditto	2/5/1 OR slightly wounded.
22nd	Working Parties ceased	2/2nd Lt. Masini Montford + Pollard arrived
23rd	Marched from BERTRANCOURT. Leaving at 9 p.m. Route ACHEUX - LOUVENCOURT - VAUCHELLES - MARIEUX - BEAUQUESNE 4 hours halt (2.15 am) west of BEAUQUESNE. Marched on to	2nd Lt. 2nd Lt. Wright + someone the Battalion from ETAPLES

(73989) W.4141-463. 400,000. 9/14. H.&J.Ltd. Forms/C. 2118/10.

Army Form C. 2118.

1st The King's Own R.

WAR DIARY
or
INTELLIGENCE SUMMARY.
(Erase heading not required.)

Instructions regarding War Diaries and Intelligence Summaries are contained in F.S. Regs., Part II and the Staff Manual respectively. Title pages will be prepared in manuscript.

Hour, Date, Place		Summary of Events and Information	Remarks and references to Appendices
	May		
BEAUMETZ.	24th	Marched off barracks route CANDAS – FIENVILLERS – BERNAVILLE BEAUMETZ. Arrived 11am.	
	25th	Marched from BEAUMETZ at 9am for YRENCH route LONGVILLERS – DOMLEGER – arriving 10 am.	
YRENCH	26th	Detachment of 40 men left for 2nd Entrenching Battn, marching to BERNEUIL under 2nd Lt Fitchett. The Battn. practised the advance in Artillery formation	
	27th	Brigade Exercise, practising the advance in Artillery formation.	
	28th	Battalion Parade 9-30 am. Fighting order, kit inspection and Gas Helmet inspection. Divisional Reserve at 3 pm.	28th 2nd Lt A. B. Montgomery, 7th Worcesters joined the Battn for instruction.
	29th	9-15 am to 11-45am Company Training. Divisional Reserve in the afternoon.	
	30th	9-30am to 11-45 am Coy Training. Rapid digging practice by Platoons.	
	31st	9-15 am to 12 noon. 2-15pm to 4-5pm Extended order drill. Companies in the attack. Drill smoke helmets were used by A & B Companies. Practice of rapid digging by platoon.	

J. W. Sandilands
Major
Commdg 1st The King's Own Regt.

12th Brigade.

4th Division.

1st BATTALION

THE KING'S OWN ROYAL LANCASTER REGIMENT

JUNE 1916

WAR DIARY or INTELLIGENCE SUMMARY.

Army Form C. 2118.

1st King's Own Royal Regt.

Vol 21 ← 22

Hour, Date, Place	Summary of Events and Information	Remarks and references to Appendices
June 1916.		
YVRENCH 1st	Morning. Company training – March by sections of ½ in drill – afternoon. At disposal of OC Companies.	
2nd	2.1.30 p.m. Divisional exercise over the training area – The Division practised the supposed coming advance – The Corps Commander was present.	
3rd	Morning. Company Training – Extend from formation. Afternoon – Battalion parade – Battalion drill and ceremonial. Preparation for Brigade sports with 2/Br. Bowley.	
4th	Brigade Church Parade 9 A.M. Roman Catholic Parade Services 7 A.M. Montgomery's Service 10 A.M. Afternoon – Battalion held for Brigade sports.	
5th	Brigade route march – moved off about 9 A.M. and marched & arrived ½ mile in very wet weather. CRAMONT – DOM LEGER – CONTEVILLE – and through MAISON PONTHIEU back to YVRENCH.	
6th	(1) Each B's and bayonet – 5 rounds were fired with the smoke helmet on (2) Initiation of Officers and other ranks in rifle wiring order (3) Company Drill (4) Bathing	Arrived 7.9.15. This was a very wet day.

Army Form C. 2118.

WAR DIARY
or
INTELLIGENCE SUMMARY.
(Erase heading not required.)

1st Bn. The King's (Liverpool Reg.)

Instructions regarding War Diaries and Intelligence Summaries are contained in F.S. Regs., Part II. and the Staff Manual respectively. Title pages will be prepared in manuscript.

Hour, Date, Place	Summary of Events and Information	Remarks and references to Appendices
YVRENCH June 7th	Brigade Parade. The Battalion moved early to the assembly trenches and once more practiced in connection with the impaired advance. The new Brigadier was present. In the afternoon Brigadier General Archie delivered a lecture to officers upon crater warfare.	
8th	Morning - Company training. 1st Rests of the Brigade Sports and boxing south helmet drill. Afternoon Brigade Sports were held. Afternoon a series of lectures were given upon a set of mobile trenches constructed by the Chaplain Capt. Burrell. It was carried by 2/Lt Lewis Gun armament was also inspected by 2/Lt. C.O. Wright, and has been adopted.	2/Lts. Kent Storey, Matthews and Hodson joined the battalion.
9th	The Battalion moved from YVRENCH via DOMLEGER to BEAUMETZ. Left 9.15 a.m. and arrived at BEAUMETZ at about noon, and took over from billets or new falls in it. Weather was warm.	
10th	Battalion left BEAUMETZ at 9.5 a.m. for BEAUVAL, by BERNAVILLE, FIENVILLERS and CANDAS. Arrived about 1 p.m. and proceeded to billets.	14 O.R. arrived

Army Form C. 2118.

WAR DIARY
or
INTELLIGENCE SUMMARY.
(Erase heading not required.)

1st Bn. The King's Own Regt.

Hour, Date, Place	Summary of Events and Information	Remarks and references to Appendices
BEAUVAL. June 11th	Church Parade in the fields at 9.30 a.m. B Coy marched to ACHEUX at 9 a.m. to report to O.C. The London Field Engineering Company. They were employed on wood cutting in the wood between ACHEUX & LOUVENCOURT. 2 Officers and 62 O.R. marched to BERTRANCOURT and reported for work to O.C. 1st Bn. Royal Warwicks. The remainder of the battalion left BEAUVAL at 6.5 p.m. and marched to BERTRANCOURT via BEAUQUESNE - MARIEUX - AUTHIE & BUS. Arrived about 11 p.m. and went into tents.	Arrival of 14 O.R. at BEAUVAL
12th	2/Lt. Molloy proceeded at 3 a.m. to take charge of detachment at Montrelet with No. 3 Entrenching Battalion. C and D coys proceeded on detachment to MAILLY-MAILLET at 3 p.m. Capt. Spring being in charge. Weather very wet.	Arrival of 16 O.R.
BERTRANCOURT 13th	11 a.m. Memorial Service to the late Field Marshal Earl Kitchener of Khartoum. Many officers & O.R. were present. Lewis gun class, also snipers and signallers. Working parties.	Arrival of 3 O.R.
14th	Working parties. Moved from BUS to BERTRANCOURT to hutments in BERTRANCOURT to time at 11 P.m. advanced to midnight.	

Army Form C. 2118.

WAR DIARY
or
INTELLIGENCE SUMMARY.
(Erase heading not required.)

1st Bn. The King's Own Regt.

Instructions regarding War Diaries and Intelligence
Summaries are contained in F.S. Regs., Part II
and the Staff Manual respectively. Title pages
will be prepared in manuscript.

Hour, Date, Place	Summary of Events and Information	Remarks and references to Appendices
BERTRANCOURT JUNE 15th 1916	Working parties day and night. Weather wet. Work chiefly carrying T.M. ammunition.	
16th	Working parties. Recce Capt. Brewis finished model of German lines opposite COLINCAMPS. Brigadier lectures Officers and NCO's upon supposed advance.	2/Lt Nelly and 41 O.R. returned from detachment at BERNEUIL. C.i.D Coys returned from MAILLY-MAILLET.
17th	Very fine weather. Working parties continue from camp. Lectures on model. Tactics.	
18th	Working parties. Lectures on model. Musketry.	
19th	Working parties. Lectures on model. Lectures mounted under company arrangements. 2/Lt MacWatters employed as sniper at the village of St Leger. King's telegram of congratulation.	2/Lts P. Clegg & Joined B.H. Banks from 10th Bn K.O. Regt at Etaples.
20th	Working parties. Afternoon Rifle bn training firing with smoke helmets on.	
21st	Weather very fine. Training - morning - study of model. Trench training. Afternoon - Rapid loading firing - Smoke helmet drill	

Army Form C. 2118.

WAR DIARY
or
INTELLIGENCE SUMMARY.
(Erase heading not required.)

1st Bn. The King's Own Regt.

Hour, Date, Place		Summary of Events and Information	Remarks and references to Appendices
BERTRANCOURT	JUNE 22nd 1916	Training - Morning - Practice in jumping trenches, and musketry. Afternoon - Lectures on musketry and working parties. Weather fine.	
"	23rd	Training. Morning - A Coy musketry. Afternoon 2-3.30 lecture under Coy Commander. Rest - working parties.	
"	24th	Training. Morning - Physical Trg. 9.15 Noon Rapid loading. Smoke Helmet drill (bayonet fighting for C Coy). Afternoon Model for all Coys. Inspection by O.C. Coy. Lecture by G.O.C. to Coy Commanders at Model.	
"	25th	Training. Model Trenches. All Coys to Coys in turn. Church parades C.E. 10:00am R.C. 7:15am Non Conf 11:30am. Smoke Helmet drill rapid loading. Baggatine. Torpedoe demonstration. BDE Orders to parade as full for Training.	
"	26th	Training. Brigade Exercise on LOUVENCOURT Training Area - The advance from Line. B. Afternoon. Rapid loading & Musketry instruction. Carrier Instruction at Model. 10% Reinforcement at Model.	

Army Form C. 2118.

WAR DIARY
or
INTELLIGENCE SUMMARY.
(Erase heading not required.)

Instructions regarding War Diaries and Intelligence Summaries are contained in F.S. Regs., Part II. and the Staff Manual respectively. Title pages will be prepared in manuscript.

Hour, Date, Place	Summary of Events and Information	Remarks and references to Appendices
BERTRANCOURT June 27th 1916	Training under Coy Commdts. Addressed by G.O.C. 4th Division 12 Noon. Afternoon Inspection of Bn in fighting order by G.O.C. Bgde.	
June 28th	Bangalore Torpedo demonstration instruction. Battn resting.	
June 29th	Bangalore Torpedo instruction. June 27 Stores etc. (very wet day)	
"	Offensive operation. Working party of 1 Officer 30 OR	
June 30th	Clearing & issuing of all supplies. Pre parts to move for trenches.	1 O.R. wounded
July 1st	No account of attack.	
July 2nd	Battalion moved into support trenches at ELLES SQUARE. Strength of Battn	Strength paraded with Bn night 30 & June Officers 41 Other ranks 984
July 3rd	Rotn support trenches. ELLES SQUARE shelled, July 7 Casualties killed.	ELLES SQUARE heavy rain
Trenches by MAILLY-MAILLET July 4th	Bn in ELLES SQUARE heavy rain	

12/4.

War Diary
of
1ᵗʰ Bn. K.O.R.L. Regt.
for
July 1916.

1/K.O.R.L. Army Form C. 2118

WAR DIARY
or
INTELLIGENCE SUMMARY.
(Erase heading not required.)

Hour, Date, Place	Summary of Events and Information	Remarks and references to Appendices
30th June to 1st July 1916.	Account of Operations on 30th June 1916 to 1st July 1916.	
	Owing to the fact that there are so few Officers now serving with the Battalion who made any substantial progress in the attack on the 1st July it is neither possible to give an account nor detailed account of the operations.	
	This account is based on information obtained from Officers and men who took part in the attack and are now serving with the Battn. Also on different categories of casualties sustained by different companies according to their different dispositions.	
BERTRANCOURT. June 30th. 10p.m	At about 10 p.m. on 30th June the Battn. was preparing to march off. The enemy commenced to shell the neighbourhood of our camp at BERTRANCOURT. At 10.54 p.m. "A" and "D" Coys moved off, "B" and "C" Coys moved in rear with 100 yds distance between platoons. The route of the Battn. was as follows :- The track running E. of the camp, across BERTRANCOURT — COURCELLES road — down the valley, thence following the white guide posts to MAILLY — SUGERRIE road, following the SUGERRIE road for 20 yds, turning S.E. along the track marked by the white guide posts to 6th AVENUE, along N. side of 6th AVENUE across the sunken road, continuing along 6th AVENUE to where ROMAN road runs under SERRE road, thence turning N.E. following white guide posts to CHEEROH AVENUE. Assembly trenches	

WAR DIARY
or
INTELLIGENCE SUMMARY.
(Erase heading not required.)

Army Form C. 2118

Hour, Date, Place	Summary of Events and Information	Remarks and references to Appendices
ASSEMBLY AREA. 1.30 a.m. July 1st.	Trenches in neighbourhood of GREEN TRENCH and BOW STREET. The Battn. was present in its assembly area at 1.30 a.m.	
July 1st	1st July. Casualties amounted to 6 w.t. to this action. Dispositions of Coys. in the attack as shewn on the programme below.	
6.41 a.m.	Frontage of 14 platoons (approximates, 500 yds.) exact dispositions of Coys. as shewn on attd. programme below. The Attack. An Officers' patrol consisting of 1 Officer (2Lt. E.C. Machell(?)) and 20 O.R. advanced as a screen extending over the whole Battn. front at 6.41 a.m. At 6.46 a.m. leading sections of the Battn. advanced from their Assembly Area. Directly the advance commenced the Batt. came under heavy machine gunfire and there seems no doubt that a large number of casualties occurred before reaching our own front line. The 10th Left Coys. seemed to have suffered most heavily up to this point. The advance still continued, however, a large number of casualties being sustained in NO MAN'S LAND from both machinegun and shellfire; this is proved by the fact that a large number of killed and wounded stretcherbearers from NO MAN'S LAND. The 10th Left Coys. again seemed to have suffered most heavily.	G.O.R.

Army Form C. 2118

WAR DIARY
or
INTELLIGENCE SUMMARY.
(Erase heading not required.)

Instructions regarding War Diaries and Intelligence Summaries are contained in F.S. Regs., Part II. and the Staff Manual respectively. Title pages will be prepared in manuscript.

Hour, Date, Place	Summary of Events and Information	Remarks and references to Appendices
July 1st	Only a small number of those Coys. reached the German front line. The two right Coys. seemed to have made substantial progress. Some men state that they actually saw men crossing the German second line. The casualties in officers of these two Coys are considerably greater than in the two left Coys. An Officer of the left centre Coy. who was only able to reach the German front line owing to his having so few men left, states that he saw no one advancing on his left, but that to his right he could see men advancing (Most of these men appeared to belong to the Seaforth Highlanders). He further states that the enemy were holding their second line directly in front of him and to his left front very strongly and that they had machine guns on the spur just in front of their second line or his left front. Three men of the two right Coys. who are now with the Batt. state that in the German second line there was a large force of all Regiments and that at	
about 12.30 a.m.	about 12.30 p.m. these men retired with the remainder of this force, practically all back to the German 1st Line, and shortly after, thence to our front line, owing to the strong bomb attacks made by the enemy which they were unable to meet owing to the shortage of bombs.	

(73989) W4141-463. 400,000. 9/14. H.&J.Ltd. Forms/C. 2118/10.

Army Form C. 2118.

WAR DIARY
or
INTELLIGENCE SUMMARY.
(Erase heading not required.)

Instructions regarding War Diaries and Intelligence Summaries are contained in F.S. Regs., Part II. and the Staff Manual respectively. Title pages will be prepared in manuscript.

Hour, Date, Place	Summary of Events and Information	Remarks and references to Appendices
July 1st	X As regards the left Coy., owing to the fact that the right Batn. 31st Division had been unable to make any headway, few of them reached the front line. There seems to be a general opinion that the Batn. lost its direction to a certain extent, advancing too much to its left so men of the Left Coy. state that when they crossed our front line there were men of the 31st Division in our front line at this point. The Brigadier of the Right Brigade 31st Division checked any further advances and ordered what men remained to	KILLED Capt. J.F.N. Young. 2nd Lt. H.P. Wells. " R.R. Wilson " C.C. Woodwalls. " P. Else " T. Hardy. " F.W. Whittaker. WOUNDED Capt. A.K. Read. 31st R.W. Susan Regt. " S.S. Skerrett " 2nd Lt. W.S. Ives " J.P. Stephenson " L.L. Morloch. " F.C. Henshaw " E.O. Wright. " B.J. Tillett " A.J. Burns. (Shell Shock) " W.R. Thompson. " L.A. Hall. (Shell Shock) " E.J. Whitworth Capt. Z.M. Brewer. R.A.M.C. MISSING Major J.N. Bromilow. Capt. A. Weatherhead. 2nd Lieut. A.H.W. Anderson.
LEG END. 4 a.m. (about)	form up in LEG END. This seems to have been about 4 A.M. but the exact time is uncertain. 120 unwounded at the end of the day and to were ordered to form up in their former Assembly trenches. (GREEN TRENCH area.) X (Diagram of Disposition of Batt: attached. colored.)	

WAR DIARY
or
INTELLIGENCE SUMMARY.
(Erase heading not required.)

Army Form C. 2118.

Hour, Date, Place	Summary of Events and Information	Remarks and references to Appendices
	Critique of Scheme and Time Table for the Attack.	
	Speaking from observation on the extreme right of the 4th Division as well as from accounts received from left of the Division there seems to have been	
	1. Lack of weight.	
	2. The fact that 11th Brigade and 31st Division were unable to capture and consolidate their first objective, enabled the enemy to man those objectives and with rifle and machine gun fire inflict heavy losses on the Battns. advancing in rear before they could even reach their own front line. They were thus by the Time Table unable even to act as a support to the 11th Brigade.	
	3. Whether or not in a position to state whether any batteries were detailed as "Sniping" had such Batteries been able to sprieon points where the enemy in rear of their front lines were seen to be using both machine gun and rifle fire, the advance would have been probably more effective. As it was it appears that the Artillery Program barrage worked strictly according to program and as was intended, thereby giving little "Artillery Support" to the rear Battns. of the Division.	
	4. Such strong points as the village of SERRE, ITS RIDGE. REDOUBT which commanded the advance inflicting heavy casualties	

Army Form C. 2118.

WAR DIARY
or
INTELLIGENCE SUMMARY.
(Erase heading not required.)

Instructions regarding War Diaries and Intelligence Summaries are contained in F. S. Regs., Part II. and the Staff Manual respectively. Title pages will be prepared in manuscript.

Hour, Date, Place	Summary of Events and Information	Remarks and references to Appendices
	with machine guns by cross fire must be captured before a considerable advance can be made. No doubt, owing to the fact that the 31st Division were unable to make any advance most of the machine guns in SERRE, by that time unmolested by Artillery fire were enabled to concentrate on the advancing troops to their left front, which seems to have been an impression in the Batt. that 5. There would be no advance by the 12th Brigade until SERRE and THIEPVAL were taken, which of course would have been the case had the programme worked out satisfactorily. 6. The Time Table was strictly adhered to throughout, and the advance carried out as a drill movement. 7. If a proportion of Officers could be kept in mine dug outs near the front line and sent up to their units directly the troops have entered the enemy trenches, even the disorder of the Brigadier General, control could be efficiently established and the position captured thoroughly consolidated and held.	

WAR DIARY
or
INTELLIGENCE SUMMARY.
(Erase heading not required.)

Army Form C. 2118

Hour, Date, Place	Summary of Events and Information	Remarks and references to Appendices
	Memo sent 11/6/16. to 12th Brigade. re above diagram.	

"Reference the attached sketch showing disposition of Batt. during/under my command during the advance.

1. Lines of sections though shewn as covering from front to rear and all in line will in reality be irregular.

2. My reasons for putting the four Coys. in line, is, that it avoids intermingling of units, and is preferred by my O.C. Coys rather than leaving two Coys. in the front line and two in support.

3. The 24 barbed wire cutters will be distributed amongst the scouts until the PUISIEUX road, and each half batt. has been instructed to ensure that 12 men in his lines of advance are specified sections to pass through in single file. On reaching the PUISIEUX road the wire cutters will be handed over to the nearest Officers or N.C.O. for redistribution to selected men.

The 64 bayonet wire cutters, and 40 wire breakers are distributed equally to the four Coys. and are all in the leading lines."

Army Form C. 2118.

WAR DIARY
or
INTELLIGENCE SUMMARY.
(Erase heading not required.)

1st/5th Bn. King's Liverpool R.

Instructions regarding War Diaries and Intelligence Summaries are contained in F.S. Regs., Part II. and the Staff Manual respectively. Title pages will be prepared in manuscript.

Hour, Date, Place	Summary of Events and Information	Remarks and references to Appendices
Trenches East of MAILLY MAILLET		
6th	Heavy rain. In support ELLES SQUARE.	
7th	ELLES SQUARE heavily shelled with lachrymatory shells in the morning. Battalion relieved in ELLES SQUARE about 2am & proceeded to huts in MAILLY MAILLY L. with about 250 to 300 as damage done to the Battalion.	
8th	First day in the trenches de arms up Company Parts in 2nd line trenches	
9th	The Corps Commander (General Sir Aylmer Hunter Weston) visited the Battalion and spoke to Coy Commanders, thanked & also congratulated them on the operations of 4th July. Bath in the afternoon.	
11th	The O.C 4/5 Bn spoke to the men by Coys contratulating them on the operations of 4th July Bn. who commenced to BERTRANCOURT in	Captain R. Mathew reported to take command of the Battalion from the 1st Bn. Staff
12th	afternoon.	
	Bn. 12th July in huts in Rufford. Inspected Musketry & uniforms. A/Lt Col Thorp commanded the	

WAR DIARY
or
INTELLIGENCE SUMMARY.
(Erase heading not required.)

Army Form C. 2118.

Hour, Date, Place	Summary of Events and Information	Remarks and references to Appendices
BEAUCOURT July (Holding)	Aeroplanes, Snipers, Bombing	
12th	Comparatively quiet and Battalion Class in contact with [?]	
13th	" "	
14th	" "	
15th	" "	Lt Colonel RussellD.S.O joined the Battalion from Commandant D. Depot
16th	" "	Lt Col Brummans to Command O.C Depot following officers posted to Battalion
16th		2/Lt H Murby 2/Lt A. Lavecomb N.D. Hipon ,, R Scott ,, CE Thomas ,, QW Cooke ,, R Stevens ,, B C Eley ,, F.A. Rostron
17th	Battalion relieved 15th Royal Warwickshire Regt in trenches ¾ mile distant of AUCHONVILLERS, being on East & North of Battalion district opposite BEAUMONT HAMEL & between Right D Coy & Gate Bar inclusive. Further in rear in PENDERO in support. A Coy in R.E. reserve Trench at rear of Battalion left, "C" Coy. TENDERLOIN Trench anywhere B. HQ. Front line by Railroad, about 350. Front line extending right with KATLIN'S STREET Southern junction of trench with NEW BEAUMONT Road	
18th	A quiet day. New trench commenced at night running forward to SUNKEN road. Enemy machine gun & Lewis guns rather active throughout night, but aeroplane active about daylight.	

WAR DIARY
or
INTELLIGENCE SUMMARY.
(Erase heading not required.)

Army Form C. 2118.

Hour, Date, Place	Summary of Events and Information	Remarks and references to Appendices
Training E of AUCHONVILLERS 19th	Continuous progress made. A certain amount of enemy artillery active by but with small effect. Held on new trench continued enemy made two separate attacks. Covering for truncheon.	1st The King leaves by [illegible]
20th	Enemy artillery opened west but with fresh from 14.2 howitzers. Weapon new trench continued. Attempt made to emplace gun. Trench completed except a number of carriettes.	
21st	5th Royal Berks Rgt. relieved 1st Battalion in trenches Bttn completed 5.15 pm. Battalion marched to billets at LOUVENCOURT. Present strength by coy to billets 8/15 am in billets 8.15 am	Lt Jemmis 2nd Lieut Swanby from pay
AUTHIEULE 22nd	Battalion marched to AUTHIEULS at 7 am arriving 10.30 am. Rested all day. Battalion marched at 10.15 pm for DOULLENS entrained at DOULLENS 62 12.30 am. Train left DOULLENS 1.30 am.	

Army Form C. 2118.

WAR DIARY
or
INTELLIGENCE SUMMARY.
(Erase heading not required.)

Instructions regarding War Diaries and Intelligence Summaries are contained in F.S. Regs., Part II. and the Staff Manual respectively. Title pages will be prepared in manuscript.

Hour, Date, Place	Summary of Events and Information	Remarks and references to Appendices
1916		1st The King's Own R.L
CASSEL } July 23(rd)	Battalion detrained CASSEL 7.30am. Breakfasts at CASSEL. Battalion marched from CASSEL 10.15am to HERZEELE, arrived there 2.30pm. Companies billeted in farms round the village. Very comfortable billets.	
HERZEELE 24th	Company training. Classes of instruction opened. Specialists. C.O.'s inspection of billets.	
" 25th	Company training	
" 26th	Arrivals Parade & Company training	
" 27th	Battalion marched from HERZEELE at 12.30pm and bivouacked in wood about 2 miles west of POPERINGHE (close to PROVEN).	
D. Camp N.E. of POPERINGHE	28th Battalion marched 9.15am to hut in D Camp, about 2 miles N.E. of POPERINGHE, about 1 mile from POPERINGHE—YPRES Rd.	
	29th Company training	
	30th Do Do	
		O.C. Smellie W. O. A.J.K. Cmdg 1st Bn. The King's Own R.L.R

(73989) W4141—463. 400,000. 9/14 3/ H.&J.Ltd. Forms/C. 2118/10.

Disposition of 1st Batt. The King's Own Regt.

July 1st 1916.

REMARKS

Scouts. Four patrols of five men commanded by selected Scout. Composed of 16 trained snipers, scouts and increased to 30 with specially selected men who have been trained at WRENCH.

Fighting Patrols. Two fighting patrols composed of a Lewis Machine Gun with 9 men, the team and assisted by 6 Scouts. Scout Officer 2/Lt. MacWalter in centre with 2 runners, 2 signallers and his own observer.

A Lewis Machine Gun has been detached from both B & C Coy for this purpose. Remainder of Gun teams will advance with right sectors of the front line, B & C Coy. The pair of scouts accompanying Lewis M.G. will carry a telescope and telescopic rifle. There will also be another telescope & rifle with each fighting patrol.

Front Line. One sector from each of the 2 leading platoons of the 4 Coys. O.C. Coys. will send the most reliable Platoon commander into the front line & L.M.G. team will advance with section immediately in rear.

Reinforcements Front Line. The platoon commander will remain at the head of these reinforcements until all are in the firing line. The last section of each platoon being a grenade section will not carry rifles.

Supports. Two platoons from each Coy., the rear section of each platoon being the grenade section.

D Coy. C Coy. B Coy. A Coy.

Batt. H.Qrs.

- ⊙ O.C. Coy.
- ○ Platoon Commander
- ⊙ Scout Officer
- ||| Lewis Gun
- P Pair of Signallers
- | Section
- M.G. Vickers Gun
- X Special Scouts
- . Supplementary Scouts

Batt. H.Q. consist of :-
C.O. and Adjt.
L.M.G. Officer 2/Lt. Robinson.
Signal Officer. 2/Lt. Rowley.
Signallers. 5.
Runners. 16.
Carriers.- L.M.G. ammunition who are trained in filling drums - 16.

Army Form C. 2118.

WAR DIARY
or
INTELLIGENCE SUMMARY.

(*Erase heading not required.*)

Instructions regarding War Diaries and Intelligence Summaries are contained in F.S. Regs., Part II. and the Staff Manual respectively. Title pages will be prepared in manuscript.

Hour, Date, Place	Summary of Events and Information	Remarks and references to Appendices

(73989) W4141—463. 400,000. 9/14. H.&J.Ltd. Forms/C. 2118/10.

7th DIVISION.

B. H. Q.

91st INFANTRY BRIGADE.

APRIL 1918.

12th Brigade.

4th Division.

1st BATTALION

THE KING'S OWN ROYAL LANCASTER REGIMENT

AUGUST 1916

1 K.O.R Lance Regt!
1st Bn King's Own

Army Form C. 2118.

WAR DIARY
or
INTELLIGENCE SUMMARY.
(Erase heading not required.)

Place	Date	Hour	Summary of Events and Information	Remarks and references to Appendices
D Aug N.E. of POPERINGHE	July 30th 1916		Training	1923
	Aug 1st		"	
	" 2nd		"	
	" 3rd	4pm	12th Brigade relieved 10th Brigade in the line. Battalion in Brigade Reserve. A.B Coys as 2 Platoons on CANAL BANK, close to No 4 BRIDGE. HQ, C&D Coys in CHATEAU DES TROIS TOURS 1 Mile West of BRIELEN.	
CHATEAU DES TROIS TOURS. CANALDOMA	" "	5th	Working Parties, amounting to about 200 pr night.	
		6th	Working Parties upon 5th	
		7th	" "	
		8th	Battalion relieved and came to rest here. Gas attack by enemy on Divisional front and heavy artillery barrage seem to point to further hostility towards Retaliation during the twelve hours Retaliation artillery	Captain F.K Hervey York & Lancaster Regt joined for duty

H. 20 pm

WAR DIARY
or
INTELLIGENCE SUMMARY.

Army Form C. 2118.

Hour, Date, Place	Summary of Events and Information	Remarks and references to Appendices
Aug 8th 1916	intermixed with relief completed 2.80 a.m. Battalion billeted in Franvin.	1/5 The King's Liverpool Rgt
Aug 9th	About 10.30 pm the Germans threw bombs into M SRTAL & ESTAMINET, but our reply put them with close.	3 O.R. wounded
Aug 10th	German Battery fired 31 rounds of 4.2 into BOAR LANE of which 27 were stated blind. Enemy machine guns very active.	Lieut W.C.B Brown died No 10 C.C.S of appendicitis. 2 O.R. killed
August 11th	Enemy very quiet. Very little machine gun fire as if thought they were relieving.	
August 12th	At 9.45 pm the Batt started being relieved by the 2nd Bn Lancashire Fusiliers owing to a new organization which	

WAR DIARY
or
INTELLIGENCE SUMMARY.
(Erase heading not required.)

Army Form C. 2118.

Instructions regarding War Diaries and Intelligence Summaries are contained in F.S. Regs., Part II and the Staff Manual respectively. Title pages will be prepared in manuscript.

Hour, Date, Place	Summary of Events and Information	Remarks and references to Appendices
August 13th	directed that only ½ Batt. would be across CANAL at the one time. The relief was not completed till 2.30 a.m. HQrs. A and B Coys to TROIS TOURS C, D to CANAL BANK. Battalion found 200 men for digging in front and support lines	
August 14	Battalion found 200 men to digging HQrs of A & B companies moved from TROIS TOURS to Strong point L 8 (map 28 N.W. H5 central). Everyone is very strong dug outs.	1 OR wounded
August 15	200 men digging	
August 16	200 men digging	7 OR arrived

WAR DIARY
or
INTELLIGENCE SUMMARY.

(Erase heading not required.)

Hour, Date, Place	Summary of Events and Information	Remarks and references to Appendices
August 17.	The Battalion relieved the 2nd Devonshire Fusiliers in the Trenches on held 8.13. Gun Cont on.	
18.	Quiet day, some bombing about 10.30 pm on a sap held by C company.	
19.	Battalion relieved by 16th Rl West Regt, the Welsh Leads company arrived at 11 pm, but the relief was not complete till 4 am. The Battalion entrance at the ASYLUM and went into Billets in the Rue DEFURNES Hippenen, POPERINGHE. The men were in a very good condition, having received leave from + ber fine	

Lee Hartest
Lt Col

WAR DIARY
or
INTELLIGENCE SUMMARY.
(Erase heading not required.)

Instructions regarding War Diaries and Intelligence Summaries are contained in F.S. Regs., Part II. and the Staff Manual respectively. Title pages will be prepared in manuscript.

Hour, Date, Place	Summary of Events and Information	Remarks and references to Appendices
August 20th	Some three before the day was spent by the men in cleaning themselves + kit inspection etc.	
21st	Lecture by General Brodie on Crater Snatching for all Officers + Platoon sergeants	
22nd	Companies route marched	
23rd	The Battalion moved to camp D	
	Map 28' b 24 d 2.2. and took over from the 1st Canadian how the Rifles, being in divisional Reserve.	
24. 25. 26.	Company trans. ditto.	
27	Sunday. Services for C of E + R.C.	
28	Battalion relieved 8th in the trenches	

WAR DIARY
or
INTELLIGENCE SUMMARY.

(Erase heading not required.)

Army Form C. 2118.

Hour, Date, Place	Summary of Events and Information	Remarks and references to Appendices
August 29th Continued	ammunition RAVINE to the trenches N & NE. Trenches from 30 to 150 yards distance.	
August 30.	During the afternoon the Germans replied to our 2" trench mortars by a heavy Artillery fire on our front and support lines. About 10.30 pm the S.O.S. Alarm was sounded, but it proved to be a mistake.	2 Lieut. R.S. Tanner killed. 1 OR wounded
August 31st.	The Battalion was relieved by the 9th Bn Australian Infantry, on relief which was complete about 2 am the Bn entrained at the ASYLUM ----- to POPERINGHE	

12th Brigade

4th Division.

---- ---

1st BATTALION

THE KING'S OWN ROYAL LANCASTER REGIMENT

SEPTEMBER 1 9 1 6.

WAR DIARY
or
INTELLIGENCE SUMMARY.
(Erase heading not required.)

Army Form C. 2118.

1 R R Lanc R 4/12

7E

329c
S13

Hour, Date, Place	Summary of Events and Information	Remarks and references to Appendices
September 1st	Battalion in Billets in PLACE BERTENS POPERINGHE. Three billets were so unsanitary that the Bn moved to billets in the RUE DE FURNES.	
September 2nd September 3rd	Company Training. The Billets were shelled by an 8 inch gun, at 5 minute intervals, the men were moved clear of the area being shelled and suffered no casualties.	
September 4th	Bn moved H.Q. and R coys to camp at BRANDHOEK, C & D coys to 3 gun huts running from EYPRES to MACMAHON FARM, relieving the	

Army Form C. 2118.

WAR DIARY
or
INTELLIGENCE SUMMARY.
(Erase heading not required.)

Instructions regarding War Diaries and Intelligence Summaries are contained in F.S. Regs., Part II. and the Staff Manual respectively. Title pages will be prepared in manuscript.

Hour, Date, Place	Summary of Events and Information	Remarks and references to Appendices
September 5th	14th Bn to the Welch Regiment. The two coys at BRAVO & HOEK found 150 men for trench digging on the 38th Div front, ½ Battalion trench digging cable.	2B. P.R. HEALD to hospital. 2.O. O.R. joined 2 Lieut J.S. STEWART 2 Lieut E.R. 25ALLBY joined Bn from 10th Bn
6th	" "	
7th	" "	
8th	" "	
9th	" "	
10		
5	½ Bn Brurijus cable.	
15th		
16.	At 9 am orders came that the Battalion was to entrain that evening, at 12.15 P.M. the Corps Commander General	

930C
EB

Army Form C. 2118.

WAR DIARY
or
INTELLIGENCE SUMMARY.
(Erase heading not required.)

Hour, Date, Place	Summary of Events and Information	Remarks and references to Appendices
17.	Hunter Weston instructs the ½ Bn at BRANDHOEK and informs that they were to go South again. The 2 companies from L. coys marched into camp about 10 hrs having left a cave taking party to hand over the work. The Bn marched off from camp 4 am Strength of Bn and entrained at HOUPOUTRE at Officers 33, 5.45 a.m. Bn detrained at SALEUX O.R. 569 at 5 km, marched to POULAINVILLE via AMIENS, distance 9 miles. Arrived POULAINVILLE 12 midnight and billeted there.	Strength of Bn Officers 33 O.R. 569

Army Form C. 2118.

WAR DIARY
or
INTELLIGENCE SUMMARY.
(Erase heading not required.)

Instructions regarding War Diaries and Intelligence Summaries are contained in F.S. Regs., Part II. and the Staff Manual respectively. Title pages will be prepared in manuscript.

Hour, Date, Place	Summary of Events and Information	Remarks and references to Appendices
18th	Bn employed cleaning themselves and men's buttons owing to very wet weather.	19 OR arrived 370. OR for draft Regiment arrived
19.	Company Training in morning, Route march in afternoon.	
20.	do	
21	do	
22	do	
23		
24		
25	Battalion moved to ALLONVILLE and Billeted there for the night, distance of march 4 miles.	

Army Form C. 2118.

WAR DIARY
or
INTELLIGENCE SUMMARY.
(Erase heading not required.)

Instructions regarding War Diaries and Intelligence Summaries are contained in F.S. Regs., Part II. and the Staff Manual respectively. Title pages will be prepared in manuscript.

Hour, Date, Place	Summary of Events and Information	Remarks and references to Appendices
Sept 27	Battalion marched to CORRIE, distance 9 miles	
Sept 27th	Battalion Training on ground N.W. of LA NEUVILLE. The attend a march data was practiced	
Sept 28	ditto	
Sept 29th	Battalion training and rapid dressing	
Sept 30th	Sunday Church Parade, No other Parades	

O.C. Bousfield
1/the King's Regt.
Comdg.

12th Brigade.

4th Division.

1st BATTALION

THE KING'S OWN ROYAL LANCASTER REGIMENT

OCTOBER 1 9 1 6

1 R Lanc Regt
12/4
Vol 25

WAR DIARY
or
INTELLIGENCE SUMMARY.
(Erase heading not required.)

Army Form C. 2118.

8E

Hour, Date, Place	Summary of Events and Information	Remarks and references to Appendices
1916 October 1st.	Church Parade at LA NEUVILLE, Lancashire Fusiliers & Surround Band attended.	
Oct 2nd	Battalion Training. The attack on the village was practiced. The Battalion attacked the village of LAHOUSSOYE, leaving billets 9 am & returning 5pm.	
Oct 3rd	Bn Training	
Oct 4th	The day was very wet, and the Battalion was left in Billets.	
Oct 5th	The Bn formed part of a divisional Attack on FRANVILLERS	
Oct 6th Oct 7th	Battalion Training, Battalion employed in arranging the ground for the attack	Captain R. A. Ray to 4th Army School as instructor.

Army Form C. 2118.

WAR DIARY
or
INTELLIGENCE SUMMARY.
(Erase heading not required.)

Hour, Date, Place	Summary of Events and Information	Remarks and references to Appendices
Oct 8.	Battalion marched at 7am to CITADEL camp across country via MORLANCOURT and FRICOURT. The ground was very heavy and a marche continued. At CITADEL camp the Battalion were very crowded in small wooden huts.	Strength of Bn Officers 31 O.R. 947.
Oct 9.	Battalion marched at 8am across country to BERNAFAY WOOD reaching them at 8.3(pm); at 4pm orders were received that the Battalion was to proceed and occupy reserve trenches at T8 Central. The journey to the trenches owing to the rough ground occupied 4 hours, everyone was in the trenches	

Army Form C. 2118.

WAR DIARY
or
INTELLIGENCE SUMMARY.
(Erase heading not required.)

Instructions regarding War Diaries and Intelligence Summaries are contained in F.S. Regs., Part II and the Staff Manual respectively. Title pages will be prepared in manuscript.

Hour, Date, Place	Summary of Events and Information	Remarks and references to Appendices
10th Oct.	2 T8 trenches. The trenches were shelled during the morning and in the evening the Batt. moved back in BERNAFAY Wood area.	10 O.R. killed 12 O.R. wounded
11th Oct.	Bn in dugouts near BERNAFAY Wood.	
12th Oct.	ditto	
13th Oct.	Battalion moved into trenches in front of LE TRANSLOY relieving 2nd Bn South of Wellington Regt.	
14th Oct.	Battalion in trenches. 1 company front line 1 support and 2 reserve. B company attempted to raid the head of SPECTRUM trench held by the Germans. About 60 yards of the trenches were unoccupied	wounded 24 O.R. 6 O.R. killed

Army Form C. 2118.

WAR DIARY
or
INTELLIGENCE SUMMARY.
(Erase heading not required.)

Instructions regarding War Diaries and Intelligence Summaries are contained in F.S. Regs., Part II and the Staff Manual respectively. Title pages will be prepared in manuscript.

Hour, Date, Place	Summary of Events and Information	Remarks and references to Appendices
15th Oct.	In trenches. B company front line, A company support, C and D companies in reserve	
16th Oct	About 5pm the Germans put a heavy barrage on the front line and attacked but were repulsed. B company relieved B company in the front line.	
17th Oct	There was an attack timed to take place at 3.30 am on the Army front to secure the trench SPECTRUM TRENCH and enemy trenches to the right. The attack was not a complete success.	Officers killed 2 Lt A.J. Harris 2 Lt J.S. Stennet wounded Lt R.H. Hodgson 2 Lt P.A. Bailey 2 Lt W. Saye killed 11 wounded 69.
18th Oct	The Germans made a counter attack and shelled our trenches on left side	

(7.3989) W4141-463. 400,000. 9/14. H.&J. Ltd. Forms/C. 2118/10.

Army Form C. 2118.

WAR DIARY
or
INTELLIGENCE SUMMARY.
(Erase heading not required.)

Instructions regarding War Diaries and Intelligence Summaries are contained in F.S. Regs., Part II and the Staff Manual respectively. Title pages will be prepared in manuscript.

Hour, Date, Place	Summary of Events and Information	Remarks and references to Appendices
19th Oct.	In trenches. Battalion relieved by the 2nd Battn. of Welch Regt. and marched to BERNAFAY WOOD area	
20th Oct.	In BERNAFAY WOOD area	
21st Oct.	ditto	
22nd Oct.	Battalion moved to trenches and occupied assembly trenches and during the night the men were employed making steps and deepening the trenches. In case of attack was to be in front line. A & B in support to them. In Bouzincourt.	
23rd	reported all ready. The original line	

WAR DIARY or INTELLIGENCE SUMMARY

Army Form C. 2118.

Hour, Date, Place	Summary of Events and Information	Remarks and references to Appendices
	For the assault was 11.30 a.m. Fifth leavy hours at 8.30 a.m. Zero hour was altered to 2.30 hrs. At 2.30 hrs the artillery put down a creeping barrage and Coy HQ went forward, followed at Zero + 10 (?) by A & B Coys. Coy C upon reaching the heart of SPECTRUM TRENCH held Os to Germans and our 1 waves & 2 waves formed on the SUNKEN ROAD and reached their objective. They were then subjected to very heavy machine gun fire from Regelbaus	Strength of Bn in assault. 11 Officers 436 N.C.O. & men

WAR DIARY or INTELLIGENCE SUMMARY.

Army Form C. 2118.

(Erase heading not required.)

Instructions regarding War Diaries and Intelligence Summaries are contained in F.S. Regs., Part II. and the Staff Manual respectively. Title pages will be prepared in manuscript.

Hour, Date, Place	Summary of Events and Information	Remarks and references to Appendices
	from the right flank and as the Battalion in the right were under orders to advance they were forced to fall back on Spectrum Trench. Shed they continued to with in 70 yards of the Road. A & B companies on the left were crown (?) but suffered heavy casualties and were unable to advance though C & D companies made a feeble counter attack which was easily driven the Germans.	Casualties killed Captain A.D.M. Brown OC C company 2 Lieut. W.E Doney 2 Lieut R.H. Banks D Lieut L Woods A Wounded Capt. J.O.C. Cuke B 2/Lt. R.T. Somerville B OR. 26 killed 118 Wounded 43 missing

Forms/C. 2118/10.

Army Form C. 2118.

WAR DIARY
or
INTELLIGENCE SUMMARY.
(Erase heading not required.)

Hour, Date, Place	Summary of Events and Information	Remarks and references to Appendices
Oct 24th	Bn relieved by 1st Bn the Liverpool Regt and proceeded to BERNAFAY WOOD area for breakfasts. The relief was	
Oct 25	not complete until 5 A.M. The march was then resumed to CITADEL CAMP, where we occupied bivouacs. We rested on the way up.	
Oct 26th	The Battalion handed at 2 pm from camp to VILLG-Sur-ANCRE, arrived about 5 pm and billeted themselves. Battalion resting and cleaning themselves.	
Oct 27th		
Oct 28th	At VILLG-sur-Ancre.	
Oct 29	Battalion entrained at 12 noon at MERICOURT, in the same train	

Army Form C. 2118.

WAR DIARY
or
INTELLIGENCE SUMMARY.
(Erase heading not required.)

Instructions regarding War Diaries and Intelligence Summaries are contained in F.S. Regs., Part II and the Staff Manual respectively. Title pages will be prepared in manuscript.

Hour, Date, Place	Summary of Events and Information	Remarks and references to Appendices
	were Bn. Hrs, Lewisham, Franklin Barks of Wellington & Essex Regt. detrained at 9.30 pm at ALLERY and billeted.	
30th Oct.		
31st Oct	Battalion rested and cleaning trenches. Conference at Bn. Hd of O.C. companies	

12th Brigade.

4th Division.

1st BATTALION

THE KING'S OWN ROYAL LANCASTER REGIMENT

NOVEMBER 1916

Army Form C. 2118.

Vol 26

WAR DIARY
or
INTELLIGENCE SUMMARY.
(Erase heading not required.)

Instructions regarding War Diaries and Intelligence Summaries are contained in F. S. Regs., Part II. and the Staff Manual respectively. Title pages will be prepared in manuscript.

Hour, Date, Place	Summary of Events and Information	Remarks and references to Appendices
November 1st.	Battalion at ALLERY. Company Training	Strength of Bat. Officers 19. O.R. 608.
2nd	ditto	
3rd	Battalion moved to Billets in MARTAINVILLE. distance of march 9 miles	
4th	Battalion Company Training	
5th	Church Parade. Company Training	
6th	Company Training	

Army Form C. 2118.

WAR DIARY
or
INTELLIGENCE SUMMARY.
(Erase heading not required.)

Instructions regarding War Diaries and Intelligence Summaries are contained in F.S. Regs., Part II. and the Staff Manual respectively. Title pages will be prepared in manuscript.

Hour, Date, Place	Summary of Events and Information	Remarks and references to Appendices
8.	Brigade Route March.	
9.	Company Training	2/Lieut Broadhurst
		2 Lieut C.N. Barker
		2 Lieut G.R.P. Harran
		Joined Battalion
10.	Company Training	
11.	Battalion Training	
12.	Church Parade.	30. O.R. joined from
		23rd I.B.D.
13.	Company Training	Major J.M. Young joined
14.	Company Training	Battalion.
	No. 18000 Pt Service	
15.	Brigade Route March. Awarded Militia held.	LETRANSLAY AINFRAY
	Attached Aeros Ft Open to MARTINVILLE.	

WAR DIARY
or
INTELLIGENCE SUMMARY.
(Erase heading not required.)

Army Form C. 2118.

Hour, Date, Place	Summary of Events and Information	Remarks and references to Appendices
Nov 16.	Company Training. Rifle range constructed E. of village. 1 Company on range.	
17.	Company Training. Night Operations	
18.	Company Training.	2 Lieut. R L PURWELL joined Battalion. 4th Manchester Battalion
19.	Company Training confined to held hut of den on account of wet.	2 Lieut. J. McRoostt. & 2 Lieut. L. Dickinson joined Battalion
20.	Church Parade.	

Army Form C. 2118.

WAR DIARY
or
INTELLIGENCE SUMMARY.
(Erase heading not required.)

Instructions regarding War Diaries and Intelligence Summaries are contained in F.S. Regs., Part II. and the Staff Manual respectively. Title pages will be prepared in manuscript.

Hour, Date, Place	Summary of Events and Information	Remarks and references to Appendices
Nov 21st	Company Training	
22nd	Company Training	
23	ditto	
24	Company Training. Night Operations	
25	Company Training	
26	Church Parade.	
27	Battalion Training. Route March	
28	Battalion Training. Night Operations	
29		
30		22 O.R. joined

12th Brigade.

4th Division.

1st BATTALION

THE KING'S OWN ROYAL LANCASTER REGIMENT

DECEMBER 1916

SECRET.

WAR DIARY.

of

1st Bn. _The King's Own_ Regt.

From : 1st _December_ 1916
To : 31st _December_ 1916

VOLUME

Date.
4 January 1917

[signature]
Lt. Colonel,
Commanding
1st Bn. _The King's Own_ Regt.

WAR DIARY
or
INTELLIGENCE SUMMARY.
(Erase heading not required.)

Army Form C. 2118.

Instructions regarding War Diaries and Intelligence Summaries are contained in F.S. Regs., Part II and the Staff Manual respectively. Title pages will be prepared in manuscript.

Hour, Date, Place	Summary of Events and Information	Remarks and references to Appendices
1916 December 1. MARTAINNEVILLE	Battⁿ at MARTAINNEVILLE – Training.	
" 2. —	" " "	
" 3. —	Battⁿ marched at 4 a.m. to OISEMONT and entrained. Detrained at MERICOURT and marched to Camp No 112.	
" 4. Camp 112	Marched from Camp 112 to Camp 16 – 104 O.R. joined Battⁿ.	
" 5. Camp 16	Battⁿ remained at Camp 16.	
" 6. MAUREPAS HALTE	Battⁿ marched from camp 16 to MAUREPAS HALTE (Coys C & D)	
" 7. SAILLY-SAILLISEL	Battⁿ marched to trenches at SAILLY-SAILLISEL and took over from the French "A" (20th Reserve Corps) – Relief complete 10.30 pm. No much material available. Trenches in a bad condition in the Company in close support – 1 O.R. killed. These Companies in forward trenches. Capt H.R. SMITH (R.A.M.C.) wounded. 7 O.R. wounded.	
" 8. —	—	
" 9. —	In trenches – Heavy rain fell making the trenches in a very bad state. 2/Lieut R.L. PORNELL helped rest 4 O.R. wounded.	
" 10. —	In trenches – Very heavy rain causing further falling in of trenches & Battⁿ relieved in trenches by Lancashire Fusiliers & marches support	
" 11. SUPPORT TRENCHES	trenches near BERTRAND - PERONNE road.	

Army Form C. 2118.

WAR DIARY
or
INTELLIGENCE SUMMARY.
(Erase heading not required.)

Instructions regarding War Diaries and Intelligence Summaries are contained in F. S. Regs., Part II. and the Staff Manual respectively. Title pages will be prepared in manuscript.

Hour, Date, Place	Summary of Events and Information	Remarks and references to Appendices
December 12 SUPPORT TRENCHES COMBLES	In Support trenches — Two companies moved to dugouts in tunnel from Bn. H.Q. & one company moved to COMBLES.	—
13 "	In support —	—
14 "	In support — 3 o.r. killed 12 o.r. wounded.	—
15 SAILLY-SAILLISEL	Battn. marched from support to front line trenches and took over from Lancashire Fusiliers. Trenches in very bad state (mud) no communication trench, very heavy shelling, front & communication trenches	—
16 "	Enemy quiet — Relief complete 10 p.m. had 2 coys in front line 1 coy in Sunken Way in the trenches	—
17 "	In trenches — Front line manned by a series of "posts" on account of the bad condition of the trenches. By mutual arrangement for withdrawal of troops available for withdrawal of troops	—
18 "	In trenches 2/Lieut. W.W.D. REDWOOD joined battalion. 3 o.r. killed 12 o.r. wounded.	—
19 FREGICOURT	Battn. relieved by Lancashire Fusiliers and marched to reserve trenches at FREGICOURT —	—
20 "	In reserve trenches — 2/Lieuts G.J. WILDING and R.A. HILDYARD Killed — 3 o.r. killed 2 o.r. wounded.	—
21 "	In reserve trenches. 2 o.r. wounded.	—

WAR DIARY
or
INTELLIGENCE SUMMARY.

(Erase heading not required.)

Army Form C. 2118.

Instructions regarding War Diaries and Intelligence Summaries are contained in F.S. Regs., Part II. and the Staff Manual respectively. Title pages will be prepared in manuscript.

Hour, Date, Place	Summary of Events and Information	Remarks and references to Appendices
December 22nd FREICOURT	In recent trenches 2 O.R. wounded	
23rd "	Relieved by Irish Fusiliers and marched into Divisional Reserve to Camp 107. 1 O.R. wounded	
Camp 107		
24th "	At rest in Camp 107 (Divisional Reserve)	
25th "	" " " "	
26th "	" " " "	
27th "	" " " "	
28th BELAIR	Marched from Camp 107 to BELAIR	
29th "	Battalion at BELAIR – all available men used for Railway unloading fatigue	
30th "	" " "	
31st "	" " "	

4th Division

12th Infantry Bde.

1st K. O. R. L.
_____

January to December

1917
_____

3-2-17

Secret

WAR DIARY
of
1st Bn The Kings Own Regt

From 1st January 1917

To 31st January 1917

VOLUME
No 1

Vol 2

J H Hardy
Captain

Comdg 1st Bn The Kings Own Regt

WAR DIARY
or
INTELLIGENCE SUMMARY.
(Erase heading not required.)

Army Form C. 2118.

Hour, Date, Place	Summary of Events and Information	Remarks and references to Appendices
Monday Jan 1st	Battalion in wooden huts at BELLAIR RAIL HEAD. Employed on unloading railway trucks and loading motor lorries	Captain R.J. Halton
Jan 2nd	2 Companies employed Platoon Training	Captain R.J. [illeg]
3rd	All men on working parties	Captain [illeg] Capt [illeg] S [illeg] Capt R.J. [illeg]
4th	2 Companies employed Platoon Training	
5th	All available men working	
6th	All available men working	
7th	Go to Division was in line on Divis day this day was celebrated as Xmas day by the 4th Division. No working parties.	113. OR joined Bn.
8th	Working parties as usual.	Captain R.J. [illeg]

Army Form C. 2118.

WAR DIARY
or
INTELLIGENCE SUMMARY.
(Erase heading not required.)

Instructions regarding War Diaries and Intelligence Summaries are contained in F.S. Regs., Part II. and the Staff Manual respectively. Title pages will be prepared in manuscript.

Hour, Date, Place	Summary of Events and Information	Remarks and references to Appendices
Jan 9"	Working parties as usual.	4th Gr. Joined Bn
Jan 10"	ditto	
Jan 11"	Battalion moved to Camp 12 c near CHIPILLY. Very poor accommodation.	
Jan 12.	Platoon training. 2 Coys & Lewis gunners on 100 yards range.	
Jan 13.		
Jan 14.	No Parades. Church Service.	
Jan 15.	Moved into huts line Camp 12 a. Great improvement.	Strength of Battalion 30 Officers 840 OR
Jan 16	Platoon training. 70 men on road working party.	
Jan 17	Platoon training	Bathing
Jan 18	Too wet, working parties except for evacuation	

Army Form C. 2118.

WAR DIARY
or
INTELLIGENCE SUMMARY.
(Erase heading not required.)

Instructions regarding War Diaries and Intelligence
Summaries are contained in F.S. Regs., Part II
and the Staff Manual respectively. Title pages
will be prepared in manuscript.

Hour, Date, Place	Summary of Events and Information	Remarks and references to Appendices
Jan 19"	Company training	[signature]
20	ditto	[signature]
21	Church Parade. Bde Rifle meeting, Jumping Cmpt.	[signature]
22	Company Training	[signature]
23	Moved to Camp 112 on BRAY - MÉAULTE road.	[signature]
24"	Moved to Camp 13. E of SUZANNE	32 O.R. joined Batt. [signature]
25"	Company Training	Captain V.O. TODD [signature]
26.	ditto	to H.Q.S.
27	ditto	2/Lt. CASSELL [signature]
28	Church Parades	Strength of Batt. 909. [signature]

Army Form C. 2118.

WAR DIARY
or
INTELLIGENCE SUMMARY.
(Erase heading not required.)

Instructions regarding War Diaries and Intelligence Summaries are contained in F.S. Regs., Part II. and the Staff Manual respectively. Title pages will be prepared in manuscript.

Hour, Date, Place	Summary of Events and Information	Remarks and references to Appendices
Jan 29th	Platoon Training.	
30	Platoon Training.	
31st	Platoon Training. Presentation of medal ribbons by I.C. to Coy Commander & Captain V.A. Hansr. Military Cross.	

SECRET

WAR DIARY
OF
1st Bn THE KING'S OWN REGT.

FROM :- 1st FEBRUARY 1917
TO :- 28th

VOLUME 3

J.C. Bromett
Lt Colonel
Commanding 1st Bn The King's Own Regt.

Army Form C. 2118.

WAR DIARY
or
INTELLIGENCE SUMMARY.
(Erase heading not required.)

Instructions regarding War Diaries and Intelligence Summaries are contained in F. S. Regs., Part II. and the Staff Manual respectively. Title pages will be prepared in manuscript.

Hour, Date, Place	Summary of Events and Information	Remarks and references to Appendices
1-2-17	Battalion in huts at Camp 18 move at 3.30 p.m. to relieve 1st Hampshire Reg't in front line trenches at BOUCHAVESNES. Three Companies front line One Company support.	2nd Lieut: G.W.WYLIE joined 1 Battalion WJG WJG
2. 2. 17	In front line trenches.	
3. 2. 17	In front line trenches. At 5 a.m. a party of Germans attempted under cover of a heavy barrage to raid the portion of trench held by D Company. They succeeded in entering the trench but were ejected at once leaving one prisoner in our hands and six dead	2nd Lieut: K. HINDE Killed in action. WJG
4. 2. 17	In front line trenches.	Eight O.R. Killed in action. WJG
5. 2. 17	Relieved by 2nd Lancashire Fus. moved to Brigade support. Two Companies Juncture Wood. Two Companies Curlu.	WJG

(73989) W4141—463. 400,000. 9/14. H.&J.Ltd. Forms/C. 2118/10.

Army Form C. 2118.

WAR DIARY
or
INTELLIGENCE SUMMARY.
(Erase heading not required.)

Instructions regarding War Diaries and Intelligence Summaries are contained in F.S. Regs., Part II. and the Staff Manual respectively. Title pages will be prepared in manuscript.

Hour, Date, Place	Summary of Events and Information	Remarks and references to Appendices
6.2.17	In Brigade support.	Lt Lewis O.R. joined Battalion. W/F.
7.2.17	In Brigade support.	W/F.
8.2.17	In Brigade support.	W/F.
9.2.17	Battalion moved to front line trenches BOUCHAVESNES to relieve 2nd Lancashire Fus:	W/F.
10.2.17	In front line trenches.	W/F.
11.2.17	In front line trenches.	W/F.
12.2.17	In front line trenches.	W/F.
13.2.17	Relieved by 2nd Lancashire Fus. Moved to close support.	Lieut O.R. Killed in action. W/F.

Army Form C. 2118.

WAR DIARY
or
INTELLIGENCE SUMMARY.
(Erase heading not required.)

Instructions regarding War Diaries and Intelligence Summaries are contained in F.S. Regs., Part II. and the Staff Manual respectively. Title pages will be prepared in manuscript.

Hour, Date, Place	Summary of Events and Information	Remarks and references to Appendices
14.2.17	In close support	Four O.R. joined Battalion and the following three officers:— Lieut. R.C. LEACH M.C. W.J.C. 2nd Lieut. G.W. COOMBES W.J.C. 2nd Lieut. A.C. TAYLOR W.J.C.
15.2.17	In close support.	
16.2.17	Relieved by 1st Hampshire Regt. Moved to Camp 17 in huts.	Capt. H. McGLENN joined Battn. from 1st Dukes of Wellingtons Regt. W.J.C.
17.2.17	In Camp 17	
18.2.17	In Camp 17	
19.2.17	In Camp 17	

(73989) W4141—463. 400,000. 9/14. H.&J.Ltd. Forms/C. 2118/10.

Army Form C. 2118.

WAR DIARY
or
INTELLIGENCE SUMMARY.
(Erase heading not required.)

Instructions regarding War Diaries and Intelligence Summaries are contained in F.S. Regs., Part II and the Staff Manual respectively. Title pages will be prepared in manuscript.

Hour, Date, Place	Summary of Events and Information	Remarks and references to Appendices
20.2.17	Battalion moved to Camp 117 in huts	(1)
21.2.17	Battalion moved to CORBIE; in billets; starting 9 a.m.	(2)
22.2.17	At CORBIE Training	(3)
23.2.17	At CORBIE Training	(3)
24.2.17	At CORBIE Training	(3)
25.2.17	At CORBIE Church parade	(3)
26.2.17	At CORBIE Training	2nd O.R. joined Battn.
27.2.17	At CORBIE Training	Five O.R. joined Battn.
28.2.17	At CORBIE Training	Lieut A.S. MACK joined Battn.

REPORT ON RAID BY THE ENEMY ON MORNING OF 3rd FEBRUARY 1917
EAST OF BOUCHAVESNES.

About 5.3 a.m. on 3rd February, the enemy opened a violent bombardment on Sap 16 and 17 and our front line between points C.15.d.6.8. and C 21.a.8.9. and on London Avenue, Loaf and Lodge Trenches.
At about 5.8 a.m. a party of about 20 men of the enemy dressed in white were seen advancing (by Lewis Gun sentry in Sap 18) within about 30 yards of Sap 16. He was unable to fire being too far away to distinguish who they were before they entered Sap 16.
As the enemy approached the Sap they were fired on with rifle fire.

Raiding Party entered Sap 16 and bombed down to trench and turned to right for a short distance; at 5.15 a.m. they were driven out.
They attempted to take 4 men prisoners but these men escaped during the enemy's retirement.
The enemy left 3 killed and 1 wounded in our hands, and 4 other men were shot while xxxx retiring and are lying out between the lines.

Lieut. Graham of the 1st King's Own went out and captured the wounded German and brought him from our wire.
The enemy belonged to the 177th R.I. 32nd Division.

The S.O.S. Signal was sent up at 5.12 a.m. by Company Commanders.
The Artillery opened at 5.17 a.m. but was not intense until 5.24 a.m.
A few rounds burst short but the majority burst mostly on enemy front line.

Our casualties:-
        1 Officer wounded (Since died of wounds)
        6 Other ranks killed.
        7 Other ranks wounded.
Most of the Casualties were caused by shell fire.

Casualties in other parts of the line were 5 Killed and 8 Wounded from shell fire.

Our trenches were badly damaged by enemy fire which consisted of heavy Trench Mortars, 5.9's and 77 mm shells.

Some of the enemy were armed with knives, some with rifles and bombs and were all dressed in white long coats.

                              (signed) K.A.Johnson

                                   Captain for
                                   Major-Genl.

                            Commanding 4th Division.

4th February, 1917.

Vol. 30

SECRET

WAR DIARY

OF

1ST BATTALION

THE KING'S OWN REGIMENT

FROM 1ST MARCH 1917.

TO 31ST MARCH 1917.

VOLUME 4

O.C. Arnett
Lt. Col.
Comdg 1/King's Own Regiment.

DATE 2nd APRIL 1917.

Army Form C. 2118.

WAR DIARY
or
INTELLIGENCE SUMMARY.
(Erase heading not required.)

Instructions regarding War Diaries and Intelligence Summaries are contained in F. S. Regs., Part II. and the Staff Manual respectively. Title pages will be prepared in manuscript.

Place	Date	Hour	Summary of Events and Information	Remarks and references to Appendices
CORBIE in billets	1-3-17		Training	WK
CORBIE	2-3-17		Training	WK
CORBIE	3-3-17		Training	WK
CORBIE	4-3-17		Move to VILLERS-BOCAGE	WK
VILLERS-BOCAGE in billets	5-3-17		Move to BEAUVAL	WK
BEAUVAL in billets	6-3-17		Move to VILLERS-LE-HOPITAL	Captain W. F.K. HARDY posted to 2/Y&L Regt.
VILLERS-LE-HOPITAL in billets	7-3-17		Move to FITZ-VILLEROY. H.Q's. "A" and "C" Companies at VILLEROY-SUR-AUTHIE "B" and "D" Companies at FITZ-VILLEROY	WK
VILLEROY-SUR-AUTHIE in billets	8-3-17		Training	WK

Army Form C. 2118.

WAR DIARY
or
INTELLIGENCE SUMMARY.
(Erase heading not required.)

Instructions regarding War Diaries and Intelligence Summaries are contained in F. S. Regs., Part II. and the Staff Manual respectively. Title pages will be prepared in manuscript.

Place	Date	Hour	Summary of Events and Information	Remarks and references to Appendices
VILLEROY-SUR-AUTHIE	9.3.17	Training	—	With 8 O.R. joined Battalion
VILLEROY-SUR-AUTHIE	10.3.17	Training	—	With 2nd Lt. M.C. CASSELL invalided to U.K. sick
VILLEROY-SUR-AUTHIE	11.3.17	Training	—	With 3 O.R. joined Battalion
VILLEROY-SUR-AUTHIE	12.3.17	Training	—	With
VILLEROY-SUR-AUTHIE	13.3.17	Training	—	With
VILLEROY-SUR-AUTHIE	14.3.17	Training	—	With
VILLEROY-SUR-AUTHIE	15.3.17	Training	—	With
VILLEROY-SUR-AUTHIE	16.3.17	Training	—	With
VILLEROY-SUR-AUTHIE	17.3.17	Training	—	With Captain L.R. HIBBERT and 29 O.R. joined Battalion

WAR DIARY or INTELLIGENCE SUMMARY.

Army Form C. 2118.

Place	Date	Hour	Summary of Events and Information	Remarks and references to Appendices
VILLEROY-SUR-AUTHIE	18.3.17		Training	W/h
VILLEROY-SUR-AUTHIE	19.3.17		Training	W/h
VILLEROY-SUR-AUTHIE	20.3.17		Training	W/h
VILLEROY-SUR-AUTHIE	21.3.17		Training	W/h 127 O.R. joined Battn.
VILLEROY-SUR-AUTHIE	22.3.17		Move to MARQUAY by Bus. "A" Coy at ORLENCOURT H.Qs, B, C and D Companies at MARQUAY	W/h
MARQUAY in billets	23.3.17		Training	W/h
MARQUAY	24.3.17		Training	W/h 13 O.R. joined Battalion
MARQUAY	25.3.17		Training	W/h
MARQUAY	26.3.17		Training	W/h

Army Form C. 2118.

WAR DIARY
or
INTELLIGENCE SUMMARY.
(Erase heading not required.)

Place	Date	Hour	Summary of Events and Information	Remarks and references to Appendices
MARQUAY	27.3.17		Training. The Commanding Officer wishes to place on record in the history of the King's Own Regiment the gallant conduct of 2nd Lt. R.L. BROWN. On the 27th March 1917 he was instructing a class in firing rifle grenades. A grenade did not leave the rifle although 5 seconds. He ordered all the others to push away and himself seized the bomb in his right hand and held resolutely it to analyse the force of the explosion. He thus saved the lives of several men, while sacrificing his own that. 2nd Lieut R.L. Brown has lost his right hand, and the Battalion has lost sacrifice cannot but have an excellent effect on all officers, N.C. Os and men.	2nd Lieut R.L. BROWN wounded. W.G. INGALL Lieut F. WATERHOUSE 2nd Lieut F.W. MUNYARD Adjutant Battalion
MARQUAY	28.3.17		Training	
MARQUAY	29.3.17		Training	
MARQUAY	30.3.17		Training	
MARQUAY	31.3.17		Training	

30-4-17

WAR DIARY

SECRET

1st Bn The King's
Own Regiment.

Covering period from
1st April to 30th April 1917

VOLUME
No 5

R. J. A. Hewitt
Commanding 1st Bn The King's Own Regt

1 R Lanc Regt
Vol 31
Major

Army Form C. 2118.

WAR DIARY
or
INTELLIGENCE SUMMARY.
(Erase heading not required.)

Instructions regarding War Diaries and Intelligence Summaries are contained in F. S. Regs., Part II. and the Staff Manual respectively. Title pages will be prepared in manuscript.

Place	Date	Hour	Summary of Events and Information	Remarks and references to Appendices
MARQUAY	April 1		Battalion training. Practice attack on flagged position.	12 O.R. joined
	2		do	
	3		Rifle training	
	4		Battalion training	
	5		do	
	6		Marched to Y huts, 1000 yds W. of ETRUN	
	7		Final preparation for attack	
Y CAMP HUTS	8		Final preparation for attack	
Y CAMP HUTS	9		The Battalion took part in the Battle of ARRAS. A copy of Battalion attack orders is attached.	
		5 a.m.	Left Y Camp. Strength 20 officers 658 O.R.	
		7.30 a.m.	Reached approx. the area West of St Catherine. On arrival large numbers of prisoners were seen in the Cage and during the half hour they continued to arrive in large numbers. Rec'd a very inspiring effect on the Battalion when morale was already very high. The enemy were shelling near the area also cheered the men. Hot meals and rum were supplied to the men. This was no shelling of the area by the enemy at the time spent in the area was of very great value. Advanced according to programme. The programme was carried out practically to the minute. The Battalion moved off by platoons at 2.5 yards interval	
		10.10 a.m.		

WAR DIARY
or
INTELLIGENCE SUMMARY.
(Erase heading not required.)

Army Form C. 2118.

Place	Date	Hour	Summary of Events and Information	Remarks and references to Appendices
	9th	12.10 p.m.	Passed through ROEUX, ST. LAURENT BLANGY and reached our behind Blue Line where Battalion was placed in a redoubt at A.13.b.central. While moving through the village it was being shelled and casualties amounts to 3 Officers & 40 O.R. wounded. Killed Lieut. K.G.R.P. HOWSON & Lt. A.S. MACK Wounded Lieut. C.W. BASKER. Our Battalion was up killed when behind the Blue line. TANKS were seen in action. Our Battalion arrived close up behind the Blue line considerably in advance of the infantry of the 26th Brigade, 9th Division, who passed through in gain at about 12.40 p.m.	
		1.10 p.m.	Left the area behind the Blue line and advanced in Artillery formation, C company on the right, B centre, D left, C in support. The formation was an Artillery formation. A Company on the right, B centre, D left, C in support. The formation was an extended down up to 75 yards. The Battalion S.S.135 with the supports companies closed up to 75 yards. The Battalion did not come under fire before the Plain & known lines. The Battalion moved another half and closed up to the 9th Division who were halted for the troops & left of ATHIES.	
		1.35 p.m.	turned in ATHIES and killed some enemy snipers had over the village. No casualties.	
		3.15 p.m.	Crossed Brown Line and closed up to troops.	
		3.20 p.m.	Advanced on 4th Brown System.	
		3.55 p.m.	Entered 4th Brown line with very little opposition and captured some 60 a 70 prisoners, killed about 12 enemy, and captured two 5.9" howitzers, four 5.9" howitzers and one 4.2" howitzer. I'm not seem later housed on the enemy. 5.7 p.m. All their had ammunition line and was later housed on the enemy. Our Battalion has become Brigade Reserve and dug themselves in in the world	

WAR DIARY or INTELLIGENCE SUMMARY

Army Form C. 2118.

Place	Date	Hour	Summary of Events and Information	Remarks and references to Appendices
FAMPOUX	10th		Coys of FAMPOUX while the 2/Bat of Wellingtons passed through and captured the village. They were unable to advance to the Green Line. Reported by FAMPOUX villagers that about 30 h-g enemy were not refugees to N. with the 9th position covered like clock work. We will soon have I should be relieved but the barrage (1.20 p.m.) from ATHIES to 4th Scarce System was very light and there was in front of the 4th Scarce System was unread. A great night was passed and no troops - could dislodge. During the evening the enemy shelled the SCARPE VALLEY unfortunately.	
		12.30 p.m.	Orders received for an attack to be made as soon as possible with the object of taking the village of ROEUX & the Chemical Works like the time of the advance was given as 2.30 p.m. The Battalion was ordered to move in Company to near the railway bridge on H.24.a. I am This Company moved at 2.25 p.m. & established touch with the casualties with 3 platoons on the embankment & to N. with the & of the bridge T on the Scarce being h.17.5. per they were unable to advance the 11.8. being in considerable strength along the embankment. The enemy having more considerably. At Company Commander Capt. V.O. TODD killed with 2nd Lt. ST.GEO. T.....?	
		at 2.30 p.m.	The remainder of the Battalion moved through the enemy's custombries moved now & then FAMPOUX with the object of crossing the customary under now & then	

WAR DIARY or INTELLIGENCE SUMMARY

Place	Date	Hour	Summary of Events and Information	Remarks and references to Appendices
			Company already established there. As soon as they emerged from the village the lines made heavy M.G. fire from the Chemical Works & trenches - found Maintained the Battalion H.Q. moved to the H.Q. of the Dukes in FAMPOUX. Then, at 2.40 p.m., received a message saying that the plan had been altered and that the Cavalry would move in advance being closely followed up by the Infantry, who would consolidate the ground gained by the Cavalry. Orders were at once sent to Companies - (being then & acting there) to hold their present positions but not to advance further. B & C Companies were informed.	
		4.30p.m.	Advance Guard of Cavalry arrived. The Cavalry Brigadier arrived at the H.Q. after receiving reports from O.C. King's Own, O.C. Dukes and his patrols he considered it possible to advance a few of the known opposition. Snow began to fall. Below a plan of action had been made a report was received that the enemy was in counter attack position was then up & rapid the attack & the Cavalry dismounted to assist. The attack was not thought but on news continued to fall & I am pretty dark the situation was abandoned & O.C. Dukes stating he was not pushed with the withdrew the Battalion in	

WAR DIARY
or
INTELLIGENCE SUMMARY.
(Erase heading not required.)

Place	Date	Hour	Summary of Events and Information	Remarks and references to Appendices
			Withdrew to the 4th Gun system at about 7 p.m. Enemy shelled FAMPOUX & FPL along P.L. in Coloured [?] candles fr. 9.5 to 5. from Mann 17.s O.R. A quiet night.	
	11th	9 a.m	Orders were received for Brigade to take the village of ROEUX and from there to proceed in a due Easterly direction toward PLOUVAIN, Zero hour 12 a.m. The Brigade attacked with King's own on the right supported by our Bn. Lan. Fus. and Dukes on the left. 1st objective of Bn. ROEUX village. 2nd objective DELVER WOOD at 11 a.m. the Batt. took over part of the Dukes line on the outskirts of FAMPOUX, a creeping barrage had been arranged for, the Batt. started to work but having to the marshy state of the ground considerable route had to be followed to the high by the railway embankment, they were unable to keep pace with the barrage, all observers agree that the barrage was extremely thin & great difficulty was experienced in	WK1

WAR DIARY
or
INTELLIGENCE SUMMARY

Army Form C. 2118.

Place	Date	Hour	Summary of Events and Information	Remarks and references to Appendices
			getting the Battn onto the embankment, as at least one M.G. for MOUNT PLEASANT and two for ROEUX were eightfrom the embankment, then M.G.s and all available Lewis Guns were placed in position on the embankment, and successfully covered the Infantry advance. B Coy under Capt Hibbert Lower Tween entangled in the marshes and were unable to preserve the bay was withdrawn and put in at another place up to their line it was thought that the 16th & 11th Brigade had progressed satisfactorily but it became known that the 6 Leinster works had been marines & Germans were seen to be occupy g building and trenches in front and we had Lewis with on Platoon of the Royal Warwicks in the embankment. There were new present the King's own, The Dukes and two Corps Lewis Gun detectors along the railway embankment, along the front from which the bank under MOUNT PLEASANT	

Army Form C. 2118.

WAR DIARY
or
INTELLIGENCE SUMMARY.
(Erase heading not required.)

Place	Date	Hour	Summary of Events and Information	Remarks and references to Appendices
	19th	10 am	The enemy shelled our line to a considerable extent, FAMPOUX was heavily shelled all the afternoon, it received from 4.30 onwards and was very noisy without great result. Or any sign of open a very rough night. Orders were received that the 9th Div would attack the GAIRELLE Lower and Cotton Borough the Cges at 5 pm. During morning FAMPOUX and our trenches were heavily shelled. 5 pm the 9th Division attacked without success. The 26th Brigade did not attack as the Chemical works had not been taken thus preventing its intended withdrawal of the Batln, at 11.20 pm two Coys of the Batln were withdrawn at about 12.30 am n the 13th the Batln was relieved by a Batln of the 26th Bgde and withdrawn to the BLUE LINE. During the attack by 9th Div. FAMPOUX was very heavily shelled particularly at each artily relief, compltd 5.30 am	

arrangements were then made for an infantry attack on the station Buildings. Most of the intervening but before they were complete a number of German colonists at a Batt were seen to be occupying these buildings and the tenders in front. M/c guns were also firing from the buildings and from the town, and it was known that the Byzas on our left had not succeeded, the attack was therefore abandoned, and a defensive line taken up a lew hundreds with lewis guns in the Corpse H.18.a. central, hrs. Heavy artillery opened fire on the trenches in front, and the enemy replied heavily considerably and good execution was done most lewis guns. About 9 pm information received that the Bgr of the 13th Div was at H 23 & 3.2. This placed the right flank of the Battn in the air, and its back to a river and marshy ground it was therefore withdrawn to conical - wood 12th Division Intelligence casualties this day 5 officers & 110 O. Ranks

Army Form C. 2118.

WAR DIARY
or
INTELLIGENCE SUMMARY.
(Erase heading not required.)

Place	Date	Hour	Summary of Events and Information	Remarks and references to Appendices
	13th		In the morning the Bath in the BLUE LINE, there were four casualties in ATHIES, in the afternoon moved to BLACK LINE. Total casualties during the operation.	
	14th		Moved to dug outs in original British front line.	
	15th to 18.		Dug outs original British front line. Lt. & Q.M. J.W. HOLDSWORTH joined Battn 16.4.17. During the whole of the operation after dark in the dug the weather was bitterly cold, it snowed & rained and a high E wind.	

Army Form C. 2118.

WAR DIARY
or
INTELLIGENCE SUMMARY

(Erase heading not required.)

Instructions regarding War Diaries and Intelligence Summaries are contained in F. S. Regs., Part II. and the Staff Manual respectively. Title Pages will be prepared in manuscript.

Place	Date	Hour	Summary of Events and Information	Remarks and references to Appendices
RESERVE TRENCHES BLANGY	19th		Move to original British 2nd line.	
British 2nd Line	20th		In dugouts	
do	21st		Move to MONTENESCOURT in billets	
MONTENESCOURT	22nd		Move to MANIN. Capt F.C. NAPER. Lt R.D. HODGSON. 2nd Lt J.E. WALKER. 2nd Lt W. WATSON. 2nd Lt H.S. GILBERT and seventy O.R. joined Battalion.	
MANIN	23rd		Move to ETREE-WAMIN in billets.	
ETREE-WAMIN	24th		Training.	
do	25th		do	
do	26th		do. a/Major R.J.A. HENNIKER joined Battalion from 2nd Duke of Wellington's Regt. Lt. S.T. NEWERS. Lt. F. WATERHOUSE. 2nd Lt. C.N. BASKER and 2nd Lt. T. MYERSCOUGH struck off strength of Battalion, wounded. Authority 3rd Army C.M. No 18 received 28-11-16	
do	27th		Move to SARS-LEZ-BOIS. a/Major H.W. GLENN reported to 2nd Lancashire Fusiliers Regt.	
SARS-LEZ-BOIS	28th		Move to HERMAVILLE	

Army Form C. 2118.

WAR DIARY
or
INTELLIGENCE SUMMARY

(Erase heading not required.)

Instructions regarding War Diaries and Intelligence Summaries are contained in F. S. Regs., Part II. and the Staff Manual respectively. Title Pages will be prepared in manuscript.

Place	Date	Hour	Summary of Events and Information	Remarks and references to Appendices
AGNEZVILLE	29th		Move to EAST of ST. NICHOLAS	
E. of ST. NICHOLAS	30th		in tents. Final preparation for attack. Move at 8.30pm to 4th German system	

ATTACK ORDERS by Lt. Colonel O.C. Borrett D.S.O. A.O.8
Commanding 1st Battalion The King's Own Regiment. FILE

REF: 1/20000 Map Sheet 51.b. N.W. (Edition 5.A.)

1. The XVII Corps is attacking the German position immediately North of the R.SCARPE at an hour ZERO on Z day as part of a general attack by the 3rd Army.
The date of Z day and hour Zero will be notified later.
The primary object of the operations is to establish a line along the German 3rd System of trenches (shown by the BROWN Line on the attached Tracing "A")
The 6th Corps is attacking South of the R.SCARPE.

2. The 9th Division is attacking immediately North of the R.SCARPE and is to capture the BLACK, BLUE and BROWN Lines in accordance with the Time Table in Appendix "A" attached. When the BROWN Line is captured the 4th Division is to pass through the 9th Division, capture the German 4th System of trenches and the village of FAMPOUX and establish itself on the GREEN Line (vide Tracing "A").

3. The attack by the 4th Division is to be carried out by the 12th Inf.Bde. on the right and the 11th Inf.Bde. on the left. The 10th Inf.Bde. is in Divisional Reserve.

4. 12th Inf.Bde. will attack with 3 Battalions in the line as follows:-

    Right   1st King's Own

    Centre 2nd Lan.Fus.

    Left   2nd Essex R.

5. 3 Machine Guns of 12th M.G.Co will be allotted to each of the three assaulting Battalions.
2 Stokes Mortars of the 12th T.M.Battery will be allotted to each of the 2nd Lan.Fus. and 2nd Essex R. and 4 Stokes Mortars to the 1st King's Own.

6. The Brigade Reserve will consist of the 2nd W.Rid.R. and the 12th M.G.Co (less 9 guns) under the command of the O.C 2nd W.Rid.R.

7. BATTALION BOUNDARIES.

    (1) ATHIES-FAMPOUX Road as far as curve at H.16.c.3.1.- trench junction H.16.c.9.0.- along communication trench to H.22.b.35.95 (trench inclusive to right Battalion)- Cross Roads H.17.c.3.3.- FAMPOUX)PLOUVAIN Road to H.18.a.9.2. on GREEN LINE (road inclusive to right Battalion).

8. (a) Prior to Z day the Brigade will be billeted in Y Huts about 1000 yards West of ETRUE on the ST POL-ARRAS Road.
The sections of the M.G.Company and T.M.Battery will come under the orders of Battalion Commanders at 6 p.m. the day before Z day

   (b) On the morning of Z day the Battalion will move from Y Huts via the ST POL-ARRAS Road to cross roads L.10.c.2.0 Road Junction L.10.d.2.9. ST VAAST BRIDGE- track south of the CHAUSSE BRUNERAUT to G.14.b.7.9.- thence to assembly areas via track to G.15.d. West of ST NICHOLAS.
The whole Brigade will assemble in the area G.15.d.

   (c) There will be a halt of approximately two hours in the assembly areas during which a hot meal will be issued.

   (d) The Brigade will then move up to the assaulting positions

(2)

on the BROWN LINE by the following routes:-
From G.15.d Track from G.15.b.9.1 to Road Junction G.16.a.
1.1.- Cross Roads G.16.c.6.9.- Road Junction G.16.c.5.7.
G.17.c.10.65.- track North of OIL FACTORY to G.18.a.0.0.

Both tracks will be used.
Northern track by 2nd Lan.Fus.and 2nd Essex Reg.
Southern track by 1st Bn King's Own and 2nd W.Rid.R.

(e) Detailed orders for these moves will be issued later. They will be roughly in accordance with the Time Table in Appendix "A". Battalions will wait for difinite orders before leaving assembly area.

9. (a) On reaching the BROWN LINE Battalions will form up for the assault approximately as follows:-
   1st King's Own Reg. Approximately along Eastern edge of Wood from H.21.a.8.7. to H.15.c.7.2. and thence along trench to H.15.c.5.5.
   2nd Lan.Fus. Approximate line of trenches from H.14.b.9.3. to H.15.a.1.6. and H.14.b.6.3. to H.14.b.7.6.

(b) The Battalion will form up with A Company on the right, B Company Centre, and D Company on the left. C Company will be in support. The M.Guns and T.Mortars attached to the Battalion will form up in a convenient spot in close proximity. The Battalion will attack the 4th German Line in this order. The Boundaries between Companies are the communication trenches, the C.T. on the left of each Company is inclusive to it.

10. (a) Lanes will be cut in the front of the 4th German Trench System during X and Y Days and from daylight on Z day.

(b) Between Zero + 7.40 hours and Zero + 9.40 hours every available Medium and Heavy Howitzer will bombard the German 4th System.

11. (a) The timings of the barrages are given in Appendix "B".
(b) A salvo of shrapnel will be fired from all 18 pounders to mark the start of the Infantry attack, otherwise the ammunition employed will be 50% shrapnel and 50% H.E.
(c) The Protective barrage will be placed 300 yards in advance of the line held.
(d) From the BROWN LINE to the 4th German System the creeping barrage will advance at 100 yards in two minutes, the times of starting being calculated to allow the Infantry to get within 50 yards of it. The barrage will lift off each line of trenches simultaneously along its whole length.
(e) Beyond the 4th German System there will be no creeping barrage, but fire will be concentrated on selected points lifting when the Infantry advancing at 100 yards in two minutes is within 400 -500 yards.
(f) A special Howitzer barrage will move through FAMPOUX the rate of 100 yards in 4 minutes, thus giving the Infantry passing along the Northern face time to get beyond and round it before the barrage lifts from the village.
(g) A protective gun barrage will be placed along the Western edge of FAMPOUX. It will remain until 5 minutes after the hour fixed for the advance of the Infantry to cover the latter whilst they get close up to the village.

12. The attack will be carried out in accordance with the Time Table in Appendix "A" and will be divided into two phases.
    (a) The capture of the German 4th System of trenches running North of the R.SCARPE West of FAMPOUX to H.10.d.7.0.
    (b) The capture of FAMPOUX and the establishment of a defensive line approximately from RAILWAY BRIDGE H.18.d.3.2. to HYDERABAD REDOUBT along the GREEN LINE.

13. (a) At Zero + 9.hrs 45 mins the standing barrage 500 yards in front of the BROWN LINE will commence to advance at the rate of 100 yards in two minutes North of the ATHIES-FAMPOUX Road.
    South of the road it will commence to move forward 5 minutes later and the barrage will then advance parallel throughout its whole length to the 4th German System and at the rate of 100 yards in two minutes.
    (b) The assaulting Infantry will follow the barrage as closely as possible.
    (c) The Brigade Reserve will move off at the same time as the 1st King's Own i.e. Zero + 9.hrs 50 mins.
    It will keep in touch with the 1st King's Own without actually committing itself to the attack. It will, however be prepared at any time to support the attack without further orders from Brigade H.Q.

14. As soon as the 4th German System is captured, Lewis Guns and Scouts will be pushed forward towards FAMPOUX. Trench Mortars will take up positions to silence any hostile Machine Guns which may be in or covering the village. The Machine Guns will take up positions to assist in this and cover the advance of 2nd W.Rid.R. Troops will not enter FAMPOUX at this stage.

15. (a) There will be a halt of about half an hour on the German 4th System during which the Brigade Reserve will close up on the 1st King's Own and will get into position ready to assault FAMPOUX.
    (b) While however, the closest touch should be kept with the 1st King's Own by the Brigade Reserve touch must also, be maintained with the 2nd Lan.Fus and the 2nd Essex R. and the Commander of the Brigade Reserve must be prepared on his own initiative to support either of these Battalions at any stage if necessary.

16. As soon as the Brigade Reserve has passed through them, the 1st King's Own will become Brigade Reserve and will be prepared to act in an exactly similar way.

17. The chief tasks of the Stokes Mortars allotted to the 1st King's Own will be the bombardment of FAMPOUX, but they will go forward later when the 2nd W.Rid.R. have passed through and will come under the orders of the O.C. 2nd W.Rid.R.

18. (a) At Zero + 10 hours 46 mins a special Howitzer barrage will commence to move through FAMPOUX at the rate of 100 yards in 4 minutes reaching the Eastern edge 32 minutes later.
    (b) The 2nd W.Rid.R. will advance at Zero + 10 hrs 42 mins and will follow this barrage up through the village.
    The 2nd Lan.Fus. and 2nd Essex R. will at the same time advance to the GREEN LINE leaving behind in the 4th German System their original first wave to carry on consolidation.
    (c) The 2nd West Rid.R. will detail one Company to pass rapidly along the Northern edge of FAMPOUX and to enter it from the North and East as soon as the barrage lifts.

19. As soon as the GREEN LINE is reached strong patrols will be pushed out to capture any artillery in the vicinity and to maintain touch with the enemy.
Touch will also be obtained with the VI Corps South of the River SCARPE and the 11th Inf. Bde on the left.

20. Battalions must be prepared at any time in the event of the attack being held up on either of their flanks to form and consolidate defensive flanks and to push on and endeavour to turn the obstacle.

21. The 1st King's Own and 2nd W.Rid.R. will be prepared to assist the VI Corps by sweeping the slopes South of the R.SCARPE with Machine Gun fire should favourable targets present themselves.

22. (a) The organization of a defensive line approximately along the GREEN LINE will be taken in hand at once. The line itself will be on the Eastern slopes of the ridge but posts will be pushed forward to obtain observation East of the ridge.
(b) Strong points will be constructed in rear of the GREEN LINE approximately as follows -

    2nd W.Rid.R. H.16.d.4.2.
    1st King's Own H.18.c.8.8.
    2nd Lan Fus. H.18.a.5.5.
    2nd Essex R. H.12.c.6.1.

½ Section 9th Field Company R.E. will be allotted to each Battalion for their construction. A party of 40 Infantry will also be detailed for work on each of them.
This party will be found by C Company.
(c) These R.E. detachments will come under the orders of the Battalion Commanders at Y Huts at 6 p.m. the day before Z day.

23. (e) Contact aeroplanes will receive signals from Battalion H.Q. by means of :-
    (i) Ground signal panels
    (ii) Lamps.
    (iii) From attacking Infantry by means of flares.
(f) Rockets and light signals will be used for communication with the artillery according to the following code:-

    Succession of Green lights))))))) Open fire.
    do.   White do.........Lengthen Range.

Signals will be continued until the required response is made by the artillery.
The increment by which the range will be increased will 100 yds
Flags will also be used for indicating the position of the assaulting troops to the artillery.
(g) The Brigade will establish a visual station on the BLUE LINE about H.7.d.9.0. and as the advance continues an intermediate station about H.16.c.9.1.
Battalions will arrange to maintain communication with one or other of these stations.

26. Brigade H.Q. at zero hour will be established in G.15.d.
Before the Brigade crosses the original British they will be established in G.17.a.70.45. alongside the 26th Inf.Bde H.Q.
They will move later to the BLUE LINE about H.13.b.8.9.

(5)

17. The Battalion H.Q. will be in rear of the Battalion until the final objective is reached when it will be established as close as possible to the junction of the centre communic -ation trench and Physic trench.

W J Gilbert Lieut..
A/Adjutant 1st Battn The King's Own Regt.

2nd April 1917.

Note.- Copies of the above have been distributed as follows

Copy No 1. C.Officer.
2. 2nd in Command.
3. Adjutant.
4. O.C. "A" Company
5. O.C. "B" Company.
6. O.C. "C" Company.
7. O.C. "D" Company.
8. File.

TIME TABLE.   APPENDIX A.

Moves.	9th Div.	12th Inf.Bde.
Leave Y Camp.		+0
Reach Assembly Area.		+2.30
Halt.		2 hours
Leave Assembly Area.		+4.30
Reach Area behind BLUE LINE.	+2.43	+6.40
Leave BLUE LINE.	+6.46	+7.40
Reach 3rd trench system W of BROWN LINE.	+7.32	+8.40
Arrive in or pass over BROWN LINE (N. of FAMPOUX Road)	+8.00	+9.40
(S. of Road)		+9.50
Reach 4th German Trench System		+10.12
Leave 4th German Trench System.		+10.42
Reach GREEN LINE.		+11.18

APPENDIX B.

TIME TABLE OF CREEPING & PROTECTIVE BARRAGES.

	ZERO + to ZERO +		Rate of advance.	Remarks.
Protective barrage 300 yds E of BROWN LINE.	8.00	9.40	Stationary.	
Advance till parallel to 4th German Trench System.	9.45	9.50	100 yds per 2 minutes.	Barrage remains stationary S. of FAMPOUX Road.
Advance along whole front.	9.50	10.6	100 yds per 2 minutes	
Lift off 4th German System.	10.6			
Barrage N. edge of FAMPOUX Barrage on N. & E. edge of FAMPOUX.Concentrated fire on Road Junction H.17.c.9.6. Road Junction H.17.d.6.9. HYDERABAD REDOUBT. Trench junction H. 17.b.6.9.	10.6	10.47	Protective.	
	10.6	10.42	Stationary.	
Lift off N. edge of FAMPOUX and H.17.c.9.6.	10.42			
Concentrated fire on road junction H.17.d.6.9, trench junction H.17.b.6.9.	10.42	10.50	Stationary.	See special How.creeping barrage for FAMPOUX.
FAMPOUX. Special 5" How.Barrage.				
Lift from W. edge of FAMPOUX	10.42			
Advances	10.42	11.14	100 yds per 4 minutes	
Lifts to protective positions in front of GREEN LINE.	11.14		Stationary.	

OPERATION ORDER NO. 20.

Ref. Map. 51 B N.W.   FAMPOUX.
                        11.4.17.

INTENTION.
(1) The 4th Division will continue the advance to day with 12th Brigade on right, 10th on left, and 11th in support.

OBJECT. and DISPOSITIONS
(2) The attack by 12th Brigade will be carried out by 1st King's Own on right and DUKE OF WELLINGTON'S on left.
The right of 1st KING'S OWN will rest on the River SCARPE.

FORMATIONS BEFORE ATTACK.
(3) Prior to zero hour the Bn. will form up for the attack in or immediately in rear of our front line trench between ATHIES FAMPOUX Road and the road which runs through H.18.c.o.7.
The Company holding the trenches North of ATHIES FAMPOUX Road will be relieved by 2nd LANCS. FUS. at 10.30 a.m.
The party of 1st K.O. with this party will rejoin their Bn. in Southern portion of village.

FORMATIONS IN ATTACK.
(4) The attack will be delivered in 3 waves Companies being disposed in this order from right to left.
No. 1 Right   No. 2 Centre   No. 3. left

SUPPORT.
(5) The Lewis gun Platoon of No. 4 Company will form support - This Platoon will cover advance of Bn. from the Eastern houses of FAMPOUX till the Bn. has crossed the Embankment. They will then move forward to Embankment. Bn. H.Q. Snipers will accompany this Platoon.

CARRIERS.
(6) No. 4 Coy less 1 Platoon - as soon as the Embankment is crossed x by the Bn. or earlier if needed. Carriers will move forward with S.A.A. and Bombs. O.C. No. 4 will keep in close touch with Bn. by runners.

MOVEMENT.
(7) During the forming up for attack prior to zero hour the greatest care must be taken to prevent the enemy observing this it. Men must as far as possible move along trenches or behind houses.

Action at ZERO.
(8) A Barrage will come down 100 yds. East of village for 8 mins. after ZERO hour. Under cover of this the battalion will move out in attack formations with front wave as close to barrage as possible. The front wave will follow barrage as soon as it commences to creep.

OBJECTIVES.
1st Objective.
(9) 1st KING'S OWN from River SCARPE to Northern edge of ROEUX inclusive.
DUKE OF WELLINGTON'S Northern edge of ROEUX to Chateau I.13.d.o.1. both inclusive.
2nd 1st KING'S OWN from R. SCARPE to W. edge of DELBAR Wood inclusive. DUKE OF WELLINGTON'S West of DELBAR Wood to N. (edge)

OPERATION ORDER No. 20 Contd.

edge of HANSA Wood inclusive. The Bn. will halt and dig in on this line while the Cavalry pass through.

BARRAGE. 10. Our objectives are now being dealt with by our Heavy Artillery. Our advance will be covered by an 18 pr. barrage.

	ZERO.
Barrage opens 100 yds. East of FAMPOUX	
" commences to creep	+8
" creeps at 50 yds. a minute till	+30
" Halts on first objective till	+40
" Creeps at 50 yds a minute till	+80
" Ceases .	+80

MACHINE GUNS. (11) The O. C. Machine Gun detachment attached to Bn. will arrange to cover advance from Eastern edge of FAMPOUX till Bn. has crossed Rly. Embankment. He will then move forward in rear of Bn.

TRENCH MORTARS. (12) Will move in rear of right flank of Bn. and be prepared to engage any hostile machine guns on Embankment.

ZERO. (13) ZERO hour will be 12 noon.

REPORTS. (14) Will be sent to Bn. H.Q. at MAIRIE till Embankment is crossed - after that H.Q. will be in rear of centre of Bn.

(Sgd) F.H. Fraser, Captain,

Copy No. 1 to C.O.
2 " O.C. No. 1 Coy.
3 " " 2 "
4 " " 3 "
5 " " 4 "
6 " M.O.
7 " R.S.M.
8 " Q.M.
9 WAR DIARY.
10 FILE.

S P A R.
X 115.   11.4.17.

We are held up on Railway Embankment by M.G. fire AAA We
are holding Railway Embankment AAA A man of R.I.F. 19th
Bde. reports that his Bn. is hung up after advancing 500 yds
AAA This is not confirmed AAA
Have taken 2 Officers and 3 3 O.R. (Prussians) prisoners.

                         S P E A R.

X 119 To S P A R   11.4.17.
              Am moving my Bn. H.Q. to Rly. Embmt. H.18.c.9.0. approx.
To S P A R.   S P E A R.
X 120   11.4.17.
                                                9 o
We are holding Railway Embankment from I.18.c.9.6. to
H.18.d.5.3 AAA We are still held up by M.G. fire from station
and Chemical Works AAA The R.I.F. are still in our
jumping off trenches just East of FAMPOUX AAA Our left flank
is at present in the air.
                         S P E A R.

To SEPIA
X 121.   11.4.17.
      We are holding Rly Embmt. from I 18.c.3.6. to H.18.c.9.9. AAA
Can you please join up with us our left flank is in the air AAA
The trenches in H.18.a.6-5 are British and have been held
by us for 2 days.
                         S P E A R.

To S P A R   11. 4.17.

Prisoners 18th PRUSSIAN Div. state that they arrived in the
line last night from DOUAI AAA

                         S P E A B.

S P A R   11. 4.17.
 X 126.
              During the attack the Barrage ran away from the
Infantry AAA A party of about 50 SPEAR and SPED crossed
Rly. Embmt. and are under cover of small bank but unable
to move from there as the enemy are holding strong point
MT. PLEASANT. The advance of remainder is held up by enfilade
fire from trenches West of CHEMICAL Works AAA The line
now held is as follows :-   From Rly. Bridge H.24.a.4.7. to
H.18.d.3.3. thence N.W. to H.18.d.o.6. thence to H.18.d.4.7.
Troops holding this line are SPEAR and SPIN and SPED and 1 Platoon
SEPIA. The latter party having been driven back from station
AAA If station and Chemical Works and trenches immediately
West of them are heavily shelled we can attack provided
MT. PLEASANT is engaged by some other troops AAA
MT. PLEASANT is a very strong point and needs special
treatment by Heavies.
                         S P E A R.

S P A R.
X 127.   11.4.17.
       Have gained touch with SCAN who are North of
ATHIES FAMPOUX Road AAA About 6.30 p.m. small parties of enemy
made strong attack on our left flank which rested on ATHIES
FAMPOUX Road and was then in the air - AAA Attack repulsed

K 127 Contd.   11.4.17.

   Parties of enemy seen advancing N. of ATHIES FAMPOUX Road and a few South of it.

                    S P E A R.

S P E A R.   12.30 p.m.
                        11.4.17.

   Attack held up by dropping too far behind Barrage AAA Am trying to work to Railway station along N. of Embankment - Am now in trench from H.18.d.6.8. to H.18.d.7.4. 2 - 6 p.m. Have tried to reach station with party of our own men and some of WARWICKS but was held up by M.G.s. Have sent patrols to flanks to gain touch with 10th Bde.

              (Sgd) P.S. Lambert, 2nd Lieut.

S P E A R.   12.4.17.   GREEN LINE.

   Everything O.K. with exception that we have been badly shelled by our own heavies AAA
   The heavies have now lengthened range in response to white lights AAA
   Enemy quiet and appears to have wind up.

              R. Anderton, 2nd Lieut.

OBJECTIVES AND BNS. BOUNDARIES
ON Z DAY.

Issued in connection with 35th A.C.
dated 2-4-17.

TRACING "A"

Tracing taken from Sheet 51-B. N.W.(61.5x)
of the 1/20,000 map of FRANCE.

GREEN LINE

BATTALION BOUNDARY
BATTALION BOUNDARY

BROWN LINE
BOUNDARY

BRIGADE BOUNDARY
BRIGADE BOUNDARY

BLUE LINE

BLACK LINE

A
B
H   2
G   1
6

SECRET

WAR DIARY

1st BATTN THE KINGS OWN REGT

FROM 1st MAY TO 31st MAY 1917

VOLUME NO 5

[signature] Major

Comdg. 1st Bn The King's Own Regt

2/6/17

Army Form C. 2118.

Map. Refs:- Sheet 51.3.N.W. **WAR DIARY**
TAMPOUX TRENCH MAP. (ATTACHED)
INTELLIGENCE SUMMARY.

1/5 B.n THE KING'S OWN Royal Lancaster Regt.

MAY 1917

(Erase heading not required.)

Place	Date	Hour	Summary of Events and Information	Remarks and references to Appendices
May	1st		Batt.n in assembly Trenches in 4th German System H.16.b in accordance with 12th Inf. Bde. O.O. No. 37.	Appendix A
				" B
	2nd	11pm	Batt.n moved up into assembly trenches in H.16.B., 13th Bat.n Rail.y Bde H.16.A.2.1. Batt.n H.Q through appx a.	" C
	3rd	3.45am	Batt.n commenced attack in accordance with 12th Inf. Bde. O.O. No. 38 and Batt.n O.O. No. 2. in conjunction with remainder 12th Inf. Bde. higher still very dark and in addition smoke Barrage by own Guns. Attack N. of Railway held up at once. Attack S. of Railway on 12th Bde. front successful in that 2 Coys. L.F., 2nd D. of West.n Regt. & about 50 men 1st K.O. pushed through to the BLACK LINE (N.+S. through I.14.c.central). Owing to lack of sufficiently strong mopping up parties & to the excessive pace of the barrage, buildings & ruins, chiefly CHEMICAL WORKS & craters were not mopped up, & enemy opened with rifle M.G. fire after first line had passed through. B Coy lost all three officers in advancing in front of CHEMICAL WORKS & owing to the confusion in troops in front of no. 1 each way lost between the Buildings & companies of the Batt.n Lt. MYERS & CAPT. LEASK led a party of about 40 men across the embankment & found some few men of the 10th Bde, whom they reorganised. They prepared to advance but were stopped by fire from the CHATEAU building and, being out of touch with the 10th Bde, and apparently in the air on both flanks, these two officers decided to dig in where they were (I.13c.6.7 to I.13.c.7.2) and this form a jumping off place, stores & reinforcements de trickled up. The sniping + M.G. fire from the buildings was very accurate & active throughout the day, although there were short periods when the enemy appeared to cease. During these periods wounded & prisoners	" D
				" E
				Rty

Place	Date	Hour	Summary of Events and Information	Remarks and references to Appendices
3rd (cont'd)			passed through the lines, but on some occasions the enemy shot down his own prisoners, as they passed through from the BLACK LINE. Meanwhile, the situation N. of the Railway was very obscure. The enemy barraged the line of the embankment & the road through the Railway Arch, also B.M.G. fire on itself, very heavily all day with 4.2, 5.9, & M.G. fire, so that it was only occasionally possible to get messages passed up or back. 2Lt was during a momentary lull that 2Lt SCIAMA was able by swift running & under very heavy sniping fire, to reach Lt MYERS & bring back the first information of his position. Shortly after his return again under heavy fire showing which his orderly was hit, Lt MYERS himself came back to report. This orderly was also hit, & he himself had many narrow escapes along the N. portion of the communication along. On return of Lt. Railway was impassible during the morning except during one short lull, when two orderlies managed to crawl to CAWDOR Trench under heavy fire from X roads I.13.a.9.3. Since a mixed body of about 30 men under Lt WHITEHEAD were found, they having straggled back after becoming detached from their units in the darkness, and having found the S. end of CAWDOR occupied by the enemy. About 6 p.m. a message was received from Lt. BASSETT, times 12 noon, which he had been unable to get through before owing to the fire, showing that he had been ordered by Lt. ESSEX to get over & hold CLIVES trench when a small body under Lt. BROADHURST had already (slightly) these parties had subsequently finding the houses still held by the enemy, to outflank them by the N.E.T. hour had been unable to do so, & had informed Lt. S. was then at 6.30 p.m. in OKAVADOR (N) & CAWDOR. The situation was as follows:—	Appx

Army Form C. 2118.

WAR DIARY
or
INTELLIGENCE SUMMARY.

(Erase heading not required.)

MAY. 1917

Place	Date	Hour	Summary of Events and Information	Remarks and references to Appendices
3rd con.		6.30 p.m.	CAPT. LEASK, Lt. MYERS, Lt. RUNYARD + 35 O.R. S. of the Rail. Lt. WHITEHEAD + 62 O.R. in CAWDOR. Lt. BASSETT, WATSON + BROADHURST + 70 O.R. in CLOVER. CAMBAR was held in the Northern portion by a few H.F.	P4
		7 p.m.	About 7 p.m. orders were received by runner from Brigade that the 1/R.B. would attack S. of the railway, supported by 1 Coy HANTS about 11 p.m., after which our parties under CAPT. LEASK would withdraw. This attack was arranged from information supplied by an officer of the 1/R.B., who, not having been fired on on exposing himself, concluded that the enemy had evacuated the buildings around the CHATEAU. On having this Lt. MYERS went up from B" H.Q. to arrange for a patrol to be sent into the buildings. On arrival at the trench he found that 5-men had already been sniped within the previous few minutes whilst a 6th was killed whilst he was there, & he himself was again fired on. He returned to B" H.Q. & reported this to Bde. H.Q. by phone. The R.B. attack failed, as Capt LEASK's trench was not deep, the owing to lack of runners which had been impossible to canvass it. The R.B. allowed him to withdraw, arranging for the balloting of the trench by light Howitzers. This party was, by permission of the 12th Bde, sent back to the M.C German System. Throughout a very trying day, Lt. MYERS + CAPT. LEASK acted with great coolness & judgement, & their tenacity in digging whilst under a very heavy continuous fire, enabled the Y.R.B. to form up	P4

Army Form C. 2118.

WAR DIARY
or
INTELLIGENCE SUMMARY.
(Erase heading not required.)

May 1917

Place	Date	Hour	Summary of Events and Information	Remarks and references to Appendices
3rd (cont'd)			for their attack at night without interference. Very great coolness & bravery was also displayed by the Bn Stretcher bearers who worked under continuous fire all day, made many journeys under severe persistent shell fire carrying wounded back to BAMPOUX. I/C STANBY especially distinguished himself in this bringing in over 30 CASUALTIES. 2/C Appendix F. About 80 prisoners were taken by the Battn	P/4 App. F. P/4
4th May			Situation unchanged, opening day, there shelling by enemy on support lines	
5th " "			Batn moved up night to CLOVER & CUSHION, B" HQ. 10 Quarry I.13a.2.2.	P/4
6th " "			Situation unchanged	
7th " "			" " by day. At night Battn relieved by LANCS. FUS & DUKES & moved back to vicinity of CAWNPUR WORK.	P/4
8th " "			Situation unchanged by day. At night Battn moved back into shelters in I.13.d.	P/4
9th " "			" " "	P/4
10th " "			Situation unchanged. Two recon parties in the SCARPE.	
11th " "			Battn reorganised into (4) companies under Mr LYNE & CAPT. KEASK & prepared to move at night forward.	App. G. P/4

WAR DIARY or INTELLIGENCE SUMMARY.

Army Form C. 2113.

Place	Date	Hour	Summary of Events and Information	Remarks and references to Appendices
" (cont'd)	11"		Orders were then received that the Batt" would take the places at the disposal of the 10" Inf. Bde. to support their attack and consolidation of a line just E. of the buildings & railway N. of ROEUX. 10" Inf. Bde. ordered Bat'n to move up to CRUMP & CRETE trenches by 11p.m. this was done and the Bat'n reached these trenches without loss, although enemy fire was at times very heavy. On arrival, disposition ordered were as follows:- X Coy. (Lt. Lowe) to CATE & CUSP trenches Y Coy (Capt. LEASK) to CUSP trench	P/y
	12"	3.30 a.m.	At about 3.30 a.m. Lt. Lowe supplied parties totalling 50 men to 6 officers & Bat'n to push through the buildings & occupy line of posts E. of the buildings. This was done with small loss.	P/y
		6.0 a.m.	At 6.0 a.m 11" Bde. attacked & secured line of CORONA trench. About 8 a.m. Lt. Lowe, finding some enemy still sniping from certain houses, took a party of 10 men forward & captured 28 prisoners. Enemy shelled CAT, CATE & CUSP (particularly the latter) throughout the day with 4.2 & 5.9. Our losses slight, but many men buried & dug out again.	P/y
		10.0 pm	Relief of 10" Bde. by a Bde. of 51" Div. commenced, we being relieved by 5" Gordons 1/5 Seaforth H'rs.	P/y
	13"	1.45 a.m.	Relief completed. Bat'n marched back to St. Nicholas & trains, by two's, to HERMAVILLE. Major W.A.T.B. SOMERVILLE joined Battalion.	P/y

Army Form C. 2118.

WAR DIARY
or
INTELLIGENCE SUMMARY.

(Erase heading not required.)

Instructions regarding War Diaries and Intelligence Summaries are contained in F. S. Regs., Part II. and the Staff Manual respectively. Title pages will be prepared in manuscript.

Place	Date	Hour	Summary of Events and Information	Remarks and references to Appendices
HERMAVILLE	14th May			
do	15		Resting. 2nd Lt. G. F. LAURIE joined Battalion	
do	16		Bayoneting. 8 O.R. joined Battalion	
do	17		Training.	
do	18		"	
do	19		"	
do	20		15. O.R. joined Battalion	
do	21		Church parade. 2nd/Lt. W.C. FRANCIS joined Battalion.	
do	22		Training. 29 O.R. joined Battalion	
do	23		" 4 O.R. joined Battalion	
do	24		"	
do	25		"	
do	26		" 26 O.R. joined Battalion.	
do	27		Church parade.	
do	28		Training.	

Army Form C. 2118.

WAR DIARY
or
INTELLIGENCE SUMMARY.
(Erase heading not required.)

VII

Instructions regarding War Diaries and Intelligence Summaries are contained in F. S. Regs., Part II. and the Staff Manual respectively. Title pages will be prepared in manuscript.

Place	Date	Hour	Summary of Events and Information	Remarks and references to Appendices
HERMAVILLE	29th May	Training	Captain J.P. JAMIESON joined Battalion.	
do	30th	do		
do	31st	do		

S E C R E T.   Copy No. 1...

12th Infantry Brigade Operation Order No. 38.

Ref.Map BIACHE Special Sheet 1/20,000. (Attached).- 1st May, 1917.

1. The 4th Division is taking part at an hour Zero on Z Day in a general attack on the enemy's positions covering FRESNES-LES-MONTAUBAN and PLOUVAIN.
The 9th Division is attacking on the left of the 4th Division.
As at present arranged Z Day is May the 3rd. The hour of Zero will be notified later.

2. The 4th Division is attacking with the 10th Inf.Bde on the right, the 12th Inf.Bde on the left and the 11th Inf.Bde in reserve.

3. The 12th Inf.Bde boundaries are shown dotted in the attached map and will be as follows:-
   South
   Cross Roads H.18.d.55.10 - CHEMICAL WORKS (inclusive to 12th Inf.Bde) - thence straight line to Southern edge of PLOUVAIN I.16.a.0.0.
   North
   HYDERABAD REDOUBT - CLYDE - CUT (all inclusive to 9th Division) thence straight line from Junction of CUBA & CASH to Station in I.9.c.

4. The Objectives of the Division will be (3.a.b.c.d.)
   (a) CHEMICAL WORKS, STATION building and cemetery, thence to track from I.8.c.3.3. to I.14.c.5.5. and buildings at Eastern end of ROEUX (BLACK LINE).

   (b) Woods in I.8.d.- CANDY, CYPRUS and CARROT Trenches (BLUE LINE)

   (c) The trenches West of PLOUVAIN from the Station to I.16.a.0.0. thence through Gun positions along the track running to I.21.b.5.0. (RED LINE).

   (d) After reaching the RED LINE a further advance may be made by reserve Division and reserve Brigade of the 4th Division if circumstances permit.

5. (a) The attack on the first objective will be carried out by the 2nd Lan.Fus on the right and the 2nd Essex R. on the left. The dividing line (Shown in RED on the attached Map) will be CAM to the ROEUX - GAVRELLE Road thence a line to Railway Junction I.13.b.8.2. thence along Railway (inclusive to 2nd Essex R.)
   The 2nd Lan.Fus will attack with 1 Company each side of the railway.
   The 2nd W.Rid.R. follow the 2nd Lan.Fus and the 1st King's Own the 2nd W.Rid.R.

   (b) For the second and third Objectives the right boundary of the 2nd Essex R. will be the railway (inclusive to 2nd Essex R. They will thus be gradually squeezed out and will form a defensive flank along the railway. They will furnish their own reserves.

   (c) On the 1st Objective the 2nd W.Rid.R. will form up on the right of the 2nd Lan.Fus either in line with them or failing that slightly in rear.
   For the attack on the 2nd Objective the boundary between the 2nd W.Rid.R. and 2nd Lan.Fus will be a line from the junction of trench and road at I.14.c.4.9. to point I.15.b.2.7. where trench cuts road.
   This line will remain the left boundary of the 2nd W.Rid.R. for the 3rd Objective.

   (d) The 1st King's Own will pass through the 2nd Lan.Fus on the

5. The following work will be taken in hand at once under
   Divisional Arrangements
       Continuation of CALABAR to CLYDE.
       CAWDOR Right extended to CAM ~~from~~ Jumping Off Line
       parallel to CALABAR.

   Under Brigade Arrangements.
       Communication Trench from front line to CALABAR extension.
       This will be under R.E. supervision.

   By 2/W.Rid.R.
       Communication Trench along Northern side of Railway
       Embankment to join up CALABAR and original GREEN LINE.

6. 1st King's Own will send on 2 Companies to report to R.E. guides at QUARRY I.13.a.1.2. at 11 p.m. They will carry 50% picks and 50% shovels.

7. Separate Administrative Instructions will be issued by the Staff Captain.

8. A Visual Receiving Station will be established at H.16.b.7.8. near the fallen Aeroplane. Messages will be received here but no answers can be sent.

9. Brigade H.Q. will close at FORESTIER REDOUBT at 7 p.m. On completion of the relief Command of the line will pass the 12th Inf.Bde at H.16.b.7.8. where completion of relief will be reported.

10. Acknowledge.

                                    Captain,

                                    Brigade Major,

                                    12th Infantry Brigade.

Issued at 3.30 p.m.
    Copies 1 to 4 Battalions.
                5. M.G. Company.
                6. T.M. Battery.
          7 to 11. Brigade H.Q.
              12. 4th Division "G".
              13. No.4 Company Train.
              14. 406/Fd Coy R.E.
              15. 11th Field Ambulance.
              16. 102nd Inf.Bde.
              17. 10th Inf.Bde.
              18. 11th Inf.Bde.

The following Appx will be taken in hand at once under
Brigade Arrangements.
1. Concentration of CANADA to CHALK.
2. CANADA might entrained to coll from Transport C? the
 travelled to CHALK.

Under Brigade Arrangements.
3. Communication trench from front line to CHALK Crescent
 T/C will be under R.E. supervision.

4. S.A.A.
 Ample supply of S.A.A. through Northern side of railway
 Embankment to lie up to VALLEY and original in DUMP.

5. Lat Line.
 Lamp line will end on C. Companies to from 11 to 5 p.m.
 guides on Coys H.Qs. at 4.30, if light, they will leave
 for close and lay a novin.

6. Through Communicative Instructions will be issued from the
 Brigade Dugouts.

7. A visual Watching station will be established at M.M.D.T.S.
 near the Well on Army lane. Messages will be received here but
 no answers can be sent.

8. Brigade M.O. will close at 10 noon on morning following the
 on completion of the relief opening of the light will
 the 18th Inf.Bde at H.45.D.2.7. where completion of relief
 will be reported.

9. No hour.....

 Captain.

 Brigadier Major.

 18th Infantry Brigade.

Signed at 5.50 p.m.

Copies 1 to 2 Battalions.
 3 C.R.C.S.
 4. Brigade
 5 to Divisional H.Q.
 6,8,9 War Diary "A"
 10 "   Company Diary.
 11,12,13 Day I.O.
 13,11,14 Field Ambulance.
 16. Light Inf.Bde.
 17. 16th Inf.Bde.
 18 19 Inf.Bde.

S E C R E T. Copy No.....

12th Infantry Brigade Operation Order No. 373

Ref. BIACHE Special Sheet 1/20,000. 30th April, 1917.

1. The 12th Inf.Bde will relieve the 102nd Inf.Bde in trenches East of FAMPOUX on the night of April 30th/May 1st.

2. Units will move off from their present position with 5 minutes interval between Companies and will proceed by the track across country to the 102nd Inf.Bde H.Q. H.16.b.7.8. where they will be met by guides. Companies will march with intervals between platoons.

3. The relief of units will be as follows:-

Unit	Unit to be relieved	Time of leaving Shelter Camp.
Brigade H.Q.	102nd Inf.Bde H.Q.	7 p.m.
2/Lan.Fus.	22nd N.F.	7.30 p.m.
2/Essex R.	21st N.F. & 27th N.F.	8 p.m.
2/W.Rid.R.	26th N.F.	8.30 p.m.
12/M.G.Coy	102nd M.G.Coy	9 p.m.
12/T.M.Battery.	102nd T.M.Battery.	9.15 p.m.
1/King's Own.	Various details.	9.30 p.m.

4. On completion of relief the line will be held as follows:-

Brigade Boundaries. Railway inclusive and CLYDE - HOARY & HECTIC exclusive.

2/Lan.Fus. CALABAR from Railway exclusive to ROEUX - GAVRELLE Road at I.13.a.9.5. and CAWDOR.

2nd Essex. ROEUX - GAVRELLE Road from I.13.a.9.5. to CLYDE exclusive and CADIZ

The boundary between Battalions will be CAM which will be available for both for communication.

2/W.Rid.R. In Brigade support in trenches in I.18. West of CAWDOR and CADIZ.
They will be prepared to make an immediate Counter Attack at any moment if necessary without further orders from Brigade H.Q.

1/King's Own. In Brigade Reserve in 4th German System.

12/M.G.Company. 1 Gun at H.18.d.1.4.
H.18.b.3.2.
H.12.d.6.1.
H.12.d.7.6.
Remainder to take over gun for gun from 102nd M.G.Company.

12/T.M.Battery. 2 guns at I.13.c.2.8.
2 guns at I.13.a.4.4.
Remainder to be got into position as soon as possible.

2.

5. Sub para d.(Cont)
the 2nd Objective to attack the 3rd Objective.

(e) On the capture of the 3rd Objective the 1st King's Own will push patrols out to the GREEN LINE.

6. Prior to the attack Battalions will be formed up in Assembly Trenches as follows:-

    2nd Lan.Fus.   CALABAR, CAWDOR and extensions of these trenches South of the Railway and NEW Trenches dug between them.

    2nd Essex R.   Present front line, new trenches in rear of it and CADIZ.

    2nd W.Rid.R.   New Trenches to be dug in H.18.d.S.of Railway.

    1st King's Own. Trenches in H.18.N.of railway and West of CAWDOR.

7. The following will be the roles of the 12th M.G.Company and 12th T.M.Battery:-

    12th M.G.Coy.   ½ Section will be detached to each Battalion.
                        ½ Section will advance and take up positions commanding the Railway Cutting.
                        1½ Sections will support the attack by indirect and overhead fire.

    12th T.M.Batty.   Supplement the Artillery barrage on the outskirts of the buildings in I.13. immediately prior to Zero.

8. Details and timings of Artillery Barrages will be notified later.

9. Strong mopping up parties will be left behind in the buildings in I.13. and consolidation will be carried out in each objective gained.

10. Acknowledge.

                                         Captain,

                                     Brigade Major,

                               12th Infantry Brigade.

Issued at 6 p.m.
    Copies 1 to 4. Battalions.
                  5. M.G.Company.
                  6. T.M.Battery.
           7 to 11. Brigade H.Q.
                 12. 4th Division "G".
                 13. 11th Field Ambulance.
                 14. Renfrew Fd Coy R.E.
                 15. C.R.E.4th Division.
                 16. 10th Inf.Bde.
                 17. 11th Inf.Bde.
                 18. 1st Rifle Brigade.

S E C R E T.   Copy No. 1.

To recipients of 12th Inf.Bde Operation Order No. 58.

2nd May, 1917.

1. The Northern boundaries of the Brigade will now run from the Junction of CUBA and CASH to the wood in I.8.d.(Wood inclusive to 9th Division).From this point the railway(inclusive to 9th Division) is the boundary.

2. The 2nd Essex R. will conform to the movements of the right Battalions of the 9th Division and will form a defensive flank along the Southern bank of the Railway Cutting from its Junction with CUPID Trench to the COPSE in H.8.d.(exclusive).

3. All units will be in their Assembly Areas by Midnight and a report that they are there will reach Brigade H.Q.by 1 a.m. The 2nd Lan.Fus are allotted 120 yards frontage South of the Railway.

4. A Machine Gun barrage will be formed from Z Hour onwards on a line 500 yards East of the Artillery ~~of the~~ Creeping Barrage. 12th M.G.Company will detail two Sections to help form this barrage under the direction of the Divisional Machine Gun Officer. These 2 Sections will move forward to help in consolidation as soon as the BLUE LINE is reached. Of the remaining 2 Sections ½ Section will be allotted to each Battalion as previously ordered.

5. The 1st Rifle Brigade are being pushed forward so as to reach Assembly Trenches vacated by the Brigade North of the Railway at Zero plus 30 minutes. The remainder of the 11th Inf.Bde will move forward and occupy our present front line as the Assembly Trenches are vacated by the Assaulting Battalions.

6. The carrying parties of all Battalions will move forward in rear of the 2nd Lan.Fus and under the orders of the O.C.that Battalion to whom they will report at 11 p.m.tonight. They will act as moppers up for the buildings in I.15.and subsequently as a garrison for them.They will not move forward from these buildings until sent for by their Battalions.

7. (a) Battalions will leave a garrison in each objective until the next objective is taken. The 2nd W.Rid.R.will take special precautions to guard their right flank.

   (b) A continuous trench will not be dug along the BLACK LINE but the 526th Fd Coy R.E.are constructing a Strong Point at the Junction of CUPID Trench with the Railway Cutting at I.14.a. 2.4.

   (c) On the BLUE LINE the R.E.are constructing Strong Points:-

      (1) At junction of CANDY and CYRIL Trenches I.15.c.3.6.

      (2) At junction of CANDY and Railway Cutting I.14.b.6.9.

   (d) Battalions are entirely responsible for consolidation of the RED LINE.
2 Sections R.E.will be sent forward to assist them in the construction of Strong Points in rear of it.
2nd W.Rid.R. and 1st King's Own will each construct 1 Strong Point and will be allotted 1 Section R.E.
Suitable positions for Strong Points appear to be the old gun positions.
A map is attached showing the Artillery Barrage Programme. Battalions will in every case follow the barrage as closely as possible.

2.

    (e) At the commencement of each advance a **salvo** Smoke Shell will be fired from all guns.

8. (a) 4" Stokes Mortars will discharge Thermite from Zero to Zero 1 on all buildings near the station.

    (b) Gas will be discharged from Livens Projectors after dark on Y Day against the village of ROEUX if the wind is favourable.

9. Contact aeroplanes will call for flares at 6.15 a.m.

10. Watches will be synchronised at 2.30 p.m. this afternoon under arrangements to be made by the Brigade Signal Section.

11. Battalions will make every endeavour to maintain touch with Brigade H.Q. by visual.

12. Zero hour will be 4.5 a.m. on May 3rd.

13. Acknowledge.

                                                      Captain,

                                          Brigade Major,

                                    12th Infantry Brigade.

APPENDIX "C"

List of Officers and strength of Battalion 3rd May, 1917.

Battalion H.Q.

A/Major	R.J.A. HENNIKER. M.C.	Commanding.
Lieut	W.J. GILBERT.	Adjutant.
Lieut	R.D. HODGSON.	L.G. Adviser.
2nd Lieut	N.G. INGALL.	Signalling Officer.
2nd Lieut	A. SCIAMA.	Attached.
Capt.	R.P. SMITH. R.A.M.C.	M.O.

A Company.

2nd Lieut	J.H. BASSETT.	Commanding.
2nd Lieut	F.W. MUNYARD.	
2nd Lieut	C.S. WHITEHEAD.	

B Company.

Capt.	F.C. NAPER.	Commanding.
2nd Lieut	G.W. COOMBES.	
2nd Lieut	J.B. BROOKS.	

C Company.

2nd Lieut	A.P. MYERS. M.C.	Commanding.
2nd Lieut	A.G.W. BROADHURST.	
2nd Lieut	W. WATSON.	

D Company.

Capt.	J.A.G. LEASK	Commanding.
2nd Lieut	H.S. GILBERT.	
2nd Lieut	T. ELWORTHY.	

Carriers.-

Lieut	R.C. Leach M.C.
2nd Lieut	J.E. WALKER.

Remained in 4th German System and then commanded details in "CLOVER" & "CUSHION" 5-5-17.- 2nd Lieut J. LOWE.

Total.- Officers, 19. Other ranks, 307. and 58 Carriers detailed to Brigade.

APPENDIX C

APPENDIX "G"   11th & 12th May, 1917.

Battalion organized as follows.-

"X" Company. (made up of A & B Coys)

    Officers.-

        2nd Lieut   J.LOWE. Commanding.

        2nd Lieut A.G.W.BROADHURST.

        2nd Lieut   A.SCIAMA.

"Y" Company. (made up of C & D Coys)

    Officers.-

        Captain. J.A.G.LEASK. Commanding.

        2nd Lieut   F.W.MUNYARD.

        2nd Lieut   C.S.WHITEHEAD.

"X" & "Y" Companies

    Other ranks.-

        224

Each Company was divided into 2 platoons, each platoon being made up from the remnants of a Company.

Battalion H.Q.

        A/Major R.J.A.HENNIKER. M.C. Commanding.

        Lieut   W.J.GILBERT.   Adjutant.

        Lieut   R.D.HODGSON.   L.G. Adviser.

Owing to lack of accomodation and number of aid posts already established, the M.O. did not accompany the Battalion.

        Casualties.-

            Officers.- NIL.

            Other ranks.-

                Killed   2
                Missing 1
                Wounded 22

                Total.- 25

APPENDIX G

APPENDIX A.

APPENDIX D

SECRET

WAR DIARY

OF

1ST BN. THE KINGS OWN REGT.

FROM 1ST JUNE 1917

TO 30TH JUNE 1917

VOLUME

VI

[signature]
a/Major
Comdg. 1st Bn. The King's Own Regt.
3/7/17

Army Form C. 2118.

WAR DIARY
or
INTELLIGENCE SUMMARY.
(Erase heading not required.)

Instructions regarding War Diaries and Intelligence Summaries are contained in F.S. Regs., Part II. and the Staff Manual respectively. Title pages will be prepared in manuscript.

Place	Date	Hour	Summary of Events and Information	Remarks and references to Appendices
HERMAVILLE	1st	Even Pd.	Training	
do	2nd		do	
do	3rd		do	
do	4th		do	
do	5th		do	
do	6th		do	
do	7th		do	
do	8th		do	
do	9th		do	
do	10th		5. O.R. joined Battalion.	
ARRAS 3	11th		Moved to ARRAS by Motor Bus. Move to Brevelau. Relieved 6th Yorkshire Scottish Borderers as per 12th Bd. Bde Operation Orders No 4/3 during afternoon between 1pm and 7.30pm in trenches E of PAMPOUX. Two companies in front line, one Company in support, one Company in Reserve and Batln H.Q. at Railway Bank — H.18.d. S.1. Relief (Sh. NW EL 5A)	
IN TRENCHES E of PAMPOUX	12th		Deepening and repairing trenches. Situation quiet. 2nd Lt FA INGATE wounded.	
do	13th		Consolidation carried on. Enemy aeroplanes active during day and Rear brick Battalion.	

Army Form C. 2118.

WAR DIARY
or
INTELLIGENCE SUMMARY.
(Erase heading not required.)

Place	Date	Hour	Summary of Events and Information	Remarks and references to Appendices
IN TRENCHES E. OF FAMPOUX	14th	Jany	Consolidation carried on.	
do	15th	"	Battalion relieved by 2nd Lancashire Fusiliers in accordance with 13th Infantry Brigade Operation Orders No 47 during afternoon between 4pm and 7pm. Marched back to FIFE CAMP in Brigade Support G.16.b.6.7.	
FIFE CAMP	16th	"	In Brigade Support. Training	
do	17th	"	Move to BROWN LINE. 3 Coys in Reserve. 1 Coy and H.B. in Support H.13.L.2.5; 1 Coy and H.B. in Support H.4.a.0.4.H.8.c.0.0.	
BROWN LINE	18th	"	Training. 2nd Lieut F.W. MUNYARD struck off strength to U.K. sick.	
do	19th	"	Move to RIFLE CAMP G.24.d.9.2.	
RIFLE CAMP	20th	"	Training	
do	21st	"	do. 25. O.R. and 2nd Lieuts D. DAVIES, R.T. SOMERVILLE and A. CARD joined Battalion.	
do	22nd	"	do. 3. O.R. joined Battalion	
do	23rd	"	do. 2nd Lieut I. SYKES joined Battalion.	
do	24th	"	do.	
do	25th	"	do. Lieut W.J. GILBERT struck off strength.	
do	26th	"	do. 7. O.R. joined Battalion (Divisional Depot)	

Army Form C. 2118.

WAR DIARY
or
INTELLIGENCE SUMMARY.

(Erase heading not required.)

Place	Date	Hour	Summary of Events and Information	Remarks and references to Appendices
RIFLE CAMP	27th	Sunday	Battalion relieved 1st Batt. Somerset Light Infantry in trenches; left sub sector R. SCARPE being our left boundary. B & D Companies in FRONT LINE; A Company in SUPPORT LINE; C Company in RESERVE and Batt. H.Q. at H.30. d.2.5.	A/49
IN TRENCHES	28th	"	2 O.R. Killed 3 O.R. wounded.	A/49
do	29th	"	3 O.R. wounded 2 to hospital sick	A/49
do	30th	"	4 O.R. wounded 2 to hospital sick	A/49

Major
Commanding 1st Batt. "King's Own R.L. Regiment"

SECRET

WAR DIARY OF

1st BN. THE KING'S OWN REGT

FROM 1st JULY TO 31st JULY 1917

VOLUME 8

[signature]
for Major
Comdg 1st Bn The King's Own Regt
3/8/17

Army Form C. 2118.

WAR DIARY
or
INTELLIGENCE SUMMARY.
(Erase heading not required.)

Instructions regarding War Diaries and Intelligence Summaries are contained in F. S. Regs., Part II. and the Staff Manual respectively. Title pages will be prepared in manuscript.

Place	Date	Hour	Summary of Events and Information	Remarks and references to Appendices
In the Field.	1st July/17		Battalion in Trenches with 1 Coy. 3/10 Middlesex Regt attached. 2 Companies in Front line. with 1 Coy 3/10 Middlesex. 1 Coy support, 1 coy, Reserve. In left Sub-sector S. Scarpe. Relieved by 2nd Lancashire Fus; in accordance with Bde. O.O. 51. 4. O.R. Wounded.	
	2nd	"	In Bde Support in HIMILAYA TRENCH East of FEUCHY. Working parties at night. 2 O.R. Wounded.	
	3rd		Do Do Do	
	4th		Do Do Do	
	5th		Relieved 2nd Lanc, Fus, in left sub-sector S. SCARPE, 1 Coy 3/10 Middlesex attached in accordance with Bde O.O. 52. 1 O.R. wounded.	
	6th		In Trenches.	
	7th		In Trenches. 2 O.R. wounded, 1 Killed.	
	8th		In Trenches. 4 O.R. wounded.	
	9th		Relieved by 2nd Lanc; Fus; in accordance with Bde O.O. 53. 2 O.R. killed. 2 O.R. wounded. In HIMILAYA TRENCH in accordance with Bde O.O. 53 moved back to Bde Support in	
	10th		In Bde Support. Working parties at night. 1 O.R. wounded	
	11th		Do. Do. Do. Do.	
	12th		Do. Do. Lt-Col O.C. Borrett D.S.O. posted to 197th Bde.	
	13th		Relieved by 1st Bn Hampshire Regt in accordance with Bde O.O. 55 moved back to Div'l Res; BALMORAL CAMP.	
	14th		TRAINING and working parties. 1 O.R. wounded.	
	15th		Do.	
	16th		Do.	
	17th		Do.	
	18th		Do.	

Army Form C. 2118.

WAR DIARY
or
INTELLIGENCE SUMMARY.

(Erase heading not required.)

Instructions regarding War Diaries and Intelligence Summaries are contained in F. S. Regs., Part II. and the Staff Manual respectively. Title pages will be prepared in manuscript.

Place	Date	Hour	Summary of Events and Information	Remarks and references to Appendices
	19th July/17.		Training and Working Parties.	
	20th		Do.	
	21st		Do.	
	22nd		TRAINING.	
	23rd		Do. 4 Officers 2nd Lt N.G. Ingall, 2nd Lt T.E. Pennington, 2nd Lt F. Price, 2nd Lt N. Pearce and 21 O.R. joined Bn from 2 2nd I.B.D.	
	24th		TRAINING.	
	25th		Do.	
	26th		Do.	
	27th		Do.	
	28th		Do. 2Nd Lieuts T.M.Marker & N.N.Hart & 4 O.R. joined Div Depot Battalion SAVY.	
	29th		BALMORAL CAMP. At night moved up to trenches and relieved the 1st Somerset L.I in the Left Sub-Sector of the PELVES Sector, as per Operation Order No 57. 2 Coy's In front line, 1in reserve and 1 Coy in support. 12th Brigade	
	30th		In Trenches 1 O.R. Wounded	
	31st		Do	

SECRET

WAR DIARY

OF

1ST BN. THE KING'S OWN REGT

FROM 1-8-17
TO 31-8-17

VOLUME No 8

[signature] Lt Col
Comdg 1st Bn The King's Own Regt
2/9/17

Army Form C. 2118.

WAR DIARY
or
INTELLIGENCE SUMMARY.

(Erase heading not required.)

Instructions regarding War Diaries and Intelligence Summaries are contained in F. S. Regs., Part II. and the Staff Manual respectively. Title pages will be prepared in manuscript.

Place	Date	Hour	Summary of Events and Information	Remarks and references to Appendices
	August. 1917.			
	1st		In Trenches in Left Sub-sector PELVES Sector. 1 O.R. Wounded.	
	2nd		" " " " " " 2 O.R. Killed, 3 O.R. Wounded.	
	3rd		" " " " " " 2nd Lt J. Fox joined Batt on 1st appointment.	
	4th		" " " " " " 2 O.R. wounded	
	5th		" " " " " "	
	6th		Relieved by 2n L.F. in accordance with Brigade O.O. 60, and movedback to HIMALAYA Trench. 2-O.R. wounded.	
	7.		In Brigade Support in HIMALAYA. Working parties up the line each night. 2 O.R. wounded.	
	8.		" " " " " "	
	9.		" " " " " "	
	10.		" " " " " "	
	11.		" " " " " " 2 O.R. Wounded.	
	12.		" " " " " " 5 - O.R. joined Battalion. from 22nd I.B.D	
	13.		In Brigade Support in HIMALAYA. Working parties up the line each night.	
	14.		Relieved by 1st Hampshire Regt and Mover back to BALMORAL Camp in Div'n Reserve.	
	15.		In BALMORAL Camp in Div'n Reserve. Working parties up the line each night. 5 O.R. Killed, 6 O.R. wounded.	
	16.		" " " " " "	
	17		" " " " " "	
	18		" " " " " "	
	19		" " " " " "	
	20		" " " " " "	
	21		" " " " " "	
	22		" " " " " "	
	23		" " " " " "	
	24		" " " " " "	
	25		" " " " " "	
	26		" " " " " "	
	27		" " " " " "	
	28.		" " " " " " 5 O.R. joined Battalion. from 22nd I.B.D	
	29		" " " " " "	
	30.		" " " " " " 4 O.R. " from 22nd I.B.D.	
	31		Relieved 1st Battn East Lancashire Regt in Left Sub-sector PELVES Sector.	

SECRET

WAR DIARY OF

1ST BN THE KING'S OWN REGT

FROM 1ST SEPT
TO 30 SEPT 1917

VOLUME

No. 9

W. Smith
Lt Col
Comdg 1st Bn The King's Own Regt

4/10/17

Army Form C. 2118.

WAR DIARY
or
INTELLIGENCE SUMMARY.
(Erase heading not required.)

Instructions regarding War Diaries and Intelligence Summaries are contained in F. S. Regs., Part II. and the Staff Manual respectively. Title pages will be prepared in manuscript.

Place	Date	Hour	Summary of Events and Information	Remarks and references to Appendices
1917. September	1st		Battalion in left sub-sector PELVES Sector. 55 O.R. joined Battn.	
	2nd		"	
	3rd		" Moved to WILDERNESS Camp. 1 O.R. wounded. 24 O.R. joined Battn. Lt	
	4th		" in WILDERNESS Camp. Training. Lt-Col W.A.T.B. Somerville D.S.O. to hospital sick.	
	5th		" in WILDERNESS Camp. Training. 1 O.R. wounded.	
	6th		" " " " " " "	
	7th		" Moved to BLAIRVILLE-HENDICOURT Camp. Lieut G. Oursman joined Batt'n.	
	8th		" in " " Training.	
	9th		" " " " "	
	10th		" " " " "	
	11th		" " " " "	
	12th		" " " " "	
	13th		" " " " "	
	14th		" " " " "	
	15th		" " " " " Church Parade.	
	16th		" " " " " Lt-Col V.A.T.B. Somerville D.S.O. joined Battalion from Hospital.	
	17th		" in BLAIRVILLE-HENDICOURT Camp Training.	
	18th		" " " " "	
	19th		" Moved by train from BNAIENY to Baselhoek and then marched to SARAWAK Camp.	
	20th		" in SARAWAK Camp Training.	
	21st		" " " " "	
	22nd		" " " " " Lieut M.J. Gilbert, 2nd Lieut W. Howarth, 2nd Lt E.J. Taylor,	
	23rd		" " " " " 2nd Lt G.G. Williams joined Battalion.	
	24th		" in SARAWAK Camp Training.	
	25th		" " " " "	
	26th		" " " " "	
	27th		" Entrained at INTERNATIONAL corner for TILLOQUE, and then marched to HULL'S Camp.	
	28th		" Moved up to SUPPORT trenches in LAGNICOURT Area.	
	29th		" In support trenches. LAGNICOURT Area.	
	30th		" Moved into front line.	

Commanding 1st Bat'n The King's Own Regt.

SECRET

War Diary of
1st Bn The King's Own Regt
from 1-10-17
to 31-10-17

VOLUME
No 10

C. Whewitt Capt
Comdg 1st Bn The King's Own Regt
4/10/17

Army Form C. 2118.

WAR DIARY
or
INTELLIGENCE SUMMARY.
(Erase heading not required.)

Instructions regarding War Diaries and Intelligence Summaries are contained in F. S. Regs., Part II. and the Staff Manual respectively. Title pages will be prepared in manuscript.

Place	Date	Hour	Summary of Events and Information	Remarks and references to Appendices
HULLS FARM CAMP. near BRIELEN.	September 28th.		12th Bde relieved a brigade of 20th Division in the Line East of LANGEMARCK. Dukes in Front Line - 1st The King's Own in Support near AU BON GITE (U.28.c.) Essex and Lan Fus in Reserve near Canal Bank. Enemy heavily gas shelled the whole area during the night. Mustard Gas was used.	RTJ
AU BON GITE	29th		In Support. Enemy's artillery active throughout the day.	RTJ
AU BON GITE	30th		In Support. Battn relieved Dukes in front line on night 30th/1st. Dukes to support.	RTJ
LANGEMARCK	October. 1st		In Front line. Our Artillery carried out bombardment of KANGAROO Trench in afternoon which drew heavy retaliation on our Front line. 11th Inf; Bde relieved 12th Inf. Bde in the line on night 1st/2nd. Battalion was relieved by Rifle Bde. and By 1 Coy Seaforths (10th Bde). Heavy enemy shelling on STEENBEEK during relief. Battalion on relief went to REDAN Camp near DAWSONS CORNER.	RTJ
REDAN CAMP	2nd to 5th.		12 Inf; Bde furnished day and night working parties throughout this period. On 3rd October the 10 & 11th Inf; Bdes carried out a successful attack East of LANGEMARCK - all objectives were taken (for boundaries and objectives see attached map A) owing to report that 11th Inf Bde had been driven back by counter-attack - the battn was ordered up to the neighbourhood of STRAY FARM in the evening. The report proved to be false, and Battn returned to REDAN Camp. Heavy rain throughout afternoon and evening.	RTJ
SARAGOSSA CAMP near CANAL BANK.	6th.		12th Infy Bde relieved 11th Inf; Bde in the line on night 7th/8th October. Essex going in on Right, Lan Fus on Left. Dukes went in Support near CANDLE Trench. 1st the King's Own were in Reserve and moved to SARAGOSSA Camp. Orders for attack by 12th Inf Bde were issued on 9th (Copy attached marked K) (For illustration of operations 9th to 13th see attached maps B & C)	RTJ

Army Form C. 2118.

WAR DIARY
or
INTELLIGENCE SUMMARY.
(Erase heading not required.)

Instructions regarding War Diaries and Intelligence Summaries are contained in F. S. Regs., Part II. and the Staff Manual respectively. Title pages will be prepared in manuscript.

Place	Date	Hour	Summary of Events and Information	Remarks and references to Appendices
LANGEMARCK	October 9th		Rain fell heavily nearly all day on 8th up to the 10 p.m. Battn marched off by Companies from SARAGOSSA Camp to assembly area near KANGAROO Trench at 11.30 p.m. Very dark night, and good deal of shelling. Reached Assembly area at 3.30 a.m. Zero hour was 5.25 a.m. Battn was heavily shelled both before and after zero hour, casualties were however slight.	P.T.
POELCAPPELLE			At 8 a.m. Battn moved to our original front line near BRAZIQUE FARM - (owing to heavy M.G. fire objectives of Essex and Lan Fus were not gained, 11th Divn on right also failed on left 29th Divn made good progress. On evening 9th line ran as shewn in red on Attached Map B. Heavy enemy artillery and rifle fire throughout day and night. Rain fell again during night which made ground into quagmire.	P.T.
"	10th.		Orders received that Household Battn and Warwicks would relieve Essex and Lan Fus respectively on night 9th/10th, these battns to go back to Canal Bank, also Dukes and King's Own to support in KANGAROO - EAGLE Trench area. Relief completed during night. Artillery fire caused many casualties especially to Household Battn.	P.T.

"	11th		Orders issued for an attack on 12th Oct (copy attached marked D) 14th Inf Bde to be composed of:-
			    Household Battn Right Assaulting Bn
			    Warwicks Left Assaulting Bn
			    King's Own Support Bn
			    Rifle Bde Reserve Bn
			 Raining again nearly all day. Household Bn & Warwicks formed up for attack east of POELCAPPEL - MILLERS HOUSE RD - King's Own on this road with two companies of Rifle Bde near EAGLE Trench. Remaining two companies of Rifle Bde behind them.
				P.T.

POELCAPPEL.	12th.		Zero hour was 5.30 a.m. Enemy put down heavy barrage on our front line, also great M.G. fire from POLCAPPEL Warwicks met with little opposition on the left, but Household Battn suffered heavy casualties by flanking M.G. fire from the village. In spite of this they took REQUETE Farm. 18th Divn of our right made no progress in the village, and so 14th Bde had to form a defensive flank. This was done by 1 Coy King's Own, and 1 Coy Rifle Bde. Counter attack forced line to retire slightly during the day near REQUETE Farm. The line as held in the evening was as shewn in the attached Map C - in red. 2 Battns of 34th Divn were sent up at night to relieve front line troops, but owing to darkness, and state of ground the relief could not be completed.	P.T.

(A7093). Wt. W18593/M1293 750,000. 1/17. D. D. & L., Ltd. Forms/C.2118 14.

Army Form C. 2118.

WAR DIARY
or
INTELLIGENCE SUMMARY.
(Erase heading not required.)

Place	Date	Hour	Summary of Events and Information	Remarks and references to Appendices
POLCAPPEL.	October. 13th		Still raining. Remains of Household Battn, Warwicks and King's Own were relieved in the evening by 2 Battalions of 34th Division and King's Own withdrew to LEIPZIG Camp (west of Canal) having spent 5 days and 5 nights in the shelled area and in the worst possible conditions of ground and weather.	RJS
	14th		Battalion moved from LEIPZIG Camp and marched to ELVERDINGHE where it entrained, proceeded to PROVEN and marched from there to PRIVETT Camp. 116 Draft of Middlesex Regt joined Battn with 4 officers - 2nd Lieut E.B. Whittall. 2nd Lt W. Gray. 2nd Lt T. Stanley. 2nd Lieut Robertshaw.	RJS
PROVEN.	15th		Battn in PRIVETT Camp near PROVEN. Engaged in general cleaning up.	RJS
"	16th		Battn marched from PRIVETT Camp to ROAD Camp at ST JAN TER BIEZEN and billetted there. 2nd Lieut S.R. Thompson joined battalion.	RJS
ST JAN TER BIEZEN	17th.		In ROAD CAMP at ST JAN TER BIEZEN. Engaged in Physical Training and general cleaning.	RJS
"	18th.		Battn in ROAD CAMP - general training. Moved at night to HOUPOUTRE to entrain.	RJS
ST JAN TER BIEZEN	19.th.		Battn entrained at HOUPOUTRE - proceeded to AUBIGNY and marched to HARBARCQ and billetted there.	RJS
HARBARCQ	20th		In Billets at HARBARCQ. Engaged in general training.	RJS
"	21st 22nd		" " " " " "	"
"	23rd		Battn moved by marched route to ACHICOURT and billetted there. Capt L.R. Hibbert proceeded to join R.F.C.	RJS
ACHICOURT	24th		Battn billetted at ACHICOURT. Engaged in General Training.	RJS
"	25th		" " " " " "	"
"	26th		" " " " " "	RJS

Army Form C. 2118.

WAR DIARY
or
INTELLIGENCE SUMMARY.
(Erase heading not required.)

Instructions regarding War Diaries and Intelligence Summaries are contained in F. S. Regs., Part II. and the Staff Manual respectively. Title pages will be prepared in manuscript.

Place	Date	Hour	Summary of Events and Information	Remarks and references to Appendices
ACHICOURT	October 27th		Battalion in billets at ACHICOURT. Engaged in general training.	PJ
"	28th		12th Inf; Bde relieved a Bde of 51st Div. 1st The King's Own Regt in Bde support. 2 Companies in Close support at M.15.d.4.4. and Batt; H.irs at 2 Companies in CARLISLE LINE. 1st Battalion The King's Own Regiment relieved 7th Bn Argyle & Sutherland Highrs. In Brigade Support. C & D Coys finding working parties; remainder gxx general training.	M
"	29th		" " " " " "	PJ
"	30th		" " " " " "	PJ
"	31st		In Brigade Support. Engaged in General Training.	

Capt.
Commanding 1st Battalion The King's Own Regiment.

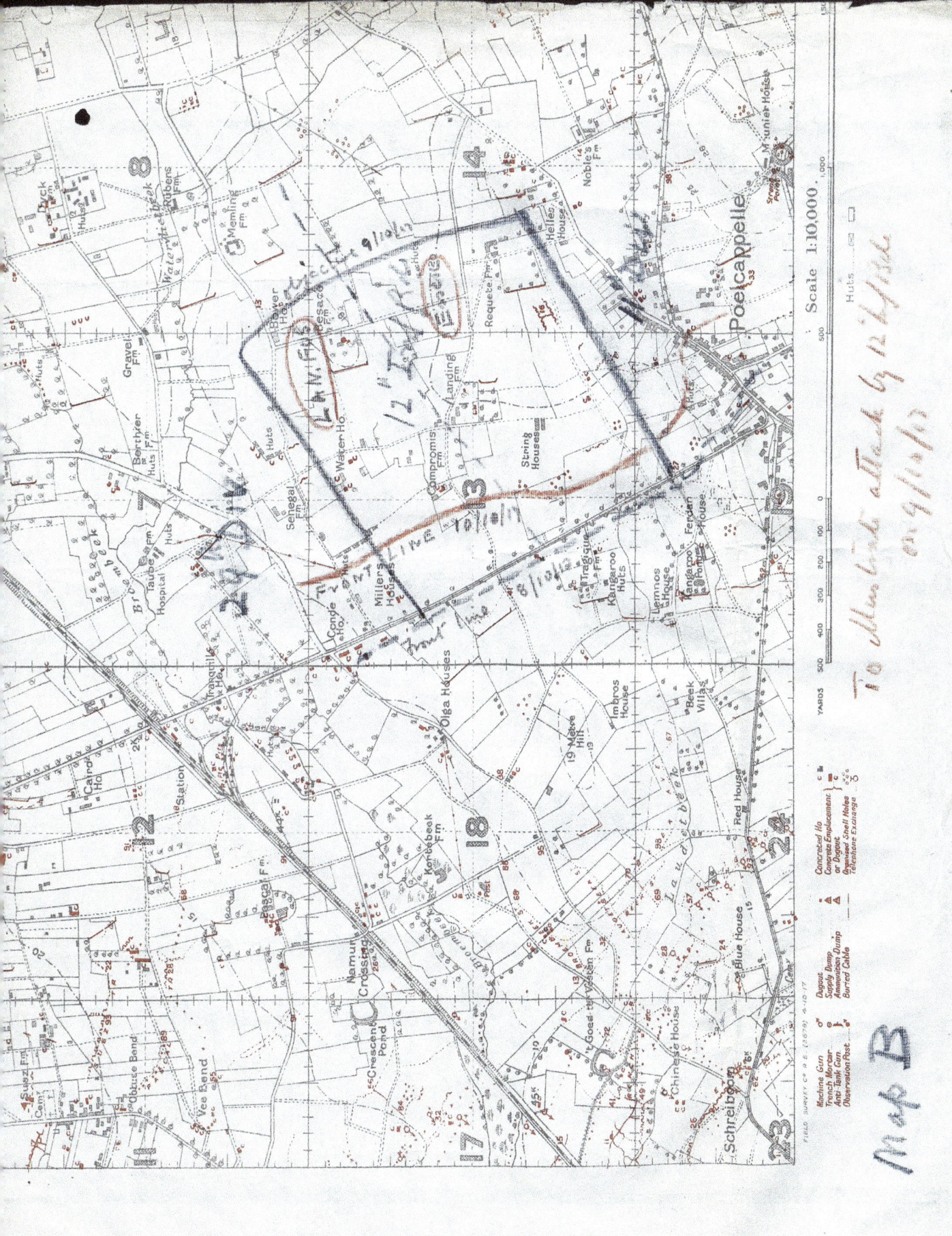

Army Form C. 2118.

WAR DIARY
or
INTELLIGENCE SUMMARY.
(Erase heading not required.)

Instructions regarding War Diaries and Intelligence Summaries are contained in F.S. Regs., Part II. and the Staff Manual respectively. Title pages will be prepared in manuscript.

Place	Date	Hour	Summary of Events and Information	Remarks and references to Appendices
November, 1917.				
ACHICOURT	1st		Battalion relieved in Bde Support in CARLISLE LINE by 21st Northumberland Fusrs, and moved back to Divn Reserve in ACHICOURT.	
"	2nd		Battn in Divn Reserve at ACHICOURT. Training. 2nd Lt C.G. Williams left Battn to join Special Brigade.	
"	3rd		Battn in Divn Reserve at ACHICOURT. Engaged in Training.	
"	4th		" " " " " " "	
"	5th		" " " " " " " and working party. 27316 Cpl Taylor and 8973 Sgt Pope awarded Distinguished Conduct Medal. Capt G.W. Wylie awarded Military Cross for Flanders Action.	
"	6th Ex		Battn in Divl Reserve at ACHICOURT. Engaged in Training and working parties.	
"	7th		" " " " " " " " " " " " Lieut R.P.F. White and 2nd Lieut R.J. Murray joined Battalion.	
"	8th		Battalion moved into line in Left Sub-sector Monchy, and relieved 1st Rifle Bde. A - C Coys front line. D Coy Support. B Company Reserve.	
"	9th		Battalion in line in left sub-sector MONCHY Sector. 1 O.R. wounded.	
"	10th		" " " " " " " " "	
"	11th		" " " " " " " 2nd Lt J.S. Nevard, 2nd Lt C. Austin, and 2nd Lt R.C. Stowell joined Battalion. 1 Prisoner 24th Saxon Regt came into our lines.	
x Durham	12th		Battalion moved to Bde Support in MONCHY DEFENCES. Relieved by 2nd Lan Fus.	
"	13th		" " " " " " " Finding working parties. Enemy sent Gas Shells over.	
"	14th		" " " " " " "	
"	15th		" " " " " " " Lan Fus made Bombing Raid.	
"	16th		Battalion moved in to front line. Relieved in support by 2nd Duke of Wellington Regt. Relieved Lan Fus in Front Line. 2nd Lt J.C. Cook, 2nd Lt A.H. Wall, 2nd Lt G.R. Adolph, and 2nd Lt R.J. Allam joined battalion.	

WAR DIARY or INTELLIGENCE SUMMARY

Army Form C. 2118.

Place	Date	Hour	Summary of Events and Information	Remarks and references to Appendices
Monchy le Preux	Nov 17		In Trenches - At 7-15 pm a party of 2 officers (2 Lieut Whele and 2 Lieut Hurst) and 2 S-OR of C Coy. any carried out a raid on the enemy's trenches. (Scheme and orders for the Raid are attached). The enemy hurriedly evacuated their trenches when the raiders entered the German trenches and secured 2 prisoners of 174' Reg't, 24 Saxon Div - 10 of the prisoners failed to reach our lines - the Left party were fired on by a Lewis M.G. and did not enter the German trenches. The response on right of the Bombing Party "Heard that Greenhay Charm 16 had killed 3 germans of the Bombing Party about their bay" and 6 OR were missing. 2/Lt Wang to their aid, went in but badly wounded - that the Lt Bay or were taken prisoner not known. 2/L and NCO 2/c Bay or were taken prisoner - hou reached the front trench. [2 Lieut Whele and 2 Lieut Hurst respectively for their part in the raid] - awarded M.C. and M.M. respectively.	
"	Nov 18		In Trenches - There was a bombardment by Corps artillery in afternoon and the Bolhe had to evacuate a remote discharge from its support trenches.	
	Nov 19		In Trenches.	
	Nov 20		In Trenches. In connection with the big attack at Cambrai a demonstration was made from the support trench at 6.30 am. Alarm rams were also sounded. About 50 OR were killed while coming over the top. - 2 Army officers killed were sent out as men R. Relieved in evening by 2 Essex. Bn moved to Brown Line	
	Nov 21			
	Nov 22, 23, 24		In Brown Line - Bn found working parties of battalion.	

Army Form C. 2118.

WAR DIARY
or
INTELLIGENCE SUMMARY.
(Erase heading not required.)

Instructions regarding War Diaries and Intelligence Summaries are contained in F. S. Regs., Part II. and the Staff Manual respectively. Title pages will be prepared in manuscript.

Place	Date	Hour	Summary of Events and Information	Remarks and references to Appendices
	November.			
	24th		Relidved in Brigade Reserve and moved back to Divn Reserve in ACHICOURT.	
	25th		In Divn Reserve in ACHICOURT. Church Parades.	
	26th		In Divn Reserve in ACHICOURT. Battn engaged in General Cleaning up.	
	27th		In Divn Reserve in ACHICOURT. Engaged in General Training. No 241475 Pte HALTON awarded	
	28th		" " " " " " " " " VICTORIA CROSS for action in FLANDERS in October.	
	29th		In Divn Reserve in ACHICOURT. Engaged in General Training.	
	30th		" " " " " " " " "	

SECRET

WAR DIARY
OF
1st Bn THE King's Own Regt

FROM 1st DEC 1917
TO 30th DEC 1917

VOLUME 12

W Cunninghame
Major
Comdg 1st Bn The King's Own Regt
3/1/18

Army Form C. 2118.

WAR DIARY
or
INTELLIGENCE SUMMARY.
(Erase heading not required.)

Instructions regarding War Diaries and Intelligence Summaries are contained in F. S. Regs., Part II. and the Staff Manual respectively. Title pages will be prepared in manuscript.

Place	Date	Hour	Summary of Events and Information	Remarks and references to Appendices
ACHICOURT	December.			
	1st.		1917. Battalion in Divn Reserve. Billetted in ACHICOURT. Church Parades.	
	2nd		Battalion moved into the line and relieved 3/10 Middlesex Regt in the Right Sub-sector MONCHY.	
	3rd		Battalion in line in Right Sub-sector MONCHY. 1 O.R. wounded.	
	4th		" " " " " " " " " "	
	5th		" " " Enemy Shelled our Trenches with Lethal Gas Shells. 2 - O.R. Killed on Patrol. 12 - O.R. Died of Gas. 30 - O.R. to Hospital suffering from Gas.	
	6th		Battalion moved back to Bde Support in FOSSE FARM and Strong points. 4 - O.R. to Hospital.	
	7th		Battalion in Bde Support in FOSSE FARM. Finding working parties.	
	8th		" " " " " " " " " " " 2nd Lt C.R. Adolph to Hospital.	
	9th		" " " " " " " " " " " 2nd Lt G.R. Adolph to Hospital. 2nd Lieut D. Davies invalided to U.K. Sick.	
	10th		Battalion moved into Line and relieved 2nd Lan Fus in Right sub-sector.	
	11th		Battalion in Line in Right sub-sector. 2nd Lt A.P. Myers M.C. 2nd Lt N.N. Smith. 2nd Lt A.P. Beresford, 2nd Lt T. Stanley, 2nd Lt J.A. Brewis transferred to 1st L.N.L. Regt.	
	12th		Battalion in Line in Right sub-sector MONCHY. 3 - O.R. wounded. Capt D.A. Ballard Killed.	
	13th		" " " " " " " " " " Lieut R.P. White and 2nd Lt T.E. Pennington to Hospital Gassed.	
	14th		Battalion moved back to Brownbine Brigade Reserve in Brown Line, South of CAMBRAI ROAD.	
	15th		Battalion in Brigade" Reserve in Brown Line. Finding"working Parties.	
	16th		" " " " " " " " " " " 2nd Lt W. Howarth	
	17th		" " " " " " " " " " transferred to 12th Trench Mortar Battery.	
	18th		Battalion moved back to Divn Reserve. Billetted in ARRAS. Batt H.Qrs in COLLEGE COMMUNAL. Lieut C.H. Hallett and 2nd Lt A.C. Adams to Hospital.	
	19th		Battalion in Divn Reserve. Billetted in ARRAS. Engaged in Training and× working parties.	
	20th		" " " " " " " " " " Engaged in General Training.	
	21st		" " " " " " " " " " " " and working parties.	
	22nd		" " " " " " " " " " " " " "	
	23rd		" " " " " " " " " " " " " "	
	24th		" " " " " " " " " " " " " "	
	25th		" " " " " " " " " " Church Parades and Chrsitmas Celebrations.	

Army Form C. 2118.

WAR DIARY
or
INTELLIGENCE SUMMARY.
(Erase heading not required.)

Instructions regarding War Diaries and Intelligence Summaries are contained in F. S. Regs., Part II. and the Staff Manual respectively. Title pages will be prepared in manuscript.

Place	Date	Hour	Summary of Events and Information	Remarks and references to Appendices
ARRAS.	DECEMBER. 1917. 26th		Battalion moved into Line and relieved 2nd Seaforth Highrs in Right Sub-sector MONCHY. Battalion H.Qtrs in CIRCLE Trench. Major W.W.S. Cuningham took command of Battalion.	
	27th		Battalion in Line in Right Sub-sector MONCHY. 3 - O.R. killed in action. 2nd Lt W. Gray wounded.	
	28th		" " " " " " "	
	29th		" " " " " " "	
	30th		" " " " " " " Lt.-Col. W.A.T.B. Somerville D.S.O. struck off strength of Battalion.	
	31st		" " " " " " "	

4TH DIVISION
12TH INFY BDE

1ST BN KING'S OWN ROY. LANCS

JAN 1918 - FEB 1919

4TH DIVISION
12TH INFY BDE

WAR DIARY
INTELLIGENCE SUMMARY
(Erase heading not required.)

Army Form C. 2118.

1 R Laws Vol 40

Place	Date	Hour	Summary of Events and Information	Remarks and references to Appendices
	May 1 to Jan 3		Battalion in support in MONCHY DEFENCES. Work Front	JK
	Jan 4 to Jan 7		Battalion in Front Line Right subsector Left sector (MONCHY) Fairly quiet tour. Hostile tube bole sniper active against MONCHY. Snipers (N.C.O.) had to go there at dawn to try to find that he had a cordlap. One camera & some riflemen were found shot.	JK
	Jan 8 to Jan 11		Battn in Brigade Reserve Left Subsector BROWN LINE Weather rather severe with snow. Working parties	JK
	Jan 12 to Jan 16		Battn in WILDERNESS CAMP near TILLOY in ↗ Corps Reserve Regimental Reserve The Battn moved up of nights of 13, 14, 15, 16 to dig new Reserve Line. in night of 15th shelled with H.E. Gas shells (5 casualties) General thaw on the 16, communication trenches nearly knee deep in mud. D Coy did very good work. Evacuation occurred by men having to go out the top.	JK
	Jan 17 to Jan 19		Battn in ARRAS Schramm Barracks. Divisional Reserve (Rear)	JK
	Jan 20 to Jan 23		Battn in FRONT LINE Right Subsector Right Sector (COMBRAI RD) Quiet tour	JK

Army Form C. 2118.

WAR DIARY
INTELLIGENCE SUMMARY.
(Erase heading not required.)

Instructions regarding War Diaries and Intelligence Summaries are contained in F. S. Regs., Part II. and the Staff Manual respectively. Title pages will be prepared in manuscript.

Place	Date	Hour	Summary of Events and Information	Remarks and references to Appendices
	Jan 24/25		Battalion in Support. Coys in Reserve Line & Strong Points. Batt'n HQrs at LA FOSSES FARM CAVES.	J.K.
	Jan 27			J.K.
	Jan 28 to Feb 1		Batt'n in Front Line Rightsector. CAMBRAI RD Quiet tour trenches good.	

3rd February 1918.   Commanding 1st Bn. The King's Own (R.L.Regt.)

[signature] Lieut. Colonel,

112th Brigade

Herewith War
Diary of this unit
for the month of
February 1918

J Kennington
for Major
Lt. Colonel.
Commdg 1st The King's Own Regmt

4/3/18

Army Form C. 2118.

1 R Kane
Vol 41

WAR DIARY
or
INTELLIGENCE SUMMARY.
(Erase heading not required.)

Instructions regarding War Diaries and Intelligence Summaries are contained in F. S. Regs., Part II. and the Staff Manual respectively. Title pages will be prepared in manuscript.

Place	Date	Hour	Summary of Events and Information	Remarks and references to Appendices
In the Field	1/2/18	—	Battalion relieved from the front line, right sub sector, and moved into Brigade reserve.	76
"	2/2/18	—	Brigade reserve	76
"	3/2/18	—	Brigade reserve	76
"	4/2/18	—	Brigade reserve, relieved in the afternoon by the 10th Scottish Rifles and moved to Billets in Arras.	76
"	5/2/18	—	Moved by march route from Arras to Berneville. Lt Col C.R. Bowler joined Bn from 10th R. Inns.	76
			Battalion at Berneville Training	76

From 6/2 to the 28/2

In the Field

12th Inf.Bde.
4th Div.

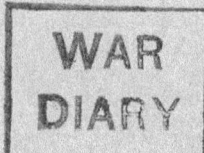

1st BATTN. THE KING'S OWN (ROYAL LANCASTER) REGIMENT.

M A R C H

1 9 1 8

Army Form C. 2118.

"12" Brigade

Place	Date	Hour	Remarks and references to Appendices
Ht BERNEVILLE	1/3/18		
	2/3/18		
	3/3/18		
	4/3/18		
	5/3/18		
	6/3/18		
	7/3/18		
	8/3/18		
	9/3/18		
	10/3/18		
	11/3/18		
	12/3/18		Training
	13/3/18		Training
	14/3/18		Lead firing at PONICOUX
	15/3/18		Training on the Range
	16/3/18		Firing on the Range

Herewith War Diary of this unit for the month of March 1918.

14th April 1918

M. V....
Lieut Colonel
Comdg 1st Bn Wilts (Duke Edin's Own) Regt

Army Form C. 2118.

INTELLIGENCE SUMMARY.
(Erase heading not required.)

Instructions regarding War Diaries and Intelligence Summaries are contained in F. S. Regs., Part II. and the Staff Manual respectively. Title pages will be prepared in manuscript.

Place	Date	Hour	Summary of Events and Information	Remarks and references to Appendices
AT BERNEVILLE	1/3/18		Company training	
	2/3/18		Brigade Field Day	
	3/3/18		Church Parade	
	4/3/18		Company training	
	5/3/18		Battalion entrained and proceeded to Tincques near TINQUES	
	6/3/18		Company training	
	7/3/18		Training & cross country run	
	8/3/18		Training	
	9/3/18		Practised march past	
	10/3/18		Inspection by G.O.C. 4th Divn. march & arrival in the evening and Billet in LEWIS 5A3	
	11/3/18			
	12/3/18		Training	
	13/3/18		Training	
	14/3/18		Lewis Gun at ACH-ICOURT	
	15/3/18		Training	
	16/3/18		Firing on the Range	

WAR DIARY
or
INTELLIGENCE SUMMARY.

Army Form C. 2118.

Place	Date	Hour	Summary of Events and Information	Remarks and references to Appendices
	17/3/18		Shelter taken for officers for counter attack from Railway Embankment at FAMPOUX.	
	18/3/18		Gathering for trench	
	19/3/18		Battalion move into the Line (GREENLAND HILL SECTOR)	
	20/3/18		In the Front Line	
	21/3/18			
	22/3/18			
	23/3/18		In Front Line. Enemy had twenty? in front line. Parted out patrols. Bde. Enemy shelled heavily	
	24/3/18		Battalion move to BLANGY	in forenoon
	25/3/18		At BLANGY. STOOD TO ut 4.30 a.m each morning in readiness	
	26/3/18		At BLANGY	
	27/3/18		Enemy raid the ESSEX Bn's R.B's	
	28/3/18		Enemy attack N of R SCARPE. Battn occupied MISSOURI, STONE & LOVIE TRS	
			both Batton heavily shelled. enemy have mastery of heights from Gavrelle. ESSEX Let Bavin, 2nd Lt. Rowsent & 1st K.O. men left w/ Coy. Two Pl in H.Q. Co. H.Q. 158mm trench	Lt. Rowe Bavin lost arm - 70 casualties in O.R.
	29/3/18		In the Line	
	30/3/18			
	31/3/18		Battn heavily shelled in day F.	

4th Division.No.G.A. 13/5.

10th Infantry Brigade.
11th Infantry Brigade.
12th Infantry Brigade.
4th Divisional Artillery.
C.R.E.
A.D.M.S.
234th M.G. Coy.
Signals.
21st West Yorks Regt.

        Will you please convey to all ranks, the G.O.C's thanks for the splendid way they have worked during the last few weeks the Division was in the line.

        The destruction of the trenches caused by the thaw was enough to dishearten anybody, but instead of it having that effect, everybody set to and worked magnificently so that we were able to hand over most of the trenches in a good condition and in many cases, in a better condition than they were in before the thaw.

        During the whole of the period, the Infantry in the front trenches never relaxed their control of the ground between our front line and that of the enemy. Several Patrol encounters took place, and several very gallant acts were recorded ending up by a final raid by the 2nd West Riding Regiment.

        The spirit evinced by all ranks of all arms during this period could not have been better. It has once more shown that the spirit which enabled the Division to save the Old Expeditionary Force from disaster during the retreat from MONS is still present, and should the necessity arise, the Germans will once more find to their cost that the 4th British Division will again defeat their efforts.

        (Sd) H. Kerslake, Lieut.Colonel,
8th February 1918.   General Staff, 4th Division.

        CERTIFIED   TRUE   COPY.

4th March 1918.   Captain,
        Adjutant 1st Bn. The King's Own Regt.

12th Brigade.
4th Division.

1st BATTALION

KING'S OWN ROYAL LANCASTER REGIMENT

APRIL 1918.

Army Form C. 2118.

WAR DIARY
or
INTELLIGENCE SUMMARY.   APRIL 1918

(Erase heading not required)

Instructions regarding War Diaries and Intelligence Summaries are contained in F.S. Regs., Part II. and the Staff Manual respectively. Title pages will be prepared in manuscript.

Place	Date	Hour	Summary of Events and Information	Remarks and references to Appendices
	1st		Battalion in the front line north of FAMPOUX	
	2nd		About 5-45 a.m. a party of the enemy, about 200 strong raided our front line. A determined attack was made the enemy bringing with him packs, barbed wire and other material as if sure of occupying the trench. He was ejected with loss, leaving in one trench 7 dead and two wounded after about an hours fighting, our casualties were 2/Lieut R.F.Rame Killed and 50 O.R. wounded.	
	3rd		In the front line.	
	4th		Relieved by the Lancashire Fusiliers and moved to Brigade support.	
	5th		Support	
	6th		Support	
	7th		In support. Relieved by the 1st Canadian Divn in the evening composing of the 7th, 8th and 10 th Battalions who took over various sectors of the line. Moved to SIMENCOURT	
	8th		At SIMENCOURT resting.	
	9th		" " "	
	10th		" " "	
	11th		" " "	
	12th		Left SIMENCOURT at 11a.m. and marched to embussing point, where the Battalion waited until 3-30 p.m. Buses proceeded via, HAUTE AVESNES, - ACQ- GAMBLAIN- BRUAY- LILLERS to a point on the LILLERS-BUSNES ROAD, S.W. of BUSNES where the Battalion debussed and occupied and outpost line. Battalion H.Q's were in a house on the left of the road (P 31 c 35.05).	
	13th		Battalion proceeded to CENSE LA VALLEE and went into billets, a line of resistance being established on the N.E., E., and S.E. of the village with posts advanced to the East of their Battalion H.Q. were at V 16 b 68.80.	
	14th		Battalion at CENSE LA VALLEE resting.	

Army Form C. 2118.

WAR DIARY
or
INTELLIGENCE SUMMARY.

(Erase heading not required.)

Place	Date	Hour	Summary of Events and Information	Remarks and references to Appendices
	15th		Reconnaissance of front line in Q 25, 26 and 32.	
	16th		Battalion took over front line from Q 33d S.W. corner of BOIS-DE- PACUET to N.W corner of RIEZ- du-VINAGE q 26 a 6.1. Right Coy "DD" Centre " "B" Left " "C" Support Coy "A" "A" coy had about 10 casualties on its way up to the trenches in the village of MONT BERNENCHON. Battalion H.Q. were at q 25 a 85.10.	
	17th		At STAND TO the enemy heavily bombarded our positions chiefly with 4:2's and 5:9's and also further back in the neighbourhood of Battalion H.Q. This lasted for about 40 minutes No infantry action followed. At 5-45 a.m. the enemy again bombarded. This continued till 5-45a.m. and the enemy then attempted to rush our front posts in the vicinity of "C" Coy. This was frustrated by rifle and Lewis Gun fire. In the evening Battalion H.Q. were moved back to the Canal bank (P 36 a 80.70.	
	18th		About 2 a.m. the enemy opened a very severe bombardment along our front, paying great attention to our back areas. What subsequently happened in somewhat obscure owing to the fact that those who were in a position to witness the course of the attackers now not available to describe it But it appears that the main force of the enemy's bombardment and of his subsequent attack was directed against the Right flank of "B" Coy and the left flank of "D" Coy. After hard fighting the enemy passed through the gap created between the two Coy's and turned S.W. thereby working round the rear of "D" Coy. The left platoon of "D" Coy was surrounded and captured. The centre platoon held their position for a short time and inflicted severe casualties on the enemy at point blank range, but finding that the enemy was closing in on their rear in large numbers, they were forced to withdraw to the Canel bank (Q 32c 70.85.) On reaching this point it was found that the bridge had been demolished and the remant of the Company made a stand on the canal bank Only a few who could swim and some others who crossed by bost or were dragged over by ropes succeeded in crossing. The rest, with whom were 2/Lieut Robertshaw and C.S.M. Batty were either killed or captured. The right platoon had been attacked in their positions about 25 yards from the BOIS-DE PACULT and were overwhelmed by weight of numbers. "B" Coy were attacked from behind the houses (QQ 26 b). The Company had suffered considerably from shell fire, but	

Army Form C. 2118.

WAR DIARY
or
INTELLIGENCE SUMMARY.
(Erase heading not required.)

Place	Date	Hour	Summary of Events and Information	Remarks and references to Appendices
	18th Cont.		except on the right flank, which were wiped out by the bombardment the line of posts was held. O.C. "B" Coy finding that his right flank had lost touch with "D" Coy sent two orderlies to "C" Coy. These orderlies appear to have got through "C" Coy's lines and encountered some Germans. They thereupon returned to O.C. "B" Coy and reported that the enemy had broken through and exposed B.Coy's left flank. Capt Broadhurst O.C. "B" Coy issued orders for the Company to fall back to the village which took palce as soon as possible. As a matter of fact "C" Coy's line had been entiœrely held throughout the engagement. Capt Broadhurst proceeded to a cottage at Q 26 d o05. O1 where he remained with a few men. Several of "B" Coy's posts were in this neighbourhood 2/Lieut Crook being with them. These subsequently joined either jamed Capt Broadhurst or "A" Coy. 2/Lieut Dobson with the remainder of his platoon withdrew and joined "A" Coy. "C" Coy held their line intact but 2/Lieut Wall and his platoon who were holding an advanced position were surrounded and either killed or captured. "A" Coy, being in support, were practically out of the attack. This Coy sent up reinforcements to "B" Coy. Subsequent to the attack and throughout the day the enemy indulged in much sniping and machine gun fire. Our men retaliated and as there was much mœvement on the part of the enemy numerous casualties wrere inflicted.

Casualties throughout the attack were :- 2/Lieut Robertshaw, 2/Lieut Nevard and 2/Lieut Wall MISSING.

Capt Broadhurst Lieut Whitehead 2/Lieut Coleman and 2/Lieut Stevens WOUNDED.

Other Ranks   262 including 149 O.R. MISSING. | |
	19th		At 8-15 p.m. that day Lieuts Dobson and Wallace with 100 O.R. assualted the Village of RIEZ-du-VINAGE behind a barrage and regained the original line, capturing a Machine gun and 19 prisoners. The Essex Regt took over this line late in the evening and the Battalion took over the line along the canal bank from P 35 b 99.85 to Q 33 a 20.40. Battalion H.Q's moved back to V 12 d 99.93.	
	20th		Enemy bombarded canal bank heavily, also MMONT BERNENCHON and LESHARISOIRS. Battalion on the Canel Bank.	
	21st		On the canal bank . 2/Lieut Battishill wounded	

Army Form C. 2118.

WAR DIARY
or
INTELLIGENCE SUMMARY.

(Erase heading not required.)

Instructions regarding War Diaries and Intelligence Summaries are contained in F. S. Regs., Part II. and the Staff Manual respectively. Title pages will be prepared in manuscript.

Place	Date	Hour	Summary of Events and Information	Remarks and references to Appendices
	22nd		Attack on BOIS du PACAUT and LA PAMERIE, in which all objectives were gained and line established along RIEZ- LA PAMERIE ROAD. In the after noon the enemy heavily bombarded the Wood and canal bank but no infantry action follwed.	
	23rd		Lancashire Fus and 2/5 Gloucesters attacked N of RIEZ and opposite BAQUEROLLES FARM and got their objectives. Battalion was by the R.Warwicks and what into billets at CENSE LA VALEE.	
	24th		Battalion at CENSE LA VALEE Lieut ROSS. 2/Lieuts Davies, Whittaker, Hargreaves and 29 O.R. joined as reinforcements.	
	25th		No 1 Coy, comprising of B and D Coy went up to the canal bank in reserve. B and C Coy's furnished and outpost line. Lieut Barber wounded.	
	26th		Reconnaissance of line at W 16 d and W 8.	
	27th		At CENSE LA VALEE resting.	
	28th		Battalion relieved 1st Hants Regt in the left Battalion front of the Right brigade, on the W edge of BOIS du PACAUT. No 1 Coy went into the front line and No 2 Coy on the Canel bank. Battalion H.Q. was at W1 a 40.55. The enemy's artillery was fairly active throughout the night	
	29th		The work of wiring in our front posts was commenced and also salvage and burying parties worked during the night. Things on the front were fairly quiet except for occasional artillery activity	
	30th		Precisely the same as the 29th.	

12th Infantry Brigade.

Herewith War Diary for the Month of May 1918.

4th June 1918.

[signature]

Lieut. Colonel,
Commdg. 1st Bn. The King's Own Regt.

1st Battalion The King's (Lancaster) Regiment.

Army Form C. 2118.

WAR DIARY
or
INTELLIGENCE SUMMARY.
(Erase heading not required.)

Instructions regarding War Diaries and Intelligence Summaries are contained in F.S. Regs., Part II. and the Staff Manual respectively. Title pages will be prepared in manuscript.

Place	Date	Hour	Summary of Events and Information	Remarks and references to Appendices
	1st		Battalion in the line. Left Sub-Sector PACAUT Sector	
	2nd			
	3rd			
	4th		X - 2 F'sep rel. 1Ko rel. 4/5.	This diary is valueless and inaccurate. See 12 Battalion.
	5th		10 B.M rel. 12 B.M. rel. 6/7.	
	6th			
	7th			
	8th			
	9th			
	10th		Brigade Reserve at CANCH LA VALLEE. 1 Company on the CANAL BANK.	
	11th			
	12th			
	13th		2/Lieut. N. Whittaker, K. in Action.	
	14th			
	15th		---- Centre Battn. VINAGR Sector. Quiet except for Enemy Barrage night of 15th.	
	16th		2/Lieut. C.J. Austin, K. in Action. 2/Lieut. J.S. Cook & 2/Lieut. R.M.J. Goldie, Wounded.	
	17th			
	18th			
	19th		2/Lieut. C.B. Meadows, M.C. K. in Action.	
	20th		Brigade Reserve, CANCHE LA VALLEE.	
	21st			
	22nd			
	23rd			
	24th		---- Centre Battalion, PACAUT Sector.	
	25th			
	26th			
	27th			

Army Form C. 2118.

WAR DIARY
1st Battalion The King's (Lancaster) Regiment.
or
INTELLIGENCE SUMMARY.
(Erase heading not required.)

Instructions regarding War Diaries and Intelligence Summaries are contained in F. S. Regs., Part II. and the Staff Manual respectively. Title pages will be prepared in manuscript.

Place	Date	Hour	Summary of Events and Information	Remarks and references to Appendices
	28th 29th 30th 31st		Enemy made small raid of "D" Company. Repulsed. Our casualties were 5 O.R. K. in Action & 1 O.R. wounded. Bentre Battn. PACAUT Sector. 10 days tour instead of 8. Battn. in PACAUT Wood.	

APPENDIX "A"

The tour in the Left Sub-Sector, PACAUT Sector was an uneventful tour of duty, though the Companies on the Canal Bank suffered a little from shell fire which fell on the bank rather frequently. The Front Line of posts was not shelled and a fair amount of work was done there on wiring. Much salvage work was done by the Battn. Very little enemy movement occurred by day, but by night hostile Machine Guns appeared to be brought forward into advanced positions and were active, as also were enemy snipers.

Gas shells were used several times, being fired on to the Canal Bank

Centre Sub Sector VINAGE Sector.

During this tour it was very quiet in the most forward area. The front posts were not shelled but the Support line was shelled occasionally by 77 m.m. and 5.9's cheifly owing to undue movement by day, and in retaliation for our harassing fire. The Canal Bank and in rear of the Canal Bank received more attention, 5.9's and Gas shells being frequently used more especially at the hours when transport was on the roads.

The enemy indulged in practically no movement by day, and our observers were only able to see a few men in posts. Enemy M.G's were not very active.

CEntre Battalion PACAUT Sector

Except for occasional shoots by enemy Light Trench Mortars and shelling of Canal Bank this tour was quiet. The enemy put a fairly heavy barrage down on the night of the 28th and attempted to raid one of our posts in D Coy. Thsi was repulsed. Our casualties being 5 O.R. killed in Action and 1 O.R. wounded. The enemy kept quiet during the day although movement was seen occasionally. A sniper in a tree was brought down by B Coy with a Lewis Gun. A considerable amount of shelling took place on the back areas at night with H.E. and Gas, and caused casualties to Transport both in men and Horses. Two Coy Q.M.Sgt were killed and 1 O.R. was wounded. The weather was very fine all the tour.

1 R Lanc Regt

WAR DIARY
or
INTELLIGENCE SUMMARY.

(Erase heading not required.)

Army Form C. 2118.

1st Battalion The King's Own Regiment.

JUNE 1918.

Place	Date 1918	Hour	Summary of Events and Information	Remarks and references to Appendices
	JUNE 1st		Battalion in the line in the Quelte and Beck Sectors. Operation Reports.	
	2nd		Battalion was relieved on the night of 1st/2nd June by the 2/5th Sherwood Foresters. Transport was also relieved.	
			Battalion moved to Camp in VALLEE BELLIF completed about midnight.	
	3rd		Devoted to general cleaning up of men. Billets. Training. Parade. Handing of Arms. Drill etc.	
	4th		— ditto —	
	5th		— ditto —	
	6th		— ditto —	
	7th		Bn. practice Platoon attack with Rifle Grenades as the leader. The Battalion proceeded on the 7th & 8th June to relieve 1st/5th & 1st/6th in the left sub-sector BARON WINAGE SECTOR. Relief A Coy in Barly 6 (B) Battn were in Rawalsies Caravan B and G. B 5 King 6(B) Bn H.Q. took over night supports Coy B & 6-S Fine & Coy. Reserve Regt with amn from Depot returned to Rawalsies.	
	9th		Normal. Enemy artillery fire was active in shelling the support lines.	0052.
	10th		Enemy aeroplane with German airman brought down by our L.G.'s & shell.	
	11th		Hostile patrol out working our line.	
	13th			
	14th			
	15th			
	16th			
	17th		Artillery activity was rather one-sided from 9 am the 11th 12th 13th etc ...	
	18th			

WAR DIARY
or
INTELLIGENCE SUMMARY

Army Form C. 2118.

1918

Place	Date	Hour	Summary of Events and Information	Remarks and references to Appendices
	June 19th		The Battalion came relieved on the night of 19/20th inst. by the 2/5th Duke of Wellingtons Regt. proceeded to huts near ONTRE LE VALLEES. A/B Coys occupied Bivouac Camp Area (C.8 Coys Garrisoned the Rear Line Defences in Canal Switch (VIRAGE SECTOR) Came under the Command of the LEFT BRIGADE (100th Bde etc.)	
	20th		B. Ch + A/B Coys in Rest Billets. Day spent in cleaning up etc.	
	21st		On CANAL BANK with C + D Coys.	
	22nd		C + D Coys went into Rest Billets. A/B Coys relieve C+D Coys on Canal Bank. Night Relief by midnight to Rt. Coy. relief to Rt. Battalion (ENSE 18 VALEE)	
	23rd		Nth + Ch Coys in Rest Billets. Day spent in cleaning up etc.	
	24th		Manual training etc.	
	25th		The Battalion proceeded to relieve the 1/5th Bn Hampshire Regt in the centre of the LEFT SECTOR PROQUET WOOD. A/B Coys (K.O) proceeded direct from C. de Buire. The relief was carried out according to will. Command in Copenaux in to front line, one in Support, one in Reserve	
	26. 27. 28. 29. 30		Nominal trench routine. Nothing of special interest to report. Usual Patrols and Standing Patrols.	

Army Form C. 2118.

WAR DIARY
or
INTELLIGENCE SUMMARY.
(Erase heading not required.)

1st.Batt.n. THE KING'S OWN REGIMENT.   JULY 1918.

Place	Date	Hour	Summary of Events and Information	Remarks and references to Appendices
	July 1.		Battalion holding trenches in the Centre Sub-Sector, PACAUT SECTOR. Enemy snipers fairly active, otherwise all quiet. Battalion Headquarters moved to Half Way House.	
	2.		A very quiet day.	
	3.		Considerable activity in sniping both by ourselves and the enemy.	
	4.		A fairly quiet day.	
	5.		Enemy rushed house held by us in BOIS de PACAUT and took possession of it. One of our men from "A" Coy. Missing.	
	6.		Enemy shelled support and reserve lines with 5.9's.	
	7.		Battalion relieved by 2nd.Bn.Duke of Wellington's Regt night of 7/8th inst. Considerable enemy shelling whilst relief was in progress, but no casualties. Battalion marched back to rest billets in CENSE LA VALLEE.	
	8. 9. 10. 11. 12. 13.		In rest billets at Cense la Vallee. Time devoted to general cleaning up, re-organisation, and the usual training.	
	14.		The Battalion proceeded to the line to relieve the 1st.Bn.THE RIFLE BRIGADE in the Centre Sub-Sector, VINAGE SECTOR. Relief was carried out successfully, there being very little enemy shelling except in the vicinity of Blackfriars Bridge.	
	15.		In the early morning the enemy heavily shelled the Canal Bank with 5.9's. Our Aircraft were very active after dawn over the enemy's lines.
Our trench system lightly shelled in the afternoon for about 15 mins. 2 Patrols left our front line during the night and reconnoitered the vicinity of THE BARN and HUN FARM.	
	16.		In the early morning the Canal Bank was again heavily shelled in the vicinity of Blackfriars Bridge and also Mont. Bernenchon. Many enemy observation balloons were up during the morning opposite our front. 2 patrols went out during the night.	
	17.		Considerable enemy shelling in the vicinity of Battn.H.Qrs causing a few casualties. Canal Bank shelled about noon with 5.9's.
At dawn, enemy shelled BLACKFRIARS BRIDGE & MONT BERNENCHON. A direct hit was obtained on the bridge, breaking the main girder. In consequence l'ECLEME BRIDGE was used for rations etc. 1 patrol went out during the night.	
	18.		Mont Bernenchon shelled about 2-0 a.m. At 2-30 p.m. a daylight raid by the 2nd/Duke of Wellington's was successfully carried out in BOIS de PACAUT. Retaliation on our sector was short and slight.	

WAR DIARY
or
INTELLIGENCE SUMMARY.

Army Form C. 2118.

1st. Battn. THE KING'S OWN REGIMENT. JULY 1918.

Sheet - 2 -

Place	Date	Hour	Summary of Events and Information	Remarks and references to Appendices
	July 19.		Considerable enemy shelling at 2-0 am. in the vicinity of Mont Bernenchon and Blackfriars Bridge.	
	20.		During the morning the enemy fired high shrapnel over between Laburnam Lodge and Bellerive. 10-30 pm. the Canal Bank was again heavily shelled. One hostile kite baloon was observed to be brought down in the forenoon.	
	21.		Between 2-30 - 3-0 am. Blackfriars Bridge and Robecq was shelled. During the morning the enemy also shelled the vicinity of Laburnam Lodge with high bursting shrapnel. 3 of our patrols went out during the night.	
	22.		At midnight 21/22nd a raid was carried out by the 14th Div. to our North. In retaliation the enemy shelled our Sector chiefly our Support Line. 2/Lieut.Park was wounded and 1 O.R. killed and 4 O.R. wounded during this shelling.	
	23.		The enemy artillery was fairly active on our trench system during the early hours of the morning. RIEZ was also shelled. 10-30 pm. Mont Bernenchon and Blackfriars Bridge was heavily shelled, during which the enemy sent over considerable amount of gas shells. The Reserve Line was visited during the day by General Birdwood.	
	24.		Intermittent shelling on our Support and Reserve Lines during the day, causing a few casualties in A.Coy. An enemy kite baloon was observed to be brought down about 9-30 pm. 4 patrols left our front during the night, and gaps were cut in our wire in preparation for a raid to be made the following day.	
	25.		Slight enemy shelling at 2-30 am. near the Canal Bank. During the afternoon the Essex raiding party came up into our front line trench. The raid took place about midnight and evoked hostile retaliation for about half an hour. Our casualties were 1 O.R.killed and 5 O.R. wounded.	
	26.		Everything very quiet during the day.	
	27.		Weather conditions very bad - no artillery activity throughout the day. The Battalion was relieved during the night by the 2/Duke of Wellington's Regt. The relief was carried out successfully with the exception of a barrell bridge over the Canal capsizing. A number of men were thrown in the water owing to this, and after being rescued, several had to be removed to Hospital. During the tour in the line the Battalion worked on deepening, widening and generally improving the trench system. The total number of groups supplied to the R.E's was 133. A belt of double apron wire was erected in front of BUTTER SUPPORT.	
	28.		In rest billets in CENSE L- VALLEE. Day spent in cleaning up etc.	
	29.		The Skeleton Scheme for manning the Brigade Reserve System was carried out.	
	30.		For instructional purposes etc the Battalion carried out the manning of the HOUCHIN-LILLERS LINE. On the return journey an open warfare scheme was carried out.	
	31.		Day spent in usual training. handling of arms etc. and re-organization of platoons etc.	

12th Inf. Brigade

Herewith War Diary of this unit for the month of August 1918.

[signature]
Lt. Colonel
Commdg. 1st. The King's Own Regmt.

[stamp: ORDERLY ROOM, No. 281, Date 1/9/18, 1st THE KING'S OWN REGT.]

1st. Battalion The King's Own Regiment. **WAR DIARY**
XXXX **INTELLIGENCE SUMMARY**
(Erase heading not required).

Army Form C. 2118.

AUGUST 1918.

Place	Date	Hour	Summary of Events and Information	Remarks and references to Appendices
Battalion in Rest Billets in Gonse La Vallee.	Augst. 1st.			
-do-	2nd.		The Village was shelled by enemy long range guns during the night.	
-do-	3rd.		The Battalion relieved the 1st.Hants.Regt.in the Centre Sub-Sector, PACAUT Sector.The relief was carried out successfully and was complete by 11-30 pm.About 12-0 mid.our left front Coy.H.Q. was shelled with T.M's. Enemy shelling near Aid Post about 10-0 pm.caused two casualties in "C" Coy. Cpl.Wallhead, though wounded, carried on with his platoon until relief was complete. At 12-15 am. Enemy Aircraft bombed the vicinity of W.1.d.with about 10 light bombs.	
	4th.		4-0 am.enemy shelled road W.2.d. with 4.5"s. Our artillery was active throughout the night and we kept up an harressing fire with M.G's. 2/Lieut.H.OGLE patrolled in front of Post 19. Owing to the enemy heavily shelling the Village of L'Eclame, the Details were moved to Burbure. During the night or 4/5th,numerous patrols went out in BOIS de PACAUT.On the whole there was little sign of settled enemy occupation. We learned that the enemy Division in front of us have been relieved by the 1st.Guards Reserve Division.	
	5th.		Patrols pushed out during the morning.Supported by L.G.Section.Progressed past H.Q.HOUSE establishing posts about 150 yards in front of this point.2/Lieut.DAVIES was in charge of this outpost line. 2/Lieut.PEACHEY went up from C.Coy.to take charge of the remainder of D.Coy. During the night the enemy shelled LES HARRISONS- CANAL BANK and round our supports in BOIS de PACAUT. We asked for retaliation.	
	6th.		During the day work was continued on establishing and consolidating posts about 200 yards N.E. of H.Q.House. The line now runs :- Q.34.d.15.48., Q 34.d.38.30., Q.34.d.33.45., Q.34.d.30.60., Q.34.d.25.65., Q.34.d.20.73., Q.34.d.17.80., Q.34.d.13.87.,-10.95., Q.34.b.03.03., Q.34.b.02.13., Q.34.a.95.25., Q.34.a.75.45.-55.55.- 20.54.-07.47.- Q.33.b.86.55.-77.60 -67.67.-55.73.-47.85.- 40.95.-27.d.37.02.- 30.20.-30.20.- 20.30-07.50.-00.60.	
	7th.		Battalion pushed forward in two bounds commencing at 8-0 am.Advanced B.H.Qrs. was established in vicinity of H.Q.House. The second halting point was reached by 10-30 am. D.Coy.Front Line - B.Coy.Support Line - C.Coy.Old Outpost Line - A.Coy.Canal Bank. A certain amount of sniping and M.G.Fire from the enemy and artillery fire on BOIS de PACAUT in vicinity of H.Q.HOUSE. At 7-20 pm.Capt.R.CARR withdrew two platoons about 200 yards on account of heavy enemy artillery fire.	
	8th.		Night of 7/8th.D.Coy.was relieved by C.Coy.on left front. Morning of 8th at "Stand To", 2/Lieut. D.DAVIES was wounded by sniper. At 3-30 pm,G.Coy.and flank Units pushed forward to a line nearer river TURBEAUTE. M.G.Fire during this operation caused some casualties.	
	9th.		Considerable enemy shelling around LES HARRISONS.Two direct hits were obtained on HALFWAY HOUSE. During the night the Battalion took over the whole of the Brigade Front and were distributed	

Army Form C. 2118.

WAR DIARY
or
INTELLIGENCE SUMMARY

(Erase heading not required.)

1st.Battalion The King's Own Regiment.

Instructions regarding War Diaries and Intelligence Summaries are contained in F.S. Regs., Part II and the Staff Manual respectively. Title pages will be prepared in manuscript.

AUGUST 1918.

Place	Date	Hour	Summary of Events and Information	Remarks and references to Appendices
	Aug. 9th.		Sheet -2- as follows:- D.Coy. Right Front., C.Coy. Centre Front., A.Coy. Left Front., B.Coy.Support. During the early afternoon the River TURBEAUTE was reconnoitred. Battalion H.Qrs.moved tp old Platoon H.Q. in BOIS de PACAUT.	
	10th.		"A" Coy.advanced their left platoon in conjunction with B.Coy.on the left. D.Coy.pushed forward to a line almost on RIVER TURBEAUTE and got into touch with the enemy on far bank.During the night three posts were pushed forward by D.Coy over River and established there.During the day C.Coy.pushed scouts and patrols forward to River and at 5-0 pm.a post was established E.of River covered by a L.G.Post just W.of River.	
	11th.		By 10-30 am. seven posts have been established E.of River. Enemy M.G.'s were very active during the time. Enemy artillery fairly quiet during the day. During the night the Battalion was relieved in the Outpost Line by the Lan,Fus.	
	12th. 13. 14.		Nothing of Special interest to report. Battalion H.Qrs.established at Half-Way House. Battn.H.Qrs.moved to STINK INN during the afternoon. A fairly quiet day. One Coy. of the 2nd ESSEX REGT.was gassed in Support Line.2/Lieut.Partington took up a platoon from A.Coy. to relieve gassed platoon.	
	15.		The Brigade was relieved by the 10th Brigade. The relief was carried out by daylight as far as the two Support Battalions were concerned. One platoon of A.Coy in Outpost Line had to wait until night for relief. B.and C.Coys.were left to man the Canal Switch on Canal Bank, and A.and D.Coys.marched back direct to rest billets in CENSE LA VALLEE.	
	16. 17. 18.		Day spent in bathing and generally cleaning up. Open Warfare Scheme carried out by the Battalion. In Billets. Usual treining etc carried out. A.and D.Coys.proceeded to the Canal Bank and relieved B.and C.Coys.The latter Coys.returned to rest billets in CENSE LA VALLEE.	
	19. 20. 21. 22. 23.		Day spent in bathing and generally cleaning up. Skeleton Manning of Defence System on Canal Bank during the evening. The Battalion (less two Coy's) fired on Range by platoons. Battalion due to return to the line, but was ordered to "Stand by" and await orders. Orders received for the Battalion to move by march route to AUCHY au BOIS. Battalion marched off at 9-0 am, in Fighting Order headed by the Band. Route:- BUSNETTES-BAS RIEUX-LILLERS-BOQUEDESQUES-PACQUEHEM-LIERES-AUCHY-au-BOIS.Destination was reached about 2-0 pm.	
	24. 25.		Day spent in usual cleaning up and resting. Warning order for move arrived during the evening. Entraining party left at 1-30 am. The Battalion moved off by march route in full marching order at 3-30 am.to entraining point - BERGUETTE. Route- GOUTE-St.HILAIRE-HAM. Detraining point - WAVRANS. March continued to SIRAUCOURT and BEAUVOIS. H.Qrs and A.Coy billeted in SIRAUCOURT..B.C. and D.Coys.in BEAUVOIS. The Bn.reached its destination by 1-30 pm.	

Army Form C. 2118.

1st. Battalion The King's Own Regiment. WAR DIARY or INTELLIGENCE SUMMARY.   AUGUST 1918.

Instructions regarding War Diaries and Intelligence
Summaries are contained in F. S. Regs., Part II.
and the Staff Manual respectively. Title pages
will be prepared in manuscript.

(Erase heading not required.)

Sheet - 3 -

Place	Date Aug.	Hour	Summary of Events and Information	Remarks and references to Appendices
	26.		At 8-30 pm, the Battalion moved off by march route in fighting order to SAVY. Route via RAMECOURT, St.POL and TINQUES. Destination was reached about 2-30 am.	
	27.		Reconnaissance of Musket Tr. and System occupied by P.P.C.LI. Situation was found to be obscure.	
	28.		The Battalion marched in fighting order to Cross Roads W. of HAUTE AVESNES and there embussed, proceeding to the vicinity of St.LAURENT BLANGY, debussing about 5-0 pm, and proceeding to the Assembly Area at Railway Triangle. Just before dark the Battalion moved to positions in Foal, Poodle, Dale, Long, Vine and Hill Trenches, near the ARRAS-CAMBRAI Road and S.Of MONCHY-le-PREUX. The Battalion distributed as follows :- A.Coy in Dale Trench., B.Coy in Highland Support., C.Coy. in Foal and Poodle Trenches and D.Coy. in Vine Trench	
	29.		Battalion ordered to move into area BADGER, SERING, OLD FRONT LINE & HOE SUPPORT. Bn.H.Q. in Spade Trench., A.Coy.Old Front Line., B.Coy.Saddle Spt., C.Coy.String Tr.D.Coy.Badger Tr. previous to this B.Coy was attached to BRUTINEL'S BRIGADE in order to escort M.G's into forward position.	
	30.			
	31.		Coy's remained in areas taken up previous day.	

Army Form C. 2118.

1st. Battalion The King's Own Regiment. WAR DIARY or INTELLIGENCE SUMMARY. AUGUST 1918.

(Erase heading not required.)

Place	Date	Hour	Summary of Events and Information	Remarks and references to Appendices
			The following congratulatory messages have been received BY THE Battalion upon its departure from the Fifth Army Command :-	
			4th.Div.H.Qrs. No.G.A. 38/7.	
			General Sir.W.Birdwood,Commanding the Fifth Army,has written a letter to the Divisional Commander dated 24/8/18 in which he says:-	
			" I must write you a line to thank you all for all the good work which you and your Division have done while I have had the privelege of having you with the Fifth Army.	
			I had much hoped to be able to have a Church parade with you to-morrow and to see at least one of your Brigades and a good many regimental officers,which,of course,is now impossible.	
			The best of good luck and good wishes to you and the whole Division in whatever may be before you, and I trust we may again be serving together one of these days."	
			(Signed) LAWRENCE CARR. Lieut-Col. G.S. 4th Div.	
	26-8-18.			
			SPECIAL ORDER by Lieutenant-General Sir T.L.N.MORLAND, K.C.B., K.C.M.G., D.S.O., Commanding XIII Corps.	
			On their departure from XIII Corps,the Corps Commander wishes to express to the G.O.C. and all ranks of the 4th Division his appreciation of the good work they have done during the last four months, and the fine spirit that they have invariably displayed.	
			In parting from them which he does with much regret,he wishes them the best of luck in the future. He is confident that when called upon,they will keep up the fine reputation of the Division.	
			H.Q., XIII Corps....24th Aug., 1918.	

To:-
   12th Infantry Brigade.

   Herewith War Diary for the month of September.

                                                        Lieut-Col.
5-10-18.   Commanding 1st.Battn.The King's Own Regiment.

Army Form C. 2118.

1st. Battalion The King's Own Regiment WAR DIARY
or
INTELLIGENCE SUMMARY.

(Erase heading not required.)

SEPTEMBER 1918.

Instructions regarding War Diaries and Intelligence Summaries are contained in F.S. Regs., Part II and the Staff Manual respectively. Title pages will be prepared in manuscript.

Place	Date	Hour	Summary of Events and Information	Remarks and references to Appendices
	Sep. 1.		During the night of 31st Aug. and 1st.Sept.the Battalion relieved the 1st.Bn.Somerset L.I. in front of ETERPIGNY.During the relief the enemy heavily bombarded the valley with gas shells,which caused a considerable number of casualties. 2/Lieut.Partington was gassed at this time.Bttn. H.Qrs was situated in front of LADY LANE.	
	2.		The Battalion attacked at 5-0 am.on DROCOURT-QUEANT LINE E. of ETERPIGNY - D.Coy to occupy furthest line.C.Coy to occupy third line - B.Coy to occupy second line and A.Coy to occupy first line. The Coys.places bombing blocks on their left flanks and at 8-0 am.began to bomb northwards with the object of taking ETAING under cover of a barrage.The attack was held up by M.G. fire from PROSPECT FARM. Casualties during this advance were - 13 killed and 36 wounded. Officers wounded :- Capt.R.Carr., M.C. DCM. Lieut.Dobson.,2/Lieut.Myers,2/LieutBarber,2/Lieut. Kennedy.2/Lieut.Rowlinson and 2/Lieut.Maywood. All the Officer casualties occurred early in the advance.At 7-30 am. A.Coy.was left without Officers and 2/Lieut.Cook (Intell.Officer at Bn.H.Qrs) went forward and took over command.	
	3.		The barrage as arrange for 8-0 am.to cover our advance on ETAING,did not materialize and heavy M.G.fire from the left prevented any attempt being made to capture the position.The enemy shelling was not intense and was somewhat scattered. Battn.H.Qrs was established about 600 yards E.of ETERPIGNY. During the advance the Battalion took about 300 prisoners . The 2nd Bn.Lan.Fus. attacked ETAING at 5-0 am under a barrage,but found that the village had been evacuated, and there was no opposition after entering the place.After entering the village the troops withdrew covering the crossings of the SENSEE. The Battalion being relieved by the 1st. Division on the night of 3/4th, the Battalion went back to the Area around SPADE TRENCH. The relief was very quiet, and the Battalion being relieved by the Northamptonshire Regt.	
	4. 5.		Day spent in generally cleaning up and re-fitting at noon the Battalion moved off by march route via the ARRAS-CAMBRAI Road, BEAURAINS to ACHICOURT and entrained there at 4-30 pm, detraining at TINQUES.Embussing there the journey was continued to La THIEULOYE arriving there about midnight.	
	6.		In billets at La THIEULOYE.Day spent in generally cleaning up, re-fitting clothing, equipment etc.	
	7.		Morning spent in training in open warfare, attacking strong points, Coy's and platoons in attack etc. Afternoon spent in organised games etc.	
	8.		-ditto-	
	9.		-ditto-	
	10.		-ditto-	
	11.		-ditto-	
	12.		-ditto-	

Army Form C. 2118.

1st. Battn. The King's Own Regiment.   WAR DIARY
or
INTELLIGENCE SUMMARY.   SEPTEMBER 1918.

Instructions regarding War Diaries and Intelligence
Summaries are contained in F.S. Regs., Part II.
and the Staff Manual respectively. Title pages
will be prepared in manuscript.

(Erase heading not required.)

Place	Date	Hour	Summary of Events and Information	Remarks and references to Appendices
	Sep. 13.		As for 7th inst.	
	14.		-do-	
	15.		-do-	
	16.		-do-	
	17.		-do-	
	18.		-do-	
	19.		-do-	
	20.		The Battalion left La THIEULOYE at 4-0 am. and marched to embussing point and proceeded to WILDERNESS CAMP arriving about 1-0 pm.	
	21.		In WILDERNESS CAMP preparing for the trenches.	
	22.		The Battalion proceeded to the ORANGE HILL Area, and moved up at 3-0 pm to Area N. of Cambrai Road.	
	23.		Usual reconnaissance of Sector held by the Hants.Regt.	
	24.		The Battalion moved in the line and relieved the 1st.Hampshire Regt in Right Sub-Sector, Left Brigade Sector. TRINQUIS BROOK and all the land near was in flood between the Battalion and the enemy. 2 platoons of the Hants Regt in the Centre Coy. could not be relieved on account of one of their posts having been scuppered during the night of the 24th.	
	25.		A.Coy. took over Right Front. B.Coy.Centre Front. C.Coy.Left Front and D.Coy. in Support.	
	26.		The Hants.did a fighting patrol over the TRINQUIS BROOK, but failed to secure any prisoners. Our Coys. carried out active patrolling in the vicinity of the bridges over the River. During a patrol by 2/Lieut. H. Ogle and Capt.A.R.Bosanquet, the enemy was encountered. 2/Lieut. H. Ogle was wounded.	
	27.		Two minor enterprises were undertaken by A. and B.Coys.C.Coy at the same time endeavouring to establish posts on the far side of the River. A. Coy were successful in establishing three posts on the N. side of the TRINQUIS. B.Coy.party under 2/Lieut. Lindsay crossed by boat and attempted to take in rear an enemy concrete work opposite the bridge. This was found impossible and the party withdrew at dawn leaving posts commanding the crossing.	
	28.		Active patrolling on the Battalion Front, but not with much success.	
	29.		-ditto-	
	30.		Several attempts made by Centre and Left Coys to cross TRINQUIS BROOK were not successful.	

Army Form C. 2118.

WAR DIARY
or
INTELLIGENCE SUMMARY.
(Erase heading not required.)

Instructions regarding War Diaries and Intelligence Summaries are contained in F. S. Regs., Part II. and the Staff Manual respectively. Title pages will be prepared in manuscript.

Place	Date	Hour	Summary of Events and Information	Remarks and references to Appendices
	Oct		Sheet - 2 -	
	20		Maj. Gen. Lucas visited Bn.H.Q. Conference of C.O's at Bde. H.Q.	appx.
	21.		Bn.H.Q. orders A.A. prepared to move to SAULZOIR. Some under orders to occupy Bde.	appx.
	22.		Bn. marched off at 1400 hours into Recces at SAULZOIR.	appx.
	23.		Reconnaissance of ground near position near RAVIN BRÛLÉ	appx.
	24.		10th & 11th Brigades attacked NOYK MONCHAUX, VERCHAIN and high ground E. of the village. Battalion moved forward to position in Sunken Rd E. of SAULZOIR	appx.
	25.		Advance continued from DOUCHY(?)	appx.
	26.		Bn. in early morning to outskirts of VERCHAIN. Bn. was attacked at 10.00hrs with high guns S. of QUERENAING outpost dispositions - 2 Rifle Coys to hold C & D line with Scotch & Cy in reserve. Artillery + Rifle MGs real ? to Rifle entrenchment the enemy fought and at 16.30 hrs 10th Bn Devon Reg. AB line held. Rifle Coys kept constant attack and for 2 businesses stat on attack Ravines. Followed Res have ??? 9 Rifle G. attack to the Kings own in support. N. of QUERENAING. A/C Coys (King's Own) lost at the divisional front Regt. The situation seems the ??? Rear Regt. Rifle Rn. C & D were from TROURS	appx.
	27.		and ??? Rifle G.s moving up in Coy support to Bn. H.Q. A/3 formed Schonnis Hautmont S of BAUMONT F3.	appx.
	28.		3rd Div. attack on our left to take HAUTMONT Enemy retreated. The ? ? ? line pushed forward to the 9 Kings of Bellas. Loss of Hampshire Regt. parties ? on Bde. to VERCHAIN. The next ? was cancelled. Pursued by enemy shell fire.	appx.
	29.		Coy of Rifle on Picket with escorts ? Battn ? into position.	appx.
	30.		In position at ? ? ? ? ?	appx.
	31.		Orders ? ? ? ? ? C.R. Coy moved ??? to ??? the station in support of ???	appx.

Army Form C. 2118.

1st Battalion The King's Own (R.L.) Regiment. WAR DIARY
or INTELLIGENCE SUMMARY.

(Erase heading not required.)

Instructions regarding War Diaries and Intelligence Summaries are contained in F. S. Regs., Part II. and the Staff Manual respectively. Title pages will be prepared in manuscript.

November 1918.

Place	Date	Hour	Summary of Events and Information	Remarks and references to Appendices
	Nov. 1.		A and C Coys moved from VERCHAIN to the Railway Embankment, in support to the 11th Brigade, who were to attack an object E. and N. of PREISEAU on the morning of 1st November. This attack was carried out successfully and C and A Coys lst The King's Own took up positions in Sunken Road in K.23.8.20.50. "B" and "D"Coys Kings Own moved from VERCHAIN to the Railway Embankment. About 1600 hrs orders were received for C & A Coys(K.O.) to relieve Coys of the Hants. and S.L.I. and to occupy an assembly position on the left of the 2nd Seaforths. A Coy took position on the right - C Coy on the left. Coys were in position about 0300 hours November 2nd. B and D Coys were in support.	
	2.		At Zero hour(0530) the Battalion attacked in conjuction with 2nd Seaforths on the right and 49th Division on the left. By 0700 hours the objective was reached and the Battalion commenced to consolidate. During the attack very little hostile resistence was encountered, the enemy surrendering freely except in a few isolated instances. Hostile M.G.fire was opened from long range on our men whilst they were consolidating inflicting several casualties particularly in in"A"Coy. C Coy reinforced A Coy with two platoons about 0730 hours. D Coy pushed forward patrols beyond the BLUE Line but were eventually held up with hostile M.G.fire. B Coy moved up in close support to C and A Coys and dug in along the Sunken Road about 2000 yards behind the BLUE LINE, with 2 platoons slightly further back. During the day the enemy continuously harrased out front line with long range M.G.fire and shells of light calibre. The Battalion was relieved during the night by the 9th SHERWOOD FORESTERS and the 6th Duke of W's, and proceeded back to rest billets in HASPRES, arriving there between midnight and 0200 hours.	
	3.		The Battalion proceeded by march route to billets in VILLERS EN CAUCHIES.	
	4.		In rest billets. Battalion parade was held during the day.	
	5.		Day spent in general cleaning up and preparing to move forward.	
	6.		The Battalion moved forward to QUERENAING by cross country track to SAULZOIR thence along main road to VERCHAIN.	
	7.		In rest billets at QUERENAING. Day spent in settling in billets and general cleaning up.	
	8.		A party was sent from the Battalion to take part in the demonstration held in VALENCIENNES. Battalion parade and usual training carried out i.e. Handling of Arms, Squad Drill etc.	
	9.		---ditto--- (Church Services in billets)	
	10.		Usual training carried out on the Battalion parade Ground.	
	11.		Brigade Ceremonial Parade on the Brigade parade Ground - Inspection by the Brigadier General and presentation of address by the MARIE of the village thanking the troops for freeing them of the enemy.	

Army Form C. 2118.

1st Battalion The King's Own (R.L.) Regiment. WAR DIARY
or
INTELLIGENCE SUMMARY.

(Erase heading not required.)

Instructions regarding War Diaries and Intelligence
Summaries are contained in F. S. Regs., Part II.
and the Staff Manual respectively. Title pages
will be prepared in manuscript.

November 1918.

Sheet No. 2.

Place	Date	Hour	Summary of Events and Information	Remarks and references to Appendices
Field.	12.		Usual parade during the morning, afternoon spent organised games.	
	13.		Many refugees were returning to the village at this time and under orders received from Brigade one Coy each day were detailed to clean up the village and help the civilians under the supervision of Captain J.A.G.Leask,M.C. A special party of slaters and tilers were also detailed to help the civilians in re-roofing their homes. A field kitchen was established to provide these refugees with soup etc.	
	14.		Baths were allotted to the Battalion at ARTRES during the morning, afternoon spent in organised games.	
	15.		Coy "attack" scheme carried out during the morning under the Commanding Officer's direction, afternoon as for previous day.	
	16.		Brigade Ceremonial Parade on the Brigade parade Ground at 0845 hours. Band and Drums in attendance. Afternoon - Football Match.	
	17.		Brigade Church parade at ARTRES at 1130 hours. Band and Drums in attendance.	
	18.		Usual morning parades including Outpost Scheme. Educational Scheme for the troops commences at 1130 hours daily. Lieut Col.G.R.Carter proceeded to Eng. on special leave	
	19.		The Battalion moved by march route to billets in St.SAULVE E. of VALENCIENNES. The march was completed by 1300 hours.	
	20.		Divisional parade on the Aerodrome Ground near SAULTAIN. Afternoon spent in organised games.	
	21.		Day spent in general cleaning up in and around billets and arranging for Company Dining Rooms also scrubbing of equipment. All salvage in the vicinity of billets collected and a dump formed.	
	22.		Usual parades on Battalion Parade Ground at 0840 hours. Commanding Officers inspection of "D" Coy at 0900 hours. One Coy detailed daily for cleaning up the village. Musketry practice carried out on the 30 yards Range under 2/Lieut.G.S.Pope.D.C.M.	
	23.		Parades as above but including one hour's drill (ceremonial).	
	24.		Battalion Church parade Service in Reading Room at 1100 hours.	
	25.		Morning P.T., Handling of Arms, and Platoon Drill. 1130 to 1230 daily Educational Training.	
	26.		Morning Training - Handling of Arms and Bayonet Fighting etc. Afternoon organised games. Special parties detailed for salvage work under Captain G.K.Lucas D.S.O.	
	27.		Morning Guard Mounting - Saluting Drill - Attacking strong points. Afternoon organised games. Inspection of the Division by the Army Commander on the Brigade Parade Ground near SAULTAIN about 1100 hours. Afternoon football match.	
	28.		Morning handling of Arms and Squad Drill - Battalion in attack. Afternoon organised games.	
	29.			
	30.		One hour's Ceremonial Drill. Rest of the morning scrubbing equipment.	

Army Form C. 2118.

1st Battn. The King's Own (R.L.) Regt.   WAR DIARY
or
INTELLIGENCE SUMMARY.   December 1918.
(Erase heading not required.)

Instructions regarding War Diaries and Intelligence Summaries are contained in F.S. Regs., Part II. and the Staff Manual respectively. Title pages will be prepared in manuscript.

Place	Date	Hour	Summary of Events and Information	Remarks and references to Appendices
Field.	Dec. 1.		Church Parades morning. Games Afternoon.	
	2.		Battalion carried out training on Parade Ground. Educational Training. Afternoon Games etc.	
	3.		Do.	
	4.		Do.	Regimental Concert
	5.		Do.	
	6.		Do.	
	7.		Do.	
	8.		Morning Ceremonial Drill.	
	9.		Church Parades.	
	10.		Battalion training.	
	11.		Do.	Visit from A.J. Godley
	12.		Brigade Ceremonial Parade. Presentation of Medal ribbands by Corps Commander.	
	13.		Battalion Bathing. When not bathing Coys carried out Physical Training and Musketry. Educational Training. Afternoon Games etc. Educational Training. Afternoon Games.	
	14.		Battalion Scheme. Route xxx march and Advance Guards.	Do.
	15.		Ceremonial Drill. Close Order Drill etc.	Do.
	16.		Church Parades.	Do.
	17.		Battalion Training. Escort and Colours arrived from England.	Do.
	18.		Do.	Do.
	19.		Battalion Outpost Scheme morning.	Do.
	20.		Battalion Bathing.	Do.
	21.		Battalion Bathing. When not bathing Close Order and Ceremonial.	Do.
	22.		Church Service.	Do.
	23.		Battalion Training.	Do.
	24.		Do.	Football Match Officers v Sergts.
	25.		Church Service.	
	26.		One hour's Physical Training, remainder of day holiday.	
	27.		Battalion Training.	Do. Regt. Concert
	28.		Company Route marches.	Do.
	29.		Church Parade. Congratulations and Greetings received from the Hon. Sir W. LAMBTON KCB.CMG.CVO.DSO. dated Egypt 9.12.18.	Do.
	30.		Bathing. Specialist training. Educational Training. Eliminating rounds Brigade Boxing Tournament.	

Army Form C. 2118.

— Sheet 2. —

WAR DIARY
or
INTELLIGENCE SUMMARY.

(Erase heading not required.)

Instructions regarding War Diaries and Intelligence Summaries are contained in F. S. Regs., Part II. and the Staff Manual respectively. Title pages will be prepared in manuscript.

Place	Date	Hour	Summary of Events and Information	Remarks and references to Appendices
Field.	Dec. 31.		Battalion Training. Educational Training. Afternoon Games etc. Finals Brigade Boxing Tournament. The Battalion won the following events;— Heavy, Light Heavy, Welter, Light, and Bantam; a total of 5 out of a possible seven, thereby winning Brigade Tournament.	RW
	January 1st 1919.			

J. Kennirelone
Lieut Colonel,
Commanding 1st Battalion The King's Own Regiment.

EXTRACT FROM THE LANCASHIRE DAILY POST DATED 13th DECEMBER 1918

RETURNING THE COLOURS.- 1st Batt. KING'S OWN ROYAL LANCASTER Rgt

Impressive ceremony at parish church.

The colours of the 1st Battalion the King's Own Royal Lancaster Regt., of which the King is Colonel-in-Chief, and General Sir Archibald Hunter the Colonel, were handed back to an escort to be conveyed to the Regiment at VALENCIENNES yesterday. The colours have had sanctuary in the King's Own Memorial Chapel at Lancaster parish Church since the Battalion went to France at the outbreak of war, and it is claimed that the Battalion was the first in action in the great war. An impressive service was conducted by the vicar, the Rev. J.U.N. Bardsley, assisted by the Revs. J.H.Dawson and V.J.H.Coles, in the presence of a large congregation. Among those present were.- Major R.N. Dobson commanding the depot of the King's Own Royal Lancaster, Mrs Dobs. the Mayor, Councillor W.Briggs, J.P., C.C., and Mayoress; Captain W.M.H Hoyle, M.C; Captain Fothergill, C.O., King's Own administration depot; Mrs. Hibbert wife of Brigadier General Hibbert; Mrs Hoyle; Mrs Hunt; Miss Booth. General Hunter and Lieut Millbank were prevented attending.

The officers acting as escort for the colours were Captain R.P.F.WHITE,M.C. and Lieut. R.T.SOMERVILLE, with C.W.M.S.Frisby, C.Q.M.S Knight, and Lance-Corporal A.Halton the Carnforth V.C. The Battalion bore itself with valour in the following principal engagement in the great war:- Le Cateau (1914), Armentieres, Second battle of Ypres The Somme, Arras(April 1917) Ypres (October 1917) Arras (March 1918) Robecq (April 1918) Drocourt, Queant (September, 1918) and Valenciennes (October 1918) The colours bear the battle honours of some of the most famous engagements in British history.

x--x

The King's Own Band under the direction of Mr. Chandler L.R. A.M., bandmaster, played the National Anthem, and the colours were borne forth to the barracks amid cheering, troops with fixed bayonets forming the guard, and the band playing the Regimental March.

-o-o-o-o-o-o-o-

SECRET.

12th Infantry Brigade

       Herewith War Diary of this unit for the Month of April 1918..

                                                     Major
                                                          for
                                                     Lieut Colonel

       Commanding 1st Battalion The King's Own Regt

4th May 1918

1st Bn KORLancs
Jan & Feby 1919

Index..............................

SUBJECT.

No.	Contents.	Date.
	~~13th DLI~~ ~~[signature]~~	

Army Form C. 2118.

1st Battalion, The King's Own Regiment.

WAR DIARY
or
INTELLIGENCE SUMMARY.

(Erase heading not required.)

Instructions regarding War Diaries and Intelligence Summaries are contained in F. S. Regs., Part II. and the Staff Manual respectively. Title pages will be prepared in manuscript.

JANUARY 1919.

Place	Date	Hour	Summary of Events and Information	Remarks and references to Appendices
Field.	Jan 1		Day spent in Recreation.	
	2		Battalion training on Battalion parade Ground. Educational Traing. Afternoons Recreation.	
	3		Cleaning up billets etc preparatory to leaving ST.SAULVE.	
	4		Battalion moved to MORLANWELZ by motor arriving about 1500 hours.	
	5		Day spent in settling down in billets.	
	6		Physical Training. Coy parades etc.	
	7		Coy Parades. Educational Training. Afternoon Games.	
	8		Battalion Training. —do—	
	9		—do— —do—	
	10		—do— —do—	
	11		—do— —do—	
	12		Devine Service. Civil reception to the Officers and men of the 12th Infantry Brigade by the civilians of Morlanwelz. The reception took place in the Town Hall Morlanwelz.	
	13		Battalion Training. Educational Training. Afternoon Games.	
	14		—do— —do—	
	15		—do— —do—	
	16		—do— & Lecture. —do—	
	17		Battalion Scheme "Advance Guards". —do—	
	18		Battalion Ceremonial Drill. Remainder of day devoted to cleaning.	
	19		Devine Service.	
	20		Battalion Training. Educational Training. Afternoon Recreation	
	21		—do— —do—	
	22		Battalion Route March. —do—	
	23		Battalion Training. —do—	
	24		Battalion Scheme "Outposts" Firing party for Belgium Soldier)	
	25		Bathing. Remainder of day cleaning.	
	26		Devine Service.	
	27		Battalion Training.	
	28		Preliminary Rounds Divisional Boxing Competition. 4 Competitors for Finals. —do—	
	29		Finals for Divisional Boxing Competition. 2 winners for the Battalion.	
	30		—do— Educational Training. Afternoon Recreation	
	31		—do— —do—	

Lieut Colonel

Command. 1st Battalion The King's Own Regiment.

1st Battalion The King's Own Regiment.

WAR DIARY
or
INTELLIGENCE SUMMARY.

(Erase heading not required.)

Army Form C. 2118/

FEBRUARY 1919.

Place	Date	Hour	Summary of Events and Information	Remarks and references to Appendices
LONDON.	1.			
	2.		Divine Service.	
	3.		Battalion Training. One Coy Trooping the Colours. Educational Training. Afternoon Recreation.	
	4.		Battalion Route March.	-do-
	5.		Training. B Coy training for Military Funeral.	-do-
	6.		Training. B Coy. Military Funeral of Pte. Devine.	-do-
	7.		Battalion Training.	-do-
	8.		Observed as a Holiday.	-do-
	9.		Divine Service.	
	10.		Battalion Training as per programme.	-do-
	11.		Battalion Route March.	-do-
	12.		Training as per programme.	-do-
	13.		-do-	-do-
	14.		Battalion Bathing.	-do-
	15.		Holiday. "B" Coy 1st The King's Own Regt. pronounced winners of Bde.Cooking Competition.	-do-
	16.		Divine Service.	
	17.		Battalion Training as per programme. Educational Training. Afternoon Recreation.	
	18.		Battalion Route March.	-do-
	19.		Battalion Training as per programme.	-do-
	20.		Battalion Parade Trooping the Colour. (cxxx)	-do-
	21.		Battalion Bathing at Herbourdes.	-do-
	22.		Observed as a Holiday.	-do-
	23.		Divine Service.	
	24.		Training as per programme.	-do-
	25.		Battalion Training and Lecture on Japan.	-do-
	26.		Training as per programme.	-do-
	27.		Battalion Trooping the Colour. (cxxx)	-do-
	28.		Training.	-do-

[signature]
Lieut Colonel.
Commanding 1st Battalion The King's Own Regiment.

WO 95/1506

12th Bde
4th Div

2 Bn Monmouthshire Regt
Jan 1916
Nov 1914 – June 1916

4th Division
War Diaries
2nd Monmouths joined from

U.K. Nov + December
1914

Oct 1915

12th Brigade.
4th Division.

Disembarked HAVRE 6.11.14.
Joined 12th Bde 20.11.14.

2nd BATTALION

MONMOUTHSHIRE REGIMENT

NOVEMBER 1 9 1 4

Army Form C. 2118.

WAR DIARY
or
INTELLIGENCE SUMMARY.
(Erase heading not required.)

Instructions regarding War Diaries and Intelligence Summaries are contained in F.S. Regs., Part II. and the Staff Manual respectively. Title pages will be prepared in manuscript.

Hour, Date, Place	Summary of Events and Information	Remarks and references to Appendices
Saturday 31st October 1914	Battalion has just occupied Billets at Churchbury Nr Ipswich when orders were received for it to proceed to join the Expeditionary Force.	ort equip't & issue of Short Rifle MMLE Mark III* by evening of Saturday 31st Nov. the Batt'n was complete.
Thursday 5th November NORTHAMPTON SOUTHAMPTON	The Battalion left NORTHAMPTON by train left 10.50 a.m. 1.30 p.m. night Embarking at SOUTHAMPTON at 11.30 p.m. & 9.30 p.m. Sailing at 11.30. Strength of Battalion including	Entraining Embarking
Friday Nov 6 HAVRE	The Transport arrived off HAVRE at 3.30 p.m. and anchored getting alongside the Quay at 11.30 p.m. The voyage was very calm & the spirits of the men were excellent	Voyage Dis-Embarkation Arrival at Rest Camp Ordnance Deficiencies
Saturday 7th Nov 14 HAVRE	Battalion disembarked at 7.30 a.m. & marches to the REST CAMP situated about 3 miles from HAVRE small deficiencies in Ordnance Stores were replaced	Bivouac
Saturday 8th Nov MAVRE	5.30 a.m. morning Battalion left for HAVRE STATION at 9 a.m. where they Knapsacks Deficiencies of Equipment & boots were here remedied. The Ordnance HAVRE had issued as far as possible. The Battalion entrained at 11 p.m. It was found to the type of train + the deficiency of were quite unused to the type of train + the deficiency of accommodation. Men were accommodated 35/45 per truck	Entraining Accommodation (train)
Sunday 9th Nov BOULOGNE/CALAIS Sunday 10th Nov	The journey was extremely slow BOULOGNE and CALAIS not being reached until early Sunday morning. Much delay was caused by viewing the train at small stations. No arrangements were made by Railway Authorities to halt the train for the purpose of nature and for cooking food, since the return to a training train at Japan station	Reviews of Rly Authorities
St OMER/WIZERNE Monday 11th Nov	The Battalion arrived at St OMER at 5.30 p.m. and there detrained, the whole marching to WIZERNE.	Arrival at first billet

(73989) W4141—463. 400,000. 9/14. H.&J.Ld. Forms/C. 2118/10.

Army Form C. 2118.

WAR DIARY
or
INTELLIGENCE SUMMARY.
(Erase heading not required.)

Instructions regarding War Diaries and Intelligence Summaries are contained in F.S. Regs., Part II. and the Staff Manual respectively. Title pages will be prepared in manuscript.

Hour, Date, Place	Summary of Events and Information	Remarks and references to Appendices
ST OMER/WIZERNE MONDAY 9th Nov WIZERNE	The detrainment took place in the dark, but everything was quickly and quietly carried out. Staff arrangements for our reception and accommodation were excellent. The Battalion reached WIZERNE at 11.30 and took about 2 hours to get to its billets, a short time considering the darkness, strangeness and new surroundings.	Detrainment Billets (arriving at)
Tuesday 10th Nov	Battalion paraded 9.30 am to watch night march of King's Saturday 9th Nov to parade 17th Nov were scenes of careful in Battalion training and Musketry. The Batt'n came under the Command of Col. A.A. Chichester Commanding Reserve Group at G.H.Q. and it is not likely the officer considered it fit to proceed to the front that the Battalion was at liberty to leave.	Parade — Night March Battalion Training Musketry Col. A.A. Chichester Command Fitness for the front
13th November	On 13th Nov 1914 the strength of the Battalion was 30 Officers 954 R + 3 Training in all Enemies counter ad whose round in Artillery but along the front was a red volume rather Discipline was rather careful and the outside the were practiced native coffee are the copies of any line in billets in actions at home. Much useful work was done at trench digging, an all-important item in this campaign.	Training - Enemy/Country Artillery/fire on our front Trench Digging Moves
Tuesday 17th Nov	The Battalion received orders to proceed by march route to HASEBROUKE and then to BAILLEUL to join the 4th Division 3rd A Corps.	Attachment Strength
Wednesday 18th Nov	Battalion paraded at 9 am (strength 30 Officers 950 R+3) and marched to HAZEBROUK. The Boots bought at NORTHAMPTON came under trial and proved to be of very bad material. A high pres has been quite the Contractor for these and there is no doubt he has taken advantage of the enormous demand	Boots (male) Price of 5 Advantage taken by Contractor

(73989) W4141–463. 400,000. 9/14. H.&J.Ltd. Forms/C. 2118/10.

WAR DIARY
or
INTELLIGENCE SUMMARY.

Army Form C. 2118.

(Erase heading not required.)

Instructions regarding War Diaries and Intelligence Summaries are contained in F.S. Regs., Part II. and the Staff Manual respectively. Title pages will be prepared in manuscript.

Hour, Date, Place	Summary of Events and Information	Remarks and references to Appendices
Wednesday 18th Nov	Lt. Scott to send in weak feet of an inferior quality. The weather was exceptionally wet and this took great [effect?] About 6 men fell out but all rejoined at HAZEBROUCK. The weather during the period 15/16 November has been very severe, gales and storms being frequent. 14 men were admitted to Hospital mostly suffering from severe cold & Rheumatism. The march of 13th miles from WIZERNE to H[AZEBROUCK] was accomplished in 5½ hours. No troubles occurred.	Boots. Weather & roads. Men falling out. Weather. 5 Admissions to Hospital. Complaints of Blisters. This march was accomplished
Thursday 19th Nov	Our 15th Brigade transport, the Cookers etc. were very bad, as much as march of 10 miles. No Cavalry at Baeliuel. A large Convoy of which hot men troops in succession, and occupied Billets in a Plenty date. Proceeded to LA BIXET	March. Billets. Sanitary conditions of Occupation reported around reporting to H.Q. Bde.
Friday 20th Nov	and reported to H Qrs 12th Brigade at LE BIZET. Companies were attached to Regular Battalions of the 12th Bde 3rd Army Corps for instruction in the trenches. This proved the first way of "blooding" them, much instruction being imparted.	Attachment to Regular Battalions
Period 21st Nov/30th/14	This period was spent at LE BIZET. Companies attached to Regular Battalions of the 12th 3rd Army Corps for instruction in the trenches. This proved the first way of "blooding" them, much instruction being imparted. Casualties were not severe being three killed and two wounded. These occurred within a day of each other being due to stray shot from the Enemy snipers. The Trenches occupied were those of the Essex Regt and the Lancashire Fusiliers.	Casualties Cause of " Trench Occupation of "

2nd Months

W4141—463. 400,000. 9/14. H.&J.Ltd. Forms/C. 2118/10.

STRENGTH RETURN.

Detail.	Officers Number.	Other ranks Number.	Remarks.
Strength of Unit on 30th Nov. 1914.	27	845	
Details, by arms attached to unit as in War establishment) A.S.C. R.A.M.C. etc.		5 6	
Total	27	856	

Signature E. B. Cuthbertson Lt. Col.

Unit OC 2nd Bn Cons Regt

Date
∎/12/1914.

URGENT.

This return to be completed and forwarded through the usual channel to reach Div. H.Q.'s by 12 M.D. on 3rd Dec. 1914.

(Sd) Y Smyth Osborne
Lt. Col.
A.A. & Q.M.G. 4th Div.

2/12/14.

12th Brigade,
4th Division.

2nd BATTALION

MONMOUTHSHIRE REGIMENT

DECEMBER 1 9 1 4

Army Form C. 2118.

WAR DIARY
or
INTELLIGENCE SUMMARY.

(Erase heading not required.)

Instructions regarding War Diaries and Intelligence Summaries are contained in F.S. Regs., Part II and the Staff Manual respectively. Title pages will be prepared in manuscript.

Hour, Date, Place	Summary of Events and Information	Remarks and references to Appendices
December 1st to December 14th	Attachment of one Company at a time to the 2 ESSEX Regt. & LANC'S F.U.S. continued until the 14th December. On this day the Battalion took over the line of trenches some 1100 yards in extent occupied by the 2 ESSEX REGT. between the N.E.RYE & from the Steenen & railway line on the road running N.W. from FRETINGHIEN. at period of 4 days in the trenches & four out. During the first two days communication with the fire trenches through unfinished trenches was very good. During the second period of 4 days communication or 10 December, communication communication trenches became impossible owing to inability to keep trenches drained owing to flatness of country. Relief became Enemy's modern staff at the country. The holes in it filled were nine and were	3? Rec'd? Killed 9 Wounded 19 2 Mins
December 14 to December 29	The Battalion continued to occupy the same line of trenches relieving the ESSEX Regiment every four days (or on occasion after five days) Most of this spent in keeping trenches dry. Great quantities of firewood & planks were sent into the trenches for this purpose. The enemy's machine guns were sometimes very active it was found however that they were temporarily silenced by our own firing on to the loopholes. The whole of the communication Christmas Day was spent in the trenches, the ESSEX taking their place in the evening it was almost impossible to use rifles & still continued to be afraid in keeping fires going to warm bombs had therefore to walk up continually in the open to the trenches. Christmas was carried on in the usual way. On Xmas day practically no firing took place by either side by mutual agreement of the troops. Anything approximately not made officers in hollow were his a wounded officer of the enemy were during this period. During the period 1st to 31st December 3 Officers & men	Killed Wounded including officers

4th Division
War Diaries
12th Infantry Brigade
2nd Battn Monmouth Regt.

January 1st October 1915

12th Inf.Bde.
4th Division.

WAR DIARY

2ND BATTN. MONMOUTHSHIRE REGT.

JANUARY

1915.

121/4329

12th Brigade

2nd Monmouthshire Regt.

Vol III. 1—31.1.15

Nil

WAR DIARY
or
INTELLIGENCE SUMMARY.

(Erase heading not required.)

Army Form C. 2118.

Instructions regarding War Diaries and Intelligence Summaries are contained in F. S. Regs., Part II. and the Staff Manual respectively. Title pages will be prepared in manuscript.

Hour, Date, Place	Summary of Events and Information	Remarks and references to Appendices

January 1st 1915
to 6th 1915

Strength of Battalion 19 Officers 752 Rank & File. Billeting arrangements being carried out every day since no advance in Divisions has not been available heavy communication trenches of E.1. are known to exist.

Jan 7th 1915
to
Jan 22, 1915

Line of trenches occupied. 9 regts. relieved and company of trenches occupied by battalion remained slight of live on new trenches known as trench 20 aspect and brought into line of the trench melees at the end of 20 aspect and we have what formed during the evening two days a second cost. Remained watching entries of nights. Remington cemetery in little time events until 9 Battalion Royal Irish Fus.

Relieve Browning R.W. near the Railway barricade. The line consists of some cottages, and it reported to be trench with 3 road, a relief was carried out quietly will it the taken the 4 platoon occupying the second trench to the East of the Railway about 100 yds on an its shelling all the service of tomb and lighting they re-intended one 163 R.E. tool & wire and 15 yards of sandbag. A 2d during the day & all quite and no casualties occurred. the relieve took out 2 P.M. the others of 6 K.O. Scott Borderers and some from the led here.

Jan 23 1915
to
Jan 31 1915

Vet names Suspect ... night. Arthur and Goodman to hospital, Suspect sprains and ... hands. Bird, Ryan,
Ferris, Legg, Nicholas, 6 servants and a corporal of Lighly Lancs. sick. Bird. Nicholas sent to Trench Station. also has ... being confined to England. 8 regt newe sent to No. 28th L. Coll. Clearing Station Rouen to England. 8 regt.
Leave Captain Woodman Lance Fus. taking 3 commanded kindly.
Nown R & sub 31st Jan I killed and Respected making one officer 2nd Lieut St Mars died since injuries. 10th admitted to 9/L.6.
Casualties 1500, 5 men admitted to 9/L.6.

W. Butcher
Lieut Col
Capt Royal Irish Fus

12th Inf. Bde.
4th Division.

WAR DIARY

2ND BATTN. MONMOUTHSHIRE REGT.

FEBRUARY

1915.

121/4610

12th Brigade

2nd Monmouths. Regt (T)

Vol IV 1 – 28.2.15

Army Form C. 2118.

WAR DIARY
or
INTELLIGENCE SUMMARY.
(Erase heading not required.)

Instructions regarding War Diaries and Intelligence Summaries are contained in F. S. Regs., Part II and the Staff Manual respectively. Title pages will be prepared in manuscript.

Hour, Date, Place	Summary of Events and Information	Remarks and references to Appendices
Le Bizet Feby 10th 1915 Feby 1st to 5th	Following same lines as heretofore; mentioning of work on the men also continued work on second line at SEVEN TREES. Line Officers wired from Reserve Battalion Capt. John W. Mins Leigh to the history, Lt D. Hornby, 2nd Lieut. W. J. Wilkins & W. J. Hythe. Capt. No.[?] Capt. A. & J. Elliot Mon M.O. returned from leave took over command from Col. Lambert having D.S.O. of the late Col. & his M.O. Lt. A. Hardy leaving in absence.	
6th	Took over a detail 155 yards extending to a farm on the North of our Line wire at SEVENTREES on reaching LYS FARM. The front connects new I-Lys trench in charge of the 2nd Party and making two new Portaloos in some platoon, who trenches the R.E. and work on Line is shortly to spread to Raerhins. Trenches in my front is also noting from over H.Q. at LYS BILET about 3 mls. battery the bob was out front from the field at SEVEN TREES a trench and the...nowhere now the fed on the other side of the Lys road, being within fire from the other side of the river south and down ground on the left	2nd Lieut
14th	14th to this date 6 wounded from poly not been under fire wounded	
20th	20th new detachment and of Lys Farm to 5th Foot Line. Some distribution of Infantry to serve instead of placed. our own Capt. Had 300 men attached and returned on operation up to Jan 6th Since being on this and line reaching from about 300 yds North from RAILWAY BRIDGE directed right bayonet East from along the bank of the RIVER to the Estuary source where we incorporated kept. The South of bridge was re-sanded at RIVIERE BIZET on the new Reserve of the Group of Houses to the W of the BIZET.	
24th 27th	Relieved by 2nd ESSEX REGT and 4th reserves to 5 letters and 3rd 300 nos. of 5th Lancs attached to relieved in close under Headquarters of our own Regt.	
28th	Received 25 officers on Draft including one new after man was killed from Feby 10th to 28th 8 NCO's & men were admitted to hospital during the month inclusive of 25 yds of men wounded. Brigadier Capt. & Miles 2nd R. Dolson (Mellor wounded Dec 30th) by Colorers (Rattleworth Dec 26th) vis Jean G McKe	MENTIONED IN DESPATCHES. DECORATIONS AWARDED [illegible]
	Leave from 2nd 6 Col. to & Battle Hon M.D.	

12th Inf. Bde.
4th Division.

WAR DIARY

2ND BATTN. MONMOUTHSHIRE REGT.

M A R C H

1 9 1 5.

137/4919

12th Brigade

1/2nd Monmouthshire Regt

Vol V 1 - 31.5.15

Nil

War Diary or Intelligence Summary

Army Form C. 2118.

LE BISET

Hour, Date, Place	Summary of Events and Information	Remarks and references to Appendices
March 1st 1915	Tillory came here of Isenhel for at Battalion 578	
March 2nd	Lt Col Reid Commanding also Read going to DESPIERRE from Lt Genl for	
	Billet at main support, two miles Welshmen ARMENTIERES who were a corps	
	of training under Col Rees digging in communication trench until relieved	
	and returned to billets	
7th	Returned to BULLETS and BISET	
8th	Went to Kemmel to labour in the South and were attached to troops	
11th	at charge of ESSEX Road who are several	
12th	Capt J.W. TAYLOR killed B3 trench station head	
13th	Returned to billets in BISET	
15th	Received an attack passing as a by formation was about 2 miles of camp	
	on PIEPRE	
16th	Received orders to go by ambulance 10 officers wounded (1) other ranks 3 killed officer billet	
	to KORTIK	19
	Went to the rear on Co B to relief the line to help HUNE HOLIDAY	
	including London Firm, No 3 Coy at 29 Royl Fusiliers attacks evening of 20th	
	225 m/gr HOOKADAY wounded also in team no. B5 trench	
17th	Col. P. RANDORS wounded	
18th	Returned to billets LE BISET	
20th	Went into trenches	
21st	Complaint in French to CENTRAL FORM to CENTRAL FORM Hospital, trained to Wyynme	
	Returning, We are also earning who of Morther	
22nd	Returned to Billits LE BISET	
30th	Casualties March 16 – 31st inclusive are 5 Nº 13 mem who Canadian Volunteer	
	to die old " " 12	
	2/ Lt. Crowher killed b 3 officers wounded Others wounded 1 Officer killed 3 Men	
	Capt. maxey R.L. Goetze	Ath Walker - Lieut
	30 R killed 38 Other ranks	for Lieut Col

12th Inf. Bde.
4th Division.

WAR DIARY

2ND BATTN. MONMOUTHSHIRE REGT.

A P R I L

1 9 1 5.

(NOTE: Includes entry for 1st/2nd May 1915)

121/81448

12th Brigade.
1/2nd Monmouth Regt.

Vol VI. 1.4. — 2.5.15.

WAR DIARY or INTELLIGENCE SUMMARY.

Army Form C. 2118.

(Erase heading not required.)

Hour, Date, Place	Summary of Events and Information	Remarks and references to Appendices
1915 – May 27th 1915	During month of April no event of importance took place in the Battalion. The Batt. was in the trenches and continued to be relieved by Essex Regt. every alternate four days. Wilts Bn. was in reserve. On 28th Bn received order that it would be relieving that night by WORCESTER. REGT. 1st, & moved to BAILLEUL. The Bn arrived at BAILLEUL at about 3am. 29th and all 12 miles no men fell out whatever an extremely good performance. an Bn was in trenches for over 800 months without any change. On 30th 9am 1st B Bde. of which Bn all form part were ordered to move to VLAMPTINGHE. which it reached about 1am & bivouacked until 7.30am. 16 VLAMPTINGHE. The march was then continued to a point 3 mile due west of VLAMPTINGHE which was very difficult... the BN again came under the enemy shell fire immediately they entered into... west of 5 miles but, arrived... on 12 May the men bivouacked the... YSER CANAL at 11pm & took up position from BN west at LA BRIQUE... about 3000yds from enemy's firing line. Here again the BN lay under shell fire from after day break on 25th the BN came under a terrific bombardment, the main portion being... date, all 9pm came the order of a terrific bombardment... pm. He enemy attempted to advance the hard pressed line Duff Kaiserkept... back... by artillery... French... action ... losing for 3 battalions (1st own Bn 3rdloms) B boy was ordered to advance... Bn B boy his memory of trenches & during that took up ride length to Bricks... advanced so resolutely good work... mention was taken in... ESSEX REGT. 2nd line Trench with... companies in support. ESSEX. REGT having opened its own line upon the Germans. We advanced from A bay... on direct to ROYAL IRISH REGT. its left... about 10 lives were lost... the enemy leaving behind 10 (5 feet 5R Kesselring) Holds & 5 kills (Reg) or slightly wounded and 10 men reported missing (12 of these during casualties) In fighting two men became the first... N.O.B. in the... Pt... and... from... the SC received the following wire from 12 Brigade on their gallant & brilliant... attack the enemy night 26/5/27 in N... & the names and... stated... S. Cushion A.R.D.B. II.5/15 from It. Butler...	

S.C.A. Rolls

12th Inf. Bde.
4th Division.

WAR DIARY

2nd BATTN. MONMOUTHSHIRE REGT.

MAY

1915.

(NOTE: See APRIL diary for entries 1st/2nd May)

12/SA/82

12th Brigade.

1/2 Worcester Regt.

Vol VII — 3 — 31.5.15

Army Form C. 2118.

WAR DIARY
or
INTELLIGENCE SUMMARY.
(Erase heading not required.)

Instructions regarding War Diaries and Intelligence Summaries are contained in F.S. Regs., Part II and the Staff Manual respectively. Title pages will be prepared in manuscript.

Hour, Date, Place	Summary of Events and Information	Remarks and references to Appendices
May 9/15	Battalion was chasing in DIV. RES. at LA BRIQUE when ordered suddenly during the day.	* Lt Col E.B Cuthbertson ⊙ Capt S.P.A Rolls
H⁺	Battn went out in support with ESSEX REGT. remainder remained in Res. at Lr. BRIQUE.	
5.15	Coloy went up to support Roya. Irish	
6	No further messages. 2nd South Lancs were heavily shelled — the Capt had withdrawn and we were ordered to reinforce them. A Coy were sent up with the C.O.* *hurriedly* in Rgl.@ A long time of heavy fighting but. Brit. were ordered to the trenches which were occupied by the Batt ... [illegible]	
	... NEUVE CHAPELLE ... Shells help them ... [large illegible paragraph] ... During the night 7th & 8th Dis Brigades were relieved ...	
8	Was ... relation ... [illegible]	

WAR DIARY or INTELLIGENCE SUMMARY.

(Erase heading not required.)

Army Form C. 2118.

Instructions regarding War Diaries and Intelligence Summaries are contained in F.S. Regs., Part II and the Staff Manual respectively. Title pages will be prepared in manuscript.

Hour, Date, Place	Summary of Events and Information	Remarks and references to Appendices
9/7	Heavy and field commenced at 5.5am and continued increasingly until 8am. At 8am the Germans moved back. The Russians retired and the ROYAL IRISH and moved to the Dugouts on the EAST bank of RIVER YSER Canal near YPRES.	
13/7	10th, 11th & 12th Batt. occupied same Dugouts during the day morning 3 snipers picked off by the R.E. at night. 8am Bn moved to Res. of the LABRIQUE (?) Valley. Bn at rest until [illegible]. Div. commanders in [illegible] to reconnoitre [illegible] of WIELTJE to [illegible] & [3pm x Platoon of WIELTJE to [illegible] of [illegible] Res. site also [illegible] in front of WIELTJE to occupy gaps in the edge of the railway lines at 10pm. ... received EAST BLANCS & occupied the line including	
15th 16/7	SHELL TRAP FARM E.16 WIELTJE & ST JEAN ROAD Occupied same trenches at 9pm 16th was relieved by SEAFORTHS + proceeded to DIV.HQ at DAMBERTINGHE at 2am. M 17,18,19,20,21,22,23,24 BILLETS at VLAMERTINGHE 20th Had bath at [illegible] baths Men marched to BOESINGHE at 10am	
24 [?]	11.40am marched on reconnoitring march to SMETHSBANK at ordi in extreme warmth of [illegible] 7miles. At 6.30pm men ordered to G.H.Q. byes at 3pm. As more trenches [illegible] it proved worse [illegible]	

WAR DIARY or INTELLIGENCE SUMMARY

Army Form C. 2118.

(Erase heading not required.)

Hour, Date, Place	Summary of Events and Information	Remarks and references to Appendices

26th — What 6.30 pm counter attack was supposed had the
Batt. without any support would have taken place at 10.30 pm
This was afterwards cancelled. The Batt. now form
a new line of trenches connecting
G.H.Q. line running due EAST. went forward to dig 1500 yds of
trenches about 200 yds S. of WIELTJE. these were successfully dug
on the outskirts of occupying. Relieved at 3.30 am 25th.
trenches held by Batt. now became front line. During the
day there was a little shelling but a great number of
casualties were caused by enemy's snipers
on trenches in vicinity of a height of about 500 ft. our
27th — enemy's vicinity of files a height of about 500 ft. our
10 am trenches frightfully all day.
Enemy's same day was relieved & shelled individually all our
men by 1st RIFLE BRIGADE —
Batt. went into Div. CHATEAU. VLAMERTINGHE. turned here about
6 am. 24th at 2 pm went onwards to form 1st & 2nd horse (?)
at 5.30 pm Batt. paraded & was made
the following farewell speech by Lt Gen. Wilson G.O.C. 6th Div.
Farewell Speech
The 18 Batt. is very sorry to lose you, but I
hope only temporarily on arriving in the Division you
[illegible] never was a finer Bn in the 18th Brigade

WAR DIARY
or
INTELLIGENCE SUMMARY.
(Erase heading not required.)

Army Form C. 2118.

Hour, Date, Place	Summary of Events and Information	Remarks and references to Appendices
	"How did you work so well as one Brigade in the fight? In the Brigade you passed me going up to the time fighting at LE TOUQUET and RAILWAY BARRIAGE stopped the ammunition of the whole army, since leaving Ypres your endurance has been magnificent under trying fire. I am glad 4th DIV. always knew that when they were in difficulty the 2nd Monmouth Regt. they knew that they were men of spirit who worked during the hard fight for with strength who fought with great tenacity (?) & who when I asked them to hold them have done his allotted number (?). I don't know how much you have suffered but will never forget you have served the Bn. in general and have distinguished themselves in fighting & in hard work. I hope the DIV. are going to have a rest (?) You may be able to attend to in shortly (?)	
28.	(W) 5.30 pm the Bn. marches from (?) POPERINGHE & arrives 12.30 pm 3. Battalion marched to HERZEELE.	
29.	The 3 Bns. were organized by G.O.C. 84th Brigade by amalgamation of the 3 Bns. Enjoying a short rest.	

Army Form C. 2118.

WAR DIARY
or
INTELLIGENCE SUMMARY.
(Erase heading not required.)

Instructions regarding War Diaries and Intelligence Summaries are contained in F.S. Regs., Part II. and the Staff Manual respectively. Title pages will be prepared in manuscript.

Hour, Date, Place	Summary of Events and Information	Remarks and references to Appendices
30/1	Same day 14th 15th casualty list on received and was obtained by O.C. 3rd Coys.	
30/1	who made urgent enquiries concerning 9th Brigade	
30/1	Billets at HERZEELE actual amalgamation took	
30/1	place at 6 pm	
3/1	Billets at HERZEELE.	
	Casualties for month.	
	Capt. Storm killed 2 other Ranks killed 31.	
	Capt. Nicholl, Marlow,	Died of wounds. y.
	Reid, Wedderburn,	Wounded 86
	2nd Lt. MacFarlane,	3
	Shiel, McWilliam	missing
	Marshall B.	
	Lost The Earle	
	of Erroll,	
	Hon H. George.	6

S.R.O. Rolls Capt H Hammersley
Comdg 2/...?

2nd Battn. Monmouthshire Regiment

June 1915 Missing

12th Inf. Bde.
4th Division.

WAR DIARY

2ND BATTN. MONMOUTHSHIRE REGT.

24TH - 31ST JULY

1915.

121/6443

4th Division

1/2nd Monmouths

Vol VIII

From 24th to 31st July 1915

WAR DIARY
or
INTELLIGENCE SUMMARY.

(Erase heading not required.)

Army Form C. 2118.

Hour, Date, Place	Summary of Events and Information	Remarks and references to Appendices
24 Sep 1915 A		
25 July 1915 D	Arrived at DOULLENS 3.30 am. Breakfast & moved to Billets at OUTRECOURT	
26 " " N	Billets in NOUVENCOURT. Company Parades	
27 " " N	Marched to FOREEVILLE 1. 0.30 am	
28 " " F	Billets FOREEVILLE	
29 " " E	Marched to AUCHONVILLERS	
30 " 1915 A	Captain A.J.M. Rose	

Army Form C. 2118.

WAR DIARY
or
INTELLIGENCE SUMMARY.
(Erase heading not required.)

Hour, Date, Place	Summary of Events and Information	Remarks and references to Appendices
30 July 1915	Company to furnish a translation. Enemy's trenches to stand to very heavy artillery and by men who has last by Germans. Very very heavy rifle fire. No casualties in our front line communication trenches. Have left all heavy clean but enemy found several of our men. Coming of trench below fire at enemy which was seen at a lot of the 66th company and over the R.E. tent near the C.O.'s by H.Q. (y) 9th Fus Coy R.E. Tent near the dug out (y) 18" of reinforced concrete on cellars. Roofing the trenches, preparing new platform. Traverse making fronts to the dug in making new splints dug outs. Each company wishes to have repair its its own sector except that 2/ men well worked on the flags. Reinforcement to arrive, 2 officers & 89 O.R. R.A.M.C. Continued Abnormal Ashmitted & sanitary R.A.M.C. arrived & at M.O.	
31 July 1915		

12th Inf. Bde.
4th Division.

WAR DIARY

2ND BATTN. MONMOUTHSHIRE REGT.

AUGUST

1915.

|2/
7439

4th Division

2nd [illegible]

[illegible]

August 15

23/[illegible]

Army Form C. 2118.

Original

WAR DIARY
or
INTELLIGENCE SUMMARY.
(Erase heading not required.)

Instructions regarding War Diaries and Intelligence Summaries are contained in F.S. Regs., Part II. and the Staff Manual respectively. Title pages will be prepared in manuscript.

Hour, Date, Place	Summary of Events and Information	Remarks and references to Appendices
Aug 1st – 12th 1915 AUCHONVILLIERS	Shoring. Working parties for reconstructing cellar roofs of new forward Covers & reconstructing trenches under R.E.	
8th	Considerable shelling (approx 50 to 60 shells)	
6th	2nd Lieut C. Lone & R.W. Sandry joined for duty	
7th	Capt. E. Edgentown joined for duty	
8th	2nd Lieut W.P. Bathill " "	
9th	2/Lr C.P. Scott & H.G. James "	
9th	2/Lt. W.H. Jones wounded	
9th	G.O.C. 4th Div. inspected A.	
9th	20 men of the Batt. joined the R.E. tunnelling Co & were kept on	
11th	Strength of Batt.	
11th	Capt. R.E. Edwards admitted to Hospital	
12th	91 NCOs & men joined for duty	
12th	Lieut Col. J. C. Jenkins joined for duty & took over command from Capt A.J.H. Bowen who was appointed Second-in-command	
13th	C.O. learning no contra arms, the village & entrenchments, they have now settled down & are looking forward to their defense at all cover in day.	

WAR DIARY
or
INTELLIGENCE SUMMARY.
(Erase heading not required.)

Army Form C. 2118

Hour, Date, Place	Summary of Events and Information	Remarks and references to Appendices
AUCHONVILLERS August 14	HQ was situated in AUCHONVILLERS overlooking the trenches & manning the defences had relieved 7/R.F. Bde and 2/15th F. Turner and H.Q. Coys were appointed & arranged details of Guards etc reported.	
" 15	The accurate weapons of the Turner & the Austrian forces caused Cpt Pritchard to inspect the village. The whole was to too. One trench, they were shown the French where & the defence & accommodation that was being carried out.	
" 17	A colonel of the French Army on inspected the village & defence & expressed his approval of the work done. He was accompanied by an officer of the 4th Divisional Staff. A lecture was made by the Senior Divisional & was arranged with [illegible] that Company Commanders should come themselves & after the work. Open section the R.E. 17 Coy were about on same work and the was carried out	

WAR DIARY
or
INTELLIGENCE SUMMARY.
(Erase heading not required.)

Army Form C. 2118.

Hour, Date, Place	Summary of Events and Information	Remarks and references to Appendices
21st–August 21 AUCHONVILLERS	A demonstration of how to combat gas was given in the village & attended by men from each Company	
23	Training has taken on different lines. Coy Com found 20 men. 2/Lt Potard proceeded to 2/Lt G.H. Hance & Lt. Potard proceeded to MESQUES for a machine gun course the Bath. Having no qualified M.G. officer. 2/Lt BOOCHER took on duties as Acting Quartermaster in place of 2/Lt A.G. DAVIES who went to hospital. Many complaints continue re water in the village & the water in the village & the drinking water reported as suspected in hospital were reported as suspected of typhoid. The water from the village sources	

WAR DIARY
or
INTELLIGENCE SUMMARY.

(Erase heading not required.)

Army Form C. 2118.

Hour, Date, Place	Summary of Events and Information	Remarks and references to Appendices
AUCHONVILLERS. August 24	Cleaning out Cooking places the Drinking water being brought from MAILLY at night. However no cases were confirmed. After making several reports the Wells were examined & condemned. Arrangements were made to lay a water pipe from the SUCRERIE. Captain E. COLQUOHOUN left the Battalion to take up duties as Adjutant 11th Suffolk Regt Battalion vice Capt H H EDWARDS who returned to take up Flying duties. The Battalion less B Coy left AUCHONVILLERS and proceeded to MAILLY in Brigade Reserve.	
7hrs 25 do	C. Coy moved into Reserve at COLINCAMPS to the 2nd ESSEX then holding the front line. One platoon was stationed at LA SIGNY FARM, another was spilt for being stalled.	
MAILLY 30 P.M.	D Coy moved into Reserve hence to the 2nd Lancs Fus. two Coys whereon holding the Front line. This move was owing to the Germans	

Army Form C. 2118.

WAR DIARY
or
INTELLIGENCE SUMMARY.
(Erase heading not required.)

Instructions regarding War Diaries and Intelligence Summaries are contained in F.S. Regs., Part II. and the Staff Manual respectively. Title pages will be prepared in manuscript.

Hour, Date, Place	Summary of Events and Information	Remarks and references to Appendices
FRANCE SOMME. MAILLY, MAILLET.	Carrying on mining operations against position known as the R.N. Capt EDWARDS fat countermine & as the Germans had been seen tamping theirs ours was not exploded at 3.30 very successfully, the enemy taking no action. Disposition of D Coy was at ELLIS SQUARE.	Various working parties being supplied.
August 26th/31st	Mr B. also recommend at MAILLY and other places in Brigade Reserve. Owing to Correspondence over acquittance rolls not having been sent in consequently orders were sent back to 11 Nov 1914 being received, an order was issued that all rolls, balance sheets issues 90 through Orderly Room. This was found to be much more satisfactory & after full accountants i.e. Company Commanders understood their duties very little work was known as to Orderly Room work.	
31st	Lt Col Seaforts went to hospital & Cptn A.J.H. Bowen took Command	

Army Form C. 2118.

WAR DIARY
or
INTELLIGENCE SUMMARY.
(Erase heading not required.)

Instructions regarding War Diaries and Intelligence Summaries are contained in F.S. Regs., Part II and the Staff Manual respectively. Title pages will be prepared in manuscript.

Hour, Date, Place	Summary of Events and Information	Remarks and references to Appendices
AUGUST 31st. MAILLY.	During August 2 officers & 99 O. Ranks were admitted to hospital sick, one officer & 2 N. O. Ranks were wounded, none were killed. The strength on the 31st August 1915 was 29 officers & 642 other ranks. No returns from hospital. Left 99 O. Ranks. No coming from England as 10 off. 1001 O. Ranks. reinforcements	

12th Inf.Bde.
4th Division.

WAR DIARY

2ND BATTN. MONMOUTHSHIRE REGT.

SEPTEMBER

1915.

121/7439

4th Bavarian

2nd Lieutenants
Vol X
Sept 16 6th Oct 15

WAR DIARY
or
INTELLIGENCE SUMMARY.
(Erase heading not required.)

Army Form C. 2118.

Hour, Date, Place	Summary of Events and Information	Remarks and references to Appendices
Sept 1st MAILLY	Considerable shelling evidently in retaliation for the mine.	
2nd "	The Battalion moved to Divisional Reserve to BEAUSSART	to BEAUSSART
3rd BEAUSSART	where we found the billets a place filthy. However Stay's here during this Leave working parties were called for to work near the front line. Most trying nights work & very unsafe as our wire working parties? through the number of bothers was high.	
	On the M.O. going on leave Lt LIPP. R.A.M.C. was temporarily attached. Burial and inquest at BEAUSSART. A lot of sanitary endeavour a large latrine erected in a field and in it the Divisional Sanitary Officer stated it was the best enn Latrine in K Divisional area.	
	Baths were at ACHEUX about 3 miles away for which the men marched every and being bathed.	
	The Army Corps Commander visited the village & Mr Billy during our stay. We started a Divisional Recreation Room in the village & in the first	OMM

WAR DIARY or INTELLIGENCE SUMMARY.

(Erase heading not required.)

Army Form C. 2118.

Hour, Date, Place	Summary of Events and Information	Remarks and references to Appendices
BUISSART Sept 8th 1915	1st Batt. 2nd Co. of Royal Dublin Fusiliers 10th Bde	
— 8th	50 N.C.O's & men joined for Duty having been discharged from Hospital	
	1 man joined Batt. for duty	
— 9th	Capt. E. Esmonde discharged from hospital & rejoined in Command	
	Capt. C. Edwards taken over duties as rejoined in Command	
	On the evening of the 9th the Batt. relieved 2nd Dublin Fusiliers (10th Bde) in the trenches front line BEAUMONT HAMEL, "C" & "D" Cos. in the trenches Nail Company being in reserve at AUCHONVILLERS	
— 10th	2 Lieut G.H. Davies was disabled to be & found & struck off the strength	
VARENNES — 16th	The Batt. was relieved in the trenches by the 2nd Dublin Fusiliers & marched to billets at VARENNES. During the tour of duty in the trenches there was no casualties. A Company of the 12th Cheshires Regt (66th Brigade) were attached to the Batt. for instruction whilst in the trenches from the 12th inst. 1 Sept. the Batt. on the 18th inst. The report of the C.O. to H.Q. 10th Brigade on their work was very good. The Batt did a tremendous amount of work whilst in the trenches in constructing traverses, improving parapets, firing steps & in digging new trenches.	
— 15th	2nd Lieut H.G. Davies admitted to Hospital	
— 5	Lieut Col J.C. Ireland transferred to England	
— 19	The Batt. paraded for march past and at ACHEUX were seen by the General Snow, Commanding the VII Army Corps. The Batt. afterwards did a practice attack in the presence of General F.G. Anley	

Army Form C. 2118.

WAR DIARY
or
INTELLIGENCE SUMMARY.
(Erase heading not required.)

Instructions regarding War Diaries and Intelligence Summaries are contained in F. S. Regs., Part II. and the Staff Manual respectively. Title pages will be prepared in manuscript.

Hour, Date, Place		Summary of Events and Information	Remarks and references to Appendices
VARENNES Sept 1915	19th	Commanding the 4th Division. The General Commanding the VII Corps and the Army for 5 days were well of the General Commanding the Division. His that the attack was very well carried out.	General G.C.
	—	921 Cpl Dupeson (Interpreter) left 4th Div. & proceeded to French Mission	
	18.	2/Lt W.A. James. Transferred to England	2nd Lt W. A. James S

Place	Date	Hour	Summary of Events and Information	Remarks and references to Appendices
VARENNES	Sept 20-21		The Battalion Company 12th Cheshires 22nd Airmen carried out a Route March on 21st. Left to march with them previous further work than an embarkan. French crew complete.	
	22		The Bn arrived and met with the French return to Ride the Battalion less 3 Coys & 2 M.G.s moved to MAILLY in Brigade Reserve on Coy B, E AUCHONVILLERS and Coy C Lewis Station to COURCELLES. 1 Platoon to LA SIGNY & 1 D Coy to ELLIS SQUARE. The march up was about 6 miles. None fell out. 2/6 D.R. Jones that evening on a Reinforced, 18 from England, 8 from the Base.	
MAILLY	23		Hd Batn remained in Brigade Reserve finding various working parties. West alley, making two steep hole on BLASTED TREES and RED COTTAGE. A & C Companies doing good work in many movements. Owing to the general expectation of an further the possibility of an advance arrangements were made to advance in case of an enemy movement. As the Battalion were Reserve, it was a Chance to obtain training when the French were up the previous. A letter was received from the Bgde or Major in which the repeated that it was the lot of Battalion to remain behind that it was	

Army Form C. 2118.

WAR DIARY
or
INTELLIGENCE SUMMARY.
(Erase heading not required.)

Place	Date	Hour	Summary of Events and Information	Remarks and references to Appendices
	Sept		entered owing to its being in Brigade Reserve. All necessary steps taken whenever men were given to each Company to make a cross an examine his intelligence. 5 Grenadiers were returned as lt. Class per Brigade grenade School. Score 50%. Three SANKEY were attended Brigade Instructor in BOMBING.	
MAILLY	29th		The Brigade being relieved by the 10th Bde; the Battalion marched to new Billets at VARENNES. Remainder have been relieving us at MAILLY.	
VARENNES	30th to October 6th		The Battalion found working party of 200 per day for work on the Corps Line near FORCEVILLE except on the 3rd when the Battalion did a route march. Avenues were deploying for a practice attack. Half General HAMBRO, G.O.C. H.E. Division rode out saw the attack carried out. The Battalion were attacked at ACHEUX given a charge of underclothing, but their uniforms were not fumigated. a large number of men were taken to the FORIES d'ACHEUX which they enjoyed very much. It was a Cinema performance Everyone was	

WAR DIARY or INTELLIGENCE SUMMARY.

(Erase heading not required.)

Army Form C. 2118.

Place	Date	Hour	Summary of Events and Information	Remarks and references to Appendices
VARENNES	Sept 30th		Coy. we'h. got chances. The Coy Comy. has lew Strength. ~~that no one xxxxxxxxxxxxxxxx~~	
	Oct 1st		During September 86 other ranks sent to Hospital, Sick. 1 other rank wounded by shrapnel. MAILLY. no men killed. On the 30th September the strength was 26 Officers 694 other Ranks. He returned from hospital 2 off. 102. O. Ranks arrived from England as reinforcements 3 off. 28. O. Ranks	

12th Inf. Bde.
4th Division.

WAR DIARY

2ND BATTN. MONMOUTHSHIRE REGT.

OCTOBER

1915.

12/737

4th Division

1/2nd Leinsters.
Oct XI
Oct 15

Army Form C. 2118.

WAR DIARY
or
INTELLIGENCE SUMMARY.
(Erase heading not required.)

Instructions regarding War Diaries and Intelligence Summaries are contained in F.S. Regs., Part II. and the Staff Manual respectively. Title pages will be prepared in manuscript.

Place	Date	Hour	Summary of Events and Information	Remarks and references to Appendices
VARENNES	Oct 1916		The Battalion was in action at VARENNES rec[eive]d Sept.	
"	6th		The B[attalio]n marched to the trenches (8 miles) taking over (same line as before) (opposite BEAUMONT-HAMEL) from the 2nd R. Dublin Fus[ilier]s. The trenches were in much the same state though access by & Lavine pit about 12' deep with airtight covers had been constructed in 8 places. The Comp[anie]s were in the front line were C on the right, A in centre & D on the left, each having 3 platoons in the front line in support, B Coy was in Reserve two platoons being at POMPADOOR TRENCH and two platoons in AUCHONVILLERS. Water has been laid on in pipes to the support line from BEAUCREQUE which was formerly brought up at first. Water was required. Patrols were sent out each night & brought in reports the enemy wire which was very strong. No hostile fire and General Surprise was taken out of the front line except for trench mortars.	Battalion in left trenches 2 Lieu Harbour joined from the 1st Batt[alio]n 2 R. Irish Rif[les] 1st Abu[?]
			ANZAC G.O.C. the Brigade inspected the trenches on Thursday & Herman ordered No B. Platoon sentry to get his platoon to stand to arms. Herman being then asleep an offer of his men stood to arms in 2½ minutes.	

2353 Wt. W2514/1454 700,000 5/15 D.D.&L. A.D.S.S./Forms/C. 2118.

WAR DIARY
INTELLIGENCE SUMMARY.
(Erase heading not required.)

Army Form C. 2118.

Place	Date	Hour	Summary of Events and Information	Remarks and references to Appendices
opposite BEAUMONT-HAMEL SOMME FRANCE.	Oct 8		The tramway line being 2 minutes	
	9		Major Gen LAMBTON, G.O.C. 4th Division inspected the trenches & forward dispositions. He received orders during the night to be prepared to advance.	
	10		On the march to the trenches, G.O.C. the Brigade watched the Battalion march past & stated that the marching was good though the Bn was probably 5 minutes early. In the trenches, no news to relieve began but the reserve trench had continued opened up on the left. "A" Coy 8th Royal Irish Rifles 86th (ULSTER) Division Cameron Scottish were very much in evidence in the trenches and in the wire way. All ranks were very keen.	
	11			
	13		The Battalion was relieved by the 2nd R Dublin Fus who took over the attached Coy 8 R.I.R. in the trenches. During the tour of the Battalion the Bn no Casualties nor did the attached company	

WAR DIARY or INTELLIGENCE SUMMARY

Army Form C. 2118.

Place	Date 1915	Hour	Summary of Events and Information	Remarks and references to Appendices
	October		In the Trench area. Types of traverse with overnight built at the been found strong, but others made in several parts of the line. Communication trenches much shrunk has done.	
BEAUSSART		13h	After relief the Battalion marched to BEAUSSART in Divisional Reserve (3½ miles). After a stay and working parties of 150/1,000 found which were in very comfortable.	
		14h	The Battalion proceeded on a Route March in full Marching Order into the transport distance 6 miles River Stand at stream, passing through BERTRANCOURT from a trench in MAILLY 1500 litres were noticed at a meadow. A field of 137 francs was taken to the men, they in getting tea flour Private found for the made whichways then in gathering apples all accounts from look men at night. Held they much appreciated, BEAUSSART the village has no reserved for having no racal at. An attempt, knowing said house was notting purposes, for the accommodation shown as a station place on affording within a brickers between & the main advance. covered in manner.	

Army Form C. 2118.

WAR DIARY
or
INTELLIGENCE SUMMARY.
(Erase heading not required.)

Place	Date 1915	Hour	Summary of Events and Information	Remarks and references to Appendices
BEAUSSART	Oct		On this day the 14th Batt. relieved the 10th Batt. and the Battalion proceeded to prepare reserve to MAILLY less 2 Coys B (Coys which had been in hole before B Coy remaining at MAILLY and A Coy going to AUCHONVILLERS	
	24		2nd Lt. COX returned from M.G. Course at WISQUES. Casualty: One man wounded by the enemy blowing up a mine of the Plateau	
	25		2nd Lt. FRASER took over duties of Brigade M.G. Officer and 2nd Lt. COX took over duties of Batt. M.G.O. One A.G. man returned sent to France to relieve damaged gun of 2nd LANCS FUSRS. The KING visited ACHEUX & inspected the 10th Brigade of the 4th Division –	
	27		Drafts arrived from base (5 M gunners) The Batt. was relieved from Brigade Reserve by R.I.F (10th Bgde) and proceeded Coundelt) to MAILLY (Divisional Reserve)	
MAILLY	30		MAILLY (Divisional Reserve) Strength of the Battalion is 26 officers & 908 otherranks. Wounded otherranks 1 – Sick officers 2. Otherranks 80 evacuated during the month. 10thers (of q.O.S.R.) joined from base total during month 1 officers & 147 a/Ranks —	

Commanding Offr 14th Batt R/W/Fus. Major

4th Division
War Diaries

1/2. Monmouths – joined
~~th~~ 12th Bde, 4-11-15
To L of C, 30-1-16.

November to January
1915 – 16

(To 29 DIV Diaries)

107th Bde
4th Division.

This Battn joined from
12th Bde 4. 11. 15.

1/2 Battn MONMOUTHSHIRE REGIMENT

NOVEMBER 1915

4th Division

1/2d Monmouth Reg

Nov / vol XII

121/7730

Joins 107 ORs from 12 Posts 4.11.15

WAR DIARY
or
INTELLIGENCE SUMMARY.
(Erase heading not required.)

Army Form C. 2118.

Place	Date	Hour	Summary of Events and Information	Remarks and references to Appendices
MAILLY	1/7/16		Divisional Reserve. Working parties found for work by day & at night digging Reserve Line	
	2/11/15		Draft of 57 other ranks joined the Battalion from England 52, Base 2. Ten men found previously sick on active service with the Battalion.	
		-2/3	No working parties were found on these dates owing to the extremely wet weather. The 12th Brigade with the exception of the 1st R. Dub Fus proceeded to join the 36th Division (temporary) The Battalion remained in the 4th Division & are attached to the 107th Brigade. Working parties were found on this date.	
	4			
	5		Working parties were found at night	
TRENCHES		7.6 p.m	The Battalion relieved the 10th Inniskillings in the trenches, the Battalion relieving the 10th Inniskillings Fus. [?] Warned for moving up the line [?] 12th [?] Brigade from the right the 2nd R.I.F. Bn [illegible] S.W. of SERRE. A.5 x D Coys [?] the Centre joined holding the [illegible] sent to [illegible] support line & the [illegible] trenches & taking up [?] positions at 7.45 p.m. Trenches were in a very bad state owing to wet weather. Two officers to the [illegible] to be evacuated to Brigade Dump [?].	
	-8		Very Wet West Unseasonable. Aerial activity fired on Bapaume Junction [?] 5 men gassed but none [illegible]. Aerial fighters during day.	[illegible]
	-9		Washed very wet trenches in bad state. The parapets in parts falling down, two men	
	-10		(wounded) Sgt Parker. A draft of 13 Other Ranks joined the Battalion.	
	-11		Raining. One Corporal Wounded any casualty Corporal [illegible] gassed and sent to [illegible]	[illegible]

WAR DIARY
or
INTELLIGENCE SUMMARY.
(Erase heading not required.)

Army Form C. 2118

Place	Date	Hour	Summary of Events and Information	Remarks and references to Appendices
TRENCHES	7/11/15		* The line occupied was about 1500 yards front Trenches 75-79 being occupied by A Coy, Nos 80-82 by B Coy + Nos 83-85 by D Coy. There is shown on the Divisional Map - Strength & the Battalion was 15 officers & 573 in the trenches as shown on the attached Return marked "B"	Map & App. 2. Strength Return marked B.
	8/11/15		On this day 2nd Lieut A.L. COPPOCK 3rd Welch Regt. attached 2/Monmouths had an apopletic fit in the trenches & was admitted to hospital	

WAR DIARY or INTELLIGENCE SUMMARY

Army Form C. 2118.

Place	Date	Hour	Summary of Events and Information	Remarks and references to Appendices
TRENCHES	12/11/15		One man wounded	
	13		" "	
BEAUSSART	14		On this night the Battalion was relieved by the 1st Warwicks. Previous to BEAUSSART the relief was hardly carried out as was the Green curing to the bad state of the trenches, the East of the Battalion arrived at Bay Bellets about 11 p.m.	
	15		During the Battalion's tour of duty in the trenches the mens' behaviour under shell & above was not bad but there was acknowledged. The work carried out was chiefly the renewing of trenches & wire, also parties to VOLIGNE to fetch up the revetting & fire trenches also. Four men were hurt to hospital at 12 that broken feet. Resting.	With 41 officers and 1100 men
	16		Finished northern shelter (the height) of a sort to a men for 9th Field Company R.E.	
	17		Working parties. Men not working had a week march.	
	18		We spent working had a week march. Patrol 7 miles - horses fell out.	
	19		Working parties	
BRIGADE RESERVE	20		The Battalion proceeded to prepare Reserve relieving the 1st Argyll Highlanders HQrs & A & B Companies at - MAILLY. C Coy to FLLSS SAUTIES & D to COLINCAMPS	
	21		Brigade Reserve - Found working parties of about 320 men per day. As the string of the 2 grs	
	22		By played a Company of 3rd R.I.F. at AUCHONVILLERS.	
BEAUSSART	26		On this date the Battalion went into Brigade Reserve at BEAUSSART being relieved by Argyll Reserve	

WAR DIARY
or
INTELLIGENCE SUMMARY.
(Erase heading not required.)

Army Form C. 2118.

Place	Date	Hour	Summary of Events and Information	Remarks and references to Appendices
BEAUSSART	26/11/15 27-30 1/12/15		The 7th A & S Highlanders - Finding Working Parties of about 200 men per day for R.E.'s	Casualties
	30/11/15		The strength of the Battalion on this date was 25 Officers & 700 other ranks. Casualties during the month were Killed 1. Wounded 1. Wounded 3. Admitted to Hospital 30/11/15. Discharged from Hospital 72. Reinforcements from England 52 in two 2 proceeded to Brigade Reserve A H Q Coy at COURCAMPS C Coy ELLES SQUARE. Hdqrs and B Coy at MAILLY relieving the 7th A & S Highlanders	
BRIGADE RESERVE	2/12/15 3-8-		Reporting Working Parties daily - Owing to bad weather C & B Companies relieved each other every two days at ELLES SQUARE	
BEAUSSART	8-		Proceeded to Divisional Reserve.	

A. S. Moore
Major
Commanding 7 Monmouth Regt

HEADQUARTERS.,
107th INFANTRY BRIGADE.

		OFFICERS	OTHER RANKS.
1.	RATION STRENGTH...................	18.	698
2.	**TRENCHES.**		
	TRENCH RIFLES........................	11.	468.
	MACHINE GUNNERS.....................	1.	49.
	STRETCHER BEARERS...................		16.
	OPERATORS...........................		23.
	BATTALION HQRS......................	2.	14.
	R.A.M.C.............................	1.	3.
	TOTAL TRENCHES.	15.	573.
3.	NOT AVAILABLE.(EMPLOYED)		
	QR.MR.STORES........................	1.	12.
	SHOEMAKERS AND TAILORS..............		5.
	TRANSPORT...........................	1.	48.
	A.S.C...............................		6.
	A.O.C...............................		1.
	R.A.M.C.(2.watercart.&.3.with.M.O...		5.
	BDE ORDERLIES.......................		4.
	MINERS (BRIGADE)....................		25.
	TUNNELLING COY.(178 R.E.)...........		16.
	4th DIV.RES.COY.....................		11.
	ON LEAVE............................	3.	19.
	COY.COOKS...........................		8.
	C.Q.M.SGTS..........................		4.
	DETACHMENTS.........................	4.	2.
	ORDERLY ROOM.CLERK..................		1.
	WATER CART CORPORAL.................		1.
	BDE GRENADE SCHOOL..................	2.	21.
	" WORKSHOPS......................		4.
	SANITARY MEN (TOWN COMMANDANT MAILLY)		3.
	TOTAL.	26.	757

MAJOR.

COMMANDING 1/2nd MONMOUTHSHIRE REGIMENT.

9/12/15.

107th Inf Bde.

4th Division.

1/2nd Battn MONMOUTHSHIRE REGIMENT

DECEMBER 1915

1/2 Mammonia Regt.
Dec.
Vol XIII

4
10 7½ Bda

Army Form C. 2118.

WAR DIARY
or
INTELLIGENCE SUMMARY.
(Erase heading not required.)

Place	Date	Hour	Summary of Events and Information	Remarks and references to Appendices
	1/12/15		Divisional Reserve.	
BRIGADE RESERVE	2/12/15		Proceeded to Brigade Reserve A & D Companies at COLINCAMPS, C Company ELLES SQUARE. A Coy & B Coy at MAILLY relieving the 7th A & S. Highlanders.	Move.
	3-4/15		Provided working parties daily. Owing to bad weather C & D Coys relieved each other every two days at ELLES SQUARE.	
BEAUSSART	8		Proceeded to Divisional Reserve.	Move
	9		Commenced Lewis Gun School under 2/Lt Rutherford. 28 Other Ranks undergoing instruction.	Lewis Gun School
	10		Found working parties, the number of men employed being 240. No men engaged in resting working parties & drawing trenches, hutting &c on the 2nd Line.	Working parties
	11		" "	
	12		" "	
	13		" "	
BRIGADE RESERVE	14		The Battalion proceeded to Brigade Reserve, C Coy & Hdqrs to MAILLY, B Coy to AUCHONVILLERS D Coy to COLINCAMPS & A Coy to ELLES SQUARE.	Move
	15		Finding working parties for the REDAN, SUCERIE ROMAN ROAD. C Coy relieved A Coy at ELLES SQUARE, A Coy coming into MAILLY.	
	16		Working Parties	
AEHUSSART	17		The Battalion was relieved by 7th A & S Highlanders. Proceeded to Divisional Reserve	Move

2353 Wt. W2544/1454 700,000 5/15 D. D. & L.   A.D.S.S./Forms/C. 2118.

Army Form C. 2118.

WAR DIARY
or
INTELLIGENCE SUMMARY.
(Erase heading not required.)

Instructions regarding War Diaries and Intelligence Summaries are contained in F.S. Regs., Part II and the Staff Manual respectively. Title pages will be prepared in manuscript.

Place	Date	Hour	Summary of Events and Information	Remarks and references to Appendices
BEAUSSART	18/12/15		2 Bombers + 3 other ranks proceeded to REAUVILLIERS to carry out course of experiments representing Authorcite Duff in making fuel out of Authracite Duff	Authorcite Duff
	19		2/Lt A.L. Cotgreave rejoined from Base	
			Finding Working parties 290 Strong for work in front trenches from 2nd R. Inn:	Working parties
	20		ditto	
BRIGADE RESERVE AUCHONVILLIERS	21		The Battalion proceeded to Brigade Reserve Hdqrs + A.C.+D Coys to MAILLY + B Coy to AUCHONVILLIERS	Move
	22		Finding Working parties 270 Strong - 150 men being employed working in Mines at the REDAN under the 252nd Tunnelling Co.	Working parties
	23		ditto	
	24		ditto	
	25		Xmas day. B Coy at AUCHONVILLIERS were relieved by A. Coy. The only working parties found were this day were for the 252nd Tunnelling Co.	
			One Casualty of other than wounded.	Casualty
	26		Working parties as usual	
	27		ditto	
	28		ditto	
	29		ditto	
	30		ditto	
			Capt. F.A. Middleway + Lieut S.R. Hockadey joined for duty.	Droppstoppers

Army Form C. 2118.

WAR DIARY
or
INTELLIGENCE SUMMARY.
(Erase heading not required.)

Place	Date	Hour	Summary of Events and Information	Remarks and references to Appendices
BRIGADE RESERVE	31/12/15		Revd. Lieut. L.P. Williams joined for duty. One man wounded. The strength of the Battalion on this date is 26 officers & 520 other ranks. The number of casualties during the month were:- Killed Nil. Wounded 3 other ranks. Accidentally gassed at the Relay Mine whilst working 4 other ranks. Injured whilst on not service forty other ranks. Admitted to Hospital sick. 79 other ranks. Discharged from Hospital 2 officers 1 other ranks 41 - Reinforcements from Systems Nil.	Strength Seventy casualties.

Casualties of the 1st Bn. Monmouth
Regt from 7.11.14. up to and including
31st Decr 1915.

Killed.
Officers   7.
Other Ranks 104   =   111.

Died of Wounds.
Officers   3.
Other Ranks 30   =   33

Died of Sickness
Officers   —
Other Ranks   6   =   6
                           ―――
                           150.

Wounded 1st time
Officers   10.
Other Ranks 349.   =   359.

Wounded 2nd Time
Officers   1.
Other Ranks   7   =   8.

Gassed.
Officers   —
Other Ranks   —   —

Injured
Officers   1.
Other Ranks   7   =   8.

Missing
Officers   —
Other Ranks   —   —

                Wounded & missing 375
                Deceased   150
                Total   525

Strength of Battalion on Arrival in France
7th Nov 1914.
Officers   31
Other Ranks 935   =   966

New men received as reinforcements
Officers   39
Other Ranks 545   =   584
                                   ――――
                                   1550

Percentage of wounded
returned 45%.
No of wounded returned 163.

107th Inf Bde

4th Division.

this Battn was Transfered
to L of C 30. 1. 1916

1/2nd Battn MONMOUTHSHIRE REGIMENT

J A N U A R Y   1 9 1 6

4

2 Monmouth Regt

Jan
Vol XIV

To A.G. 30.1.16.

Army Form C. 2118.

WAR DIARY
or
INTELLIGENCE SUMMARY.
(Erase heading not required.)

Instructions regarding War Diaries and Intelligence Summaries are contained in F. S. Regs., Part II. and the Staff Manual respectively. Title pages will be prepared in manuscript.

Place	Date	Hour	Summary of Events and Information	Remarks and references to Appendices
MAILLY	1.1.16		C Coy relieved A Coy at AUCHONVILLERS. Battalion still finding Working Parties for 252nd Tunnelling Coy R.E. who are driving a mine in REDAN. Draft arrived. Strength 81. O.R only. (18 of these have not been out before) The following were mentioned in Sir John French's despatch:— Lieut Col. E.G. Godfrey C.M.G., M.V.O.; Capt. (2nd Adjmt) A.H. Bowers; Capt. (Hony Major) P.G. Dunmore; Lieut (Camp Capt) C. Comley; Company Sgt Major Crowley No 5 Sergt August 2nd.	
"	2.1.16		Working Parties	
"	3.1.16		" "	
"	4.1.16		D Company relieved C Company at AUCHONVILLERS	
"	5.1.16		Working Parties	
"	6.1.16		" "	
"	7.1.16		2 O Ranks of Working Party with 252nd Tunnelling Coy R.E. were wounded. Just after stand down duty. The enemy shelled the REDAN point to some extent very little damage was done. The shells were small. Effect very local	
"	8.1.16		Enemy fired up a mine at REDAN which was a hoot of our Trenches. 3 of our men left working party suffering from shell shock. 2 men of the 252nd Tunnelling Coy R.E. were buried for 15 hours 1 Coy men working steadily endeavour in getting them out which was done safely.	
"	9.1.16		The Battalion was still in BDE Reserve	

2353 Wt. W2344/1454 700,000 5/15 D.D.&L. A.D.S.S./Forms/C. 2118.

WAR DIARY or INTELLIGENCE SUMMARY

Army Form C. 2118

(Erase heading not required.)

Instructions regarding War Diaries and Intelligence Summaries are contained in F.S. Regs., Part II. and the Staff Manual respectively. Title pages will be prepared in manuscript.

Place	Date	Hour	Summary of Events and Information	Remarks and references to Appendices
8/11/124	9.1.16		Lieut T.F.R Williams returned from III Army school and resumed command of D Coy. The working parties coming from the RED & N were were called when there were rearranged (cable doing duty). Band & Coy had a much needed rest, which they all enjoyed.	
"	10.1.16 (11.1.16)		Working Party left Beaufour. London Gazette Capt (Hon/Major) D.G Finnymore awarded D.S.O. Capt (Temp Major) J.H Syer D.S.O to be Temp Lieut Colonel. Lieuts A.H Edwards and L.C Edwards to be Temp Majors. Sergt Yates E (1393) and Sergt Dow White H (450) awarded the D.C.M. The following officers joined Battalion for duty:- Lieut R.B Candy, 2/Lt W Cook, 2/Lt F Deacon, 2/Lt E Taylor, and 2/Lt R Spencer.	
"	15.1.16		B Company relieved D Company at AUSHONVILLERS Working parties with the 2/5 2nd Lunch Long Coy R.E. were required by two Companies and Battalion less Ruins Regiment (Supv at Billeting tn)	
"	16.1.16 to 22.1.16 23.1.16		Brigade Reserve. Working parties being found. B Company relieved B Company at AUSHONVILLERS.	

Place	Date	Hour	Summary of Events and Information	Remarks and references to Appendices
MAILLY	23.1.16		Orders were received that an attack were to be made on map VIEWPOINT TRENCHES and FORT HOYSTED. One Company and C Company and B Company were ordered to do this by day and night respectively and the position was duly reconnoitred. The trenches being found to be in a poor condition. No ammunition store was there, so 18 bars were taken up.	
"	24.1.16		Working Parties still being found.	
"	25.1.16		"	
"	26.1.16		"	
"	27.1.16		Gas alarm sounded at 7.0 p.m Enemy having used it against 46 and 37th Division an east sect to effect on us on our front gongs beaters sheet bell rang all ranks were calm all about to ready to move without much trouble.	
"	28.1.16		Gas alarm sounded again at 1.30 am netted fires information received the enemy had mango shell, shrapnel, aphyxiating and lef. w AUCHONVILLERS Orders received that the 1 Battalion would proceed on	
"	29.1.16		to C. The Battn were inspected by Major General Lambton G.O.C. 4th Division after which he addressed the men saying that they had done good work, and he was sorry we were leaving the Division. He was given three hearty cheers were given by the men for the General.	

WAR DIARY or INTELLIGENCE SUMMARY

Army Form C. 2118.

Place	Date	Hour	Summary of Events and Information	Remarks and references to Appendices
MAILLY	29/1/16		General Anley Inspected combs fires also fires and invited the Battn good luck.	
"	30/1/16		Battn left MAILLY at 8.30 am receiving a good send off from all troops at MAILLY. The Divisional Band accompanied us to BUS-LE-ARTOIS. The weather was fine and not too warm, the men marched well and arrived at THIEVRES for dinner after which we marched to HALLOY at 2.30 pm.	
HALLOY	31/1/16		Having done 13 miles and only one left out, we sent two Bullets here for the night. CO met me by C.O. on the morning and marched by to DOULLENS. At 11am where they were to do duty. The remainder of Battn had dinner, after which at 1.15pm marched to MONDICOURT – PAS/ to entrain. B Coy to BOULOGNE D Coy CALAIS. C Coy and HQ to ETAPLES. Train left MONDICOURT 5.33pm arriving ETAPLES at midnight where C Coy and H.Q. were billeted. Casualties during month. Increase during month 28 From Hospital 63 From England 16 _____ 109 Killed — Wounded — Missing 1 Died of wounds 2 Hospitalised 55 _____ 60	A.S. Wilmer Lt Col Commdg 6th N.F.